William Hanna

The earlier years of our Lord's Life on earth by the Rev. William Hanna

William Hanna

The earlier years of our Lord's Life on earth by the Rev. William Hanna

ISBN/EAN: 9783743336810

Manufactured in Europe, USA, Canada, Australia, Japa

Cover: Foto ©Lupo / pixelio.de

Manufactured and distributed by brebook publishing software (www.brebook.com)

William Hanna

The earlier years of our Lord's Life on earth by the Rev. William Hanna

THE EARLIER YEARS

OF

OUR LORD'S LIFE ON EARTH.

BY THE

REV. WILLIAM HANNA, D.D. LL.D.

AUTHOR OF THE LIFE OF DR. CHALMERS.

EDINBURGH:
EDMONSTON AND DOUGLAS.
1864.

CONTENTS.

	PAGE
THE ANNUNCIATION—MARY AND ELISABETH,	1
THE NATIVITY,	21
THE PRESENTATION IN THE TEMPLE,	46
THE VISIT OF THE MAGI,	69
THE MASSACRE OF THE INNOCENTS, AND THE FLIGHT INTO EGYPT,	94
THE THIRTY YEARS AT NAZARETH—CHRIST AMONG THE DOCTORS,	116
THE FORERUNNER,	138
THE BAPTISM,	166
THE TEMPTATION,	188
THE FIRST DISCIPLES,	217
THE FIRST MIRACLE,	242
THE CLEANSING OF THE TEMPLE,	268
THE CONVERSATION WITH NICODEMUS,	288
THE WOMAN OF SAMARIA,	311
THE JEWISH NOBLEMAN AND THE ROMAN CENTURION,	338
THE POOL OF BETHESDA,	358
THE SYNAGOGUE OF NAZARETH,	379
FIRST SABBATH IN CAPERNAUM, AND FIRST CIRCUIT OF GALILEE,	400

I.

THE ANNUNCIATION—MARY AND ELISABETH.[1]

"IN the sixth month"—half a year from the time when, within the holy place at Jerusalem, he had stood on the right side of the altar of incense, and announced to the incredulous Zacharias the birth of the Baptist—the angel Gabriel was sent to an obscure Galilean village to announce a still greater birth,—that of the Divine Redeemer of mankind. As we open, then, the first page in the history of our Lord's earthly life, we come at once into contact with the supernatural. The spirit-world unfolds itself; some of its highest inhabitants become palpable to sense, and are seen to take part in human affairs. In the old patriarchal and prophetic ages angels frequently appeared, conversing with Abraham and Hagar,

[1] Luke i. 26-56.

and Lot and Jacob; instructing in their ignorance, or comforting in their distress, or strengthening in their weakness, Joshua and Gideon, and Elijah and Daniel and Zechariah. Excluding, however, those instances in which it was the Angel of the Covenant who appeared, the cases of angelic manifestation were comparatively rare, and lie very thinly scattered over the four thousand years which preceded the birth of Christ. Within the half century that embraced this life we have more instances of angelic interposition than in all the foregoing centuries of the world's history. At its opening and at its close angels appear as taking a special interest in events which had little of outward mark to distinguish them. Gabriel announces to Zacharias the birth of John, to Mary the birth of Jesus. An angel warns Joseph in a dream to take the young child down to Egypt. On the night of the great birth, and for the first time on earth, a multitude of the heavenly host is seen. In the garden of Gethsemane, an angel comes to strengthen our Lord in his great agony. On the morning of the Resurrection, angels appear, now sitting, now standing, within and without the sepulchre, as if they thronged around the place where the body of the Lord had lain. When from the top of Olivet the cloud carried the rising Jesus out of the apostles' sight, two angels stand beside the apostles as they gaze so steadfastly up into the heavens, and foretell his second coming. Nor do they withdraw from human sight when the ministry of our Lord has closed. Mingling with the other miraculous agency whereby the kingdom of Christ was established and extended, theirs appears. An angel releases Peter, commissions Philip, instructs Cornelius, smites Herod, stands amid the terrors of the shipwreck before Paul.

Is there aught incredible in this? If there be indeed a world of spirits, and in that world Christ fills the place our faith attributes to him; if in that world there be an innumerable company of angels; if the great design of our Lord's visit to this earth was to redeem our sinful race to God, and unite us with the unfallen members of his great family,—then it was not unnatural that those who had worshipped around his throne should bend in wonder over his cradle, stand by his side in his deep agony, roll away the stone rejoicing from his sepulchre, and attend him as the everlasting doors were lifted up, when, triumphant over death and hell, he resumed his place on the eternal throne. When the Father brought his first begotten into the world, the edict was, "Let all the angels of God worship him." Shall we wonder, then, that this worship, in one or two of its acts, should be made manifest to human vision, as if to tell us what an interest the Incarnation excited, if not in the minds of men, in another and higher branch of the great community of spirits? From the beginning angels were interested spectators of what transpired on earth. When under the moulding hand of the Great Creator the present economy of material things was spread forth—so good, so beautiful—they sang together, they shouted for joy. When sin and death made their dark entrance, angels stood by, hailing the first beams of light that fell upon the darkness, welcoming the first human spirit that made its way into the heavenly mansions. The slow development of the divine purposes of mercy in the history of human redemption, they watched with eager eye. Still closer to our earth they gathered, still more earnest was their gaze as the Son of the Eternal prepared to leave the glory he had with the Father, that he might come down and tabernacle as a man among us. And when the great event of his Incarnation at last took place, it looked for a short season as if they were to mingle visibly in the affairs of men, and of that new kingdom which the Ancient of Days set up. It was the Son of God who brought these good angels down along with him. He has mediated not only between us and the Father, but between us and that elder branch of the great commonwealth of spirits, securing their services for us here, preparing us for their society hereafter. He has taught them to see in us that seed out of which the places left vacant by the first revolt in heaven are to be filled. He has taught us to see in them our elder brethren, to a closer and eternal fellowship with whom we are hereafter to be elevated. Already the interchange of kindly offices has commenced. Though since he himself has gone they have withdrawn from human vision, they have not withdrawn from earthly service under the Redeemer. Are they not all ministering spirits sent forth to minister to them who shall be heirs of salvation? Who shall recount to us wherein that gracious ministry of theirs consists; who shall prove it to be a fancy, that as they waited to bear away the spirit of Lazarus to Abraham's bosom, they hover round the death-bed of the believer still, the tread of their footstep, the stroke of their wing unheard as they waft the departing spirit to its eternal home?

"The angel Gabriel was sent from God unto a city of Galilee, named Nazareth, to a virgin espoused to a man, whose name was Joseph, of the house of David; and the virgin's name was Mary." Little information is given in the Gospels as to the previous history either of Joseph or Mary. He, we are told, was of the house of David, of royal lineage by direct descent; but that line now fallen so low that he was but a village tradesman, a carpenter. Mary too, we have reason to believe, was also of the royal stock of David; yet in so humble a condition of life as made it natural that she should be betrothed to Joseph. This betrothal had taken place, and the new hopes it had excited agitate the youthful Mary's heart. She is alone in her dwelling, when, lifting up her eyes, she sees the form of the angel, and hears his voice say unto her: "Hail, thou that art highly favoured, the Lord is with thee: blessed art thou among women." To Zacharias he had spoken at once by name, and had proceeded without prelude to deliver the message with which he had been charged. He enters more reverently this humble abode at Nazareth than he had entered the holy place of the great Temple at Jerusalem. He stands more reverently before this youthful maiden than before the aged priest. He cannot open to her his message till he has offered her such homage as heavenly messenger never paid to any member of our race. Is it any wonder that saluted so by one who, wearing, as in all likelihood he did, our human form, was yet like no man she had ever seen, Mary should have been "troubled at his saying,"—troubled as she felt the privacy of her seclusion thus invaded, and looked upon that strange, unearthly, yet most attractive form which stood before her? She is not so troubled however as to hinder her from casting in her thoughts "what manner of salutation this should be." She receives the salutation in silence, with surprise, with awe, with thoughtful wonder. In sympathy with feelings depicted in her alarmed yet inquiring countenance, Gabriel hastens to relieve her fears, and satisfy her curiosity. "Fear not," he says, after a brief pause. "Fear not, Mary;" the very familiar mention of her name carrying with it an antidote against alarm. "Fear not, Mary; for thou hast found favour with God. And, behold, thou shalt conceive in thy womb, and bring forth a son, and shalt call his name Jesus. He shall be great, and shall be called the Son of the Highest; and the Lord God shall give unto him the throne of his father David: and he shall reign over the house of Jacob for ever; and of his kingdom there shall be no end."

There was scarce a mother in Israel, in those days, who did not cherish it as the very highest object of desire and ambition to be the mother of the promised Messiah. Mary was a mother in Judah, and the man to whom she was betrothed belonged also to that stock from which the Messiah was to spring. Perhaps the hope had already dawned that this great honour might be in store for her. Her devout and thoughtful habits had made her familiar with the old prophecies that foretold the Messiah's advent, and with the manner in which his kingdom was there spoken of. Obscure and mysterious as much of what Gabriel said may have appeared to her, she seems at once to have apprehended that it was of the birth of this great son of David that he was speaking. She does not ask, she seems not to have needed any information on that point. Nor does she hesitate to accept as true all that Gabriel had declared. She puts indeed a question which, if its meaning had not been interpreted by the manner in which Gabriel dealt with it, and by the subsequent conduct of Mary herself, we might have regarded as akin to that of Zacharias; as indicating that she too had given way to incredulity. But hers was a question of curiosity not of unbelief; a question akin, not to the one which Zacharias put about the birth of John, but to that of Abraham about the birth of

Isaac, when he said to the angel, Whereby shall I know this? a question implying no failure of faith, for we know that Abraham staggered not at the promise through unbelief, but expressive simply of a desire for further information, for some sign in confirmation of his faith. He got such a sign and rejoiced. And so with Mary: her question, like the patriarch's, springing not from the spirit of a hesitating unbelief, but from natural curiosity, and the wish to have the faith she felt confirmed. Her desire was granted. She was told that the Holy Ghost should come upon her, that the power of the Highest should overshadow her, that the child afterwards to be born was now miraculously to be conceived. And as a sign, this piece of information, new to her we may believe, was given, that her relative, the aged Elisabeth, was also to have a son. Her question having been answered, and the manner of the great event so far revealed as to throw her back simply on the promise and power of God, Mary says: "Behold the handmaid of the Lord; be it unto me according to thy word." What a contrast here between Zacharias and Mary! The aged priest had been taught from childhood in one of the schools of the prophets, and must have been familiar with all those narratives and prophecies which might have prepared him to believe, and he had besides the experience of years to give power to his trust in God. Mary was of humbler parentage; her opportunities of instruction but meagre compared with his; hers too was the season of inexperienced youth; her faith was as yet unfortified by trial. What he was asked to believe was unlikely indeed, and altogether unlooked for, yet not beyond the powers of nature. What she is asked to believe is a direct miraculous forthputting of the great power of God. Yet the old priest staggers, while the young maiden instantly confides.

In Mary's immediate and entire belief of the angel's word, a far greater confidence in God was shown than could have been shown by Zacharias, even had he received Gabriel's message as she did, without a suspicion or a doubt. She who, being betrothed, proved unfaithful, was, by the law of Moses, sentenced to be stoned to death, and though that law had now fallen into disuse, or was but seldom literally executed, yet she who was deemed guilty of such a crime stood exposed to the loss of character, and became the marked object of public opprobrium. Mary could not fail at once to perceive, and to be sensitive to the misconceptions and the perils which she would certainly incur. She might, in self-vindication, relate what Gabriel had told her, but how many would believe her word? What voucher could she give that it was actually a heavenly messenger she had seen, and that what he had said was true? Many a distressing fear as to the future,—as to the treatment she might receive from Joseph, the calumnies, the shame, the scorn to which from other quarters she might be exposed,—might have arisen, if not to check her faith, yet to hold her own acquiescence in the will of God in timid and trembling suspense; but, strong in the simplicity and fulness of her trust, she puts all fears away, and committing herself into the hands of him whose Angel she believes Gabriel to be, she says, "Behold the handmaid of the Lord; be it unto me according to thy word."

Let us notice one other element in Mary's faith: its humility, its complete freedom from that undue thought of self which so often taints the faith of the most believing. Wonderful as the announcement is, that a child born of her should, by such miraculous conception as Gabriel had spoken of, be the Son of the Highest, should be a King sitting on the throne of David,—his kingdom one that should outrival David's, of which there never should be an end,—Mary harbours no doubt, raises no question, thinks not, speaks not of her own unworthiness to have such honour conferred on her, or of her unfitness to be the mother of such a child. As if one so unworthy of the least of God's mercies had no right or title to question his doings, however great a gift it pleased him to confer, she sinks all thought of self in thought of him, and says, " Behold the handmaid of the Lord ; be it unto me according to thy word." A finer instance of simple, humble, childlike, unbroken trust, we shall scarcely find in any record human or divine. " Blessed," let us say with her cousin Elisabeth, " is she that believed : for there shall be a performance of those things which were told her from the Lord." "Thou hast found favour," said Gabriel to her, "with God." It is possible to interpret that saying without any reference to Mary's character; to rest in the explanation, which is no doubt so far true, that it was God's good pleasure to select out of all the maidens of Israel this Mary of Nazareth, to be the most honoured of the daughters of Eve. But if it be true, as we are elsewhere taught, that to him that hath it is given; that it is done unto every one according to his faith; that to him that believeth, all things are possible; if all the recorded experience of God's people confirms these general sayings of the Divine word,—are we wrong in considering the high honour conferred by God on Mary as a striking exemplification of the principle of adapting the gift to the character and capacity of the receiver?

His errand accomplished, Gabriel withdrew; and after the brief and exciting interview, Mary was left in solitude to her own thoughts. The words she had so lately heard kept ringing in her ears. She tried to enter more and more into their meaning. As she did so, into what a tumult of wonder, and awe, and hope, must she have been thrown! She longs for some one with whom she can converse, to whom she may unburden her full mind and heart. There is no one near to whom she can or dare lay open all her secret thoughts; but she remembers now what Gabriel had told her about her kinswoman Elisabeth, who may well be intrusted with the secret, for she too has been placed in something like the same condition. Eager for sympathy, thirsting for companionship and full communion of the heart, she arises in haste, and departs for the distant residence of her cousin, who lives amid the far-off hills of Judah. It is a long—for one so young and so unprotected, it might be, a perilous journey; nearly the whole length of the land—at least a hundred miles to traverse. But what is distance, what are dangers to one so lifted up with the exalted hopes to which she has been begotten! The hundred miles are quickly trodden; joy and hope make the long distance short. She reaches at last the house in which Elisabeth resides, and, with all due respect—such as is due from the inferior in station, the junior in years—she salutes the wife of the venerable priest. How filled with wonder must she have been, when, instead of the ordinary return to her salutation, Elisabeth breaks forth at once with the exclamation, "Blessed art thou among women;" the very words which the angel had so lately spoken in her astonished ear; "and blessed is the fruit of thy womb." She need not tell her secret; it is already known. What a fresh warrant this for the truth of all that Gabriel had said! It comes to confirm a faith already strong, but which might, perhaps, otherwise have begun to falter. It did not waver in the angel's presence; but had month after month gone by, with no one near to share her thoughts, or build her up in her first trust, might not that trust have yielded to human weakness, and shown some symptom of decay? Well-timed, then, the kindly aid which the strange greeting of her cousin brought with it, supplying a new evidence that there should indeed be a performance of all those things which were told of the Lord.

"And whence is this to me, that the mother of my Lord should come to me?" If in Mary we have one of the rarest exhibitions of humility towards God, of entire acquiescence in his will; in Elisabeth we have as rare and beautiful an instance of humility towards others, the entire absence of all selfish, proud, and envious feelings. Elisabeth leaves out of sight all the outer distinctions between herself and her humbler relative, forgets the difference of age and rank, recognises at once, and ungrudgingly, the far higher distinction which had been conferred by God upon Mary, and wonders even at the fact that to such a home as hers the honoured mother of her Lord should come. But now the same spirit which had enlightened her eyes, and filled her heart, and opened her lips to give such greeting to her cousin, comes in still fuller measure upon Mary, and to the wonderful salutation she gives a still more wonderful response in that strain of rapt and rhythmical praise which the Holy Catholic Church has ever treasured as the first and fullest of our Christian hymns.

It divides itself into two parts. Rising at once to God as the source of all her blessings, her soul and all that was within her being stirred up to bless him, she celebrates, in lofty strains of praise, the Lord's goodness to herself individually. "My soul doth magnify the Lord." The Lord had magnified her, by his goodness had made her great, and she will magnify the Lord. The larger his gift to her, the larger the glory she will render to his great name. "My spirit hath rejoiced in God my Saviour." She hails the coming Saviour, as one needed by her as by all sinners, and embraces him, though her own son according to the flesh, as her God and Saviour; glorying more in the connexion that she has with him in common with the entire multitude of the redeemed, than in that special maternal relationship in which she has the privilege to stand to him. Royal though her lineage, hers had been a low estate; her family poor in Judah; she among the least in her father's house; but in his great grace and infinite condescension the Lord had stooped to raise her from the dust, to set her upon a pinnacle of honour, and gratefully and gladly will she acknowledge the hand that did it. "For he hath regarded the low estate of his handmaiden." And how high had he exalted her!

The angel had called her blessed at Nazareth. Elisabeth, in the city of Judah, had repeated his saying; but Mary herself rises to the full conception and full acknowledgment of the honour the Lord had put upon her: "For, behold," she says, "from henceforth, all generations shall call me blessed." But it fills her with no pride, it prompts to no undue familiarity with God, or with his great name. She knows to whom to attribute this and every other gift and grace, and in the fulness of a devout and grateful reverence, she adds : " He that is mighty hath done to me great things ; and holy is his name."

So much about herself and all that the Lord had done for her ; but now she widens the embrace of her thanksgiving and praise, and losing all sense of her individuality, her virgin lips are touched with fire, and as poetess and prophetess of the infant church she pours forth the first triumphal song which portrays the general character of the gospel kingdom then to be ushered in.

In these strains there breathed the spirit at once of the Baptist and of Christ ; of the two children of the two mothers who stood now face to face saluting one another. It is the voice of him who cried in the wilderness, "Prepare ye the way of the Lord, make straight in the desert a highway for our God: every valley shall be exalted, and every hill shall be made low; and the crooked shall be made straight, and the rough places plain; and the glory of the Lord shall be revealed." It is the voice of him who opened his mouth on the mountain side of Galilee, and said, "Blessed are the poor in spirit: for theirs is the kingdom of heaven. Blessed are the meek: for they shall inherit the earth. Blessed are they which do hunger and thirst after righteousness: for they shall be filled." Do we not recognise the very spirit of the ministries both of John and of Jesus in the words: "He hath showed strength with his arm: he hath scattered the proud in the imagination of their hearts. He hath put down the mighty from their seats, and exalted them of low degree. He hath filled the hungry with good things; and the rich he hath sent empty away. He hath holpen his servant Israel, in remembrance of his mercy; as he spake to our fathers, to Abraham, and to his seed for ever."

II.

THE NATIVITY.[1]

It is difficult, perhaps impossible, to decide whether it was before or after her visit to Elisabeth, that Joseph was made acquainted with the condition of his betrothed. It must have thrown him into painful perplexity. He was not prepared at first to put implicit faith in her narrative, but neither was he prepared utterly to discredit it. To put her publicly away by a bill of divorce would have openly stamped her character with shame, and branded her child with infamy. He was unwilling that either of these injuries should be inflicted. To put her away privily would at least so far cover her reputation that the child might still be regarded as his; and this he had generously resolved to do, when the angel of the Lord appeared to him

[1] Luke ii. 1-20.

in a dream, removed all his doubts, and led him to take Mary as his wife. This difficulty overcome, Mary was quietly awaiting at Nazareth the expected birth. But it was not at Nazareth that the Messiah was to be born. An ancient prophecy had already designated another village, not in Galilee, but in Judea, as the destined birthplace. "But thou, Bethlehem Ephratah"—so had the prophet Micah spoken 700 years before—"though thou be little among the thousands of Judah, yet out of thee shall he come forth unto me that is to be ruler in Israel; whose goings forth have been from of old, from everlasting." To this village of Bethlehem Mary was to be guided at such a time as should secure the fulfilment of the prophecy.

A singular instrumentality was employed to gain this end. The Roman Empire had now stretched its dominion to its widest limits, its power extending from the Euphrates to the British Islands—from the Northern Ocean to the borders of Ethiopia. Amid the prevalence of universal peace, the Emperor, judging it a fit opportunity to ascertain by accurate statistics the population and resources of the different provinces of his dominions, issued an edict that a general census of the empire should be taken. It gratified his pride; it would be useful afterwards for many purposes of government, such as determining the taxes that might be imposed, or the levies that might be drawn from the different provinces. This edict of Augustus came to be executed in Judea. That country was not yet, in the outward form of its government, reduced to the condition of a Roman province; but Herod, while nominally an independent king, was virtually a Roman subject, and had to obey this as well as the other edicts of the Emperor. In doing so, however, Herod followed the Jewish usage, and issued his instructions that every family should repair forthwith to the seat of its tribe, where its genealogical records were kept. The distinction of inheritance among the Jews had long been lost, but the distinction of families and tribes was still preserved, and Herod grounded upon that distinction the prescribed mode of registration or enrolment. Joseph and Mary, being both of the house and lineage of David, were obliged to repair to Bethlehem.

The manner in which the power of the Roman Empire was thus employed to determine the birthplace of our Lord, naturally invites us to reflect upon the singular conjunction of outward circumstances, the strange timing of events that then took place. Embracing the whole sphere of reflection which thus opens to our view, let us, before fixing our attention upon the incidents of the particular narrative now before us, dwell for a little on the Divine wisdom that was displayed in fixing upon that particular epoch in the world's history as the one in which Jesus was born, and lived, and died. "When," says the inspired apostle, " the fulness of the time was come, God sent forth his Son, made of a woman, made under the law." The expression used here, " the fulness of the time," evidently implies not only that there was a set time appointed beforehand of the Father, but that a series of preparatory steps were pre-arranged, the accomplishment of which had, as it were, to be waited for, ere the season best suited for the earthly advent of our

Lord arrived. Some peculiar fitness must then have marked the time of Christ's appearance in this world. We are inclined to wonder that his appearance should have been so long delayed. Looking at all the mighty issues that hung suspended on his advent, we are apt at times to be surprised that so many thousand years should have been suffered to elapse ere the Son of God came down to save us; and yet, could the whole plan and counsels of the Deity be laid open to our eye, we cannot but believe that as there were the best and weightiest reasons why his coming should be deferred so long, there were also the best and weightiest reasons why it should be deferred no longer. To attempt on either side the statement of these reasons, would be to attempt to penetrate within the veil that hides from us the secret things of God. Taking up, however, the history of the world as it is actually before us, it can neither be unsafe nor presumptuous to consider the actual and obvious benefits which have attended the coming of the Saviour at that particular period when it happened.

In the first place, we can readily enough perceive that it has served greatly to enhance the number and the force of the evidences in favour of the Divine origin and authority of his mission. Two of the chief outer pillars upon which the fabric of Christianity as a revelation from Heaven rests, are Prophecy and Miracles. But if Christ had come in the earliest ages; had the Incarnation followed quickly upon the Fall, so far as that coming was concerned, there had been no room or scope for prophecy,—one great branch of the Christian evidences had been cut off. As it now is, when we take up that long line of predictions, extending over more than three thousand years, from the first dim intimation that the Seed of the woman should bruise the head of the serpent, down to the last prophecy of Malachi, that the Lord, whom the Jews sought, should come suddenly to his temple as the Messenger of the Covenant, whom they delighted in; when we mark the growing brightness and fulness that characterizes each succeeding prediction, as feature after feature in the life and character of the great Messiah is added to the picture; when we compare the actual events with the passages in those ancient writings, in which they were repeatedly foretold, what a strong confirmation is given thereby to our faith, that He, of whom all those things had been spoken so long beforehand, was indeed the Christ, the Son of the living God. How much, then, in regard to prophecy, should we have lost, had the interval between the Fall and the Incarnation not been long enough for that wonderful series of prophecies to be interposed.

Even as to the miracles we should have been put to great and serious disadvantage. Our faith in the reality of these miracles rests upon human testimony. That testimony is embodied in the writings of the apostles and their contemporaries. Those writings were issued at an advanced stage in the history of the world. They have come down to us through the same channel,—they come, accompanied with the same vouchers for their authenticity,—with a vast mass of other ancient writings, whose genuineness and credibility no one has ever denied. Our belief in the miracles of Jesus is thus bound up with our belief in a large portion of ancient history, for our knowledge of which we are indebted to writings of equal and greater antiquity than those of the New Testament. If we renounce the one, we must, in all fairness, renounce the other also. We must blot out all that is alleged to have happened in the world from this date upwards. It has been of the greatest possible service in the defence of Christianity against the attack of scholarly men, that the life of Jesus Christ, recorded in the four Gospels, forms part and parcel of so large a portion of the preserved literature of antiquity,—written, as it were, with the same ink, published at the same time, preserved in the same manner, so that together they must stand or together fall. How should it have stood, if, instead of being as it is, those miracles of Christ had been wrought far back in the world's history; the record of them written at some period preceding that from which any other authentic narrative had come down to us, some centuries before the date of the first acknowledged book of common history? Who does not perceive to what exceptions, just or unjust, they would, in consequence, have been exposed? Who does not perceive that, fixing his eye upon the barbarous and fabulous age in which the record originated, and upon the longer and more perilous passage that it had made, with some show at least of reason, with some apparent ground for the distinction, other ancient histories might have been received, and yet this one rejected? We have to thank God then for the wisdom of that order of things whereby, in consequence of the particular time at which Christ appeared, our faith in him as the heaven-sent Saviour rests upon the same solid basis with our faith in the best accredited facts of common history.

We can discern another great and beneficial purpose that was served by the appearance of Christ at so late a period. The world was left for a long while to itself, to make full proof of its capabilities and dispositions. Many great results it realized. There were countries unvisited by any light from heaven, upon which the sun of civilisation rose and shone with no mean lustre; where the intellect of man acted as vigorously as it has ever done on earth; where all the arts and refinements of life were brought to the highest state of culture; where taste and imagination revelled amid the choicest objects of gratification; where, in poetry and in painting, and in sculpture and in architecture, specimens of excellence were furnished which remain to this day the models that we strive to imitate. Was nothing gained by allowing Egypt, Greece, and Rome to run out their full career of civilisation, while the light from heaven was confined meanwhile to the narrow limits of Judea? Was nothing gained by its being made no longer a matter of speculation but a matter of fact, that man may rise in other departments, but in religion will not, left unaided, rise to God; that he may make great progress in other kinds of knowledge, but make no progress in the knowledge of his Maker; that he may exercise his intellect, regale his fancy, refine his taste, correct his manners, but will not, cannot purify his heart? For what was the actual state of matters in those countries unblest by revelation? We have the description drawn by an unerring hand: "They became vain in their imaginations, and their foolish heart was darkened. Professing themselves to be wise, they became fools, and changed the glory of the uncorruptible God into an image made like to corruptible man, and to birds, and four-footed beasts, and creeping things; who changed the truth of God into a lie, and worshipped and served the creature more than the Creator, who is blessed for ever." We should have lost that exhibition of the greatest refinement coupled with the grossest idolatry, had the light of Revelation mingled universally from the first with the light of ordinary civilisation.

Let us look a little more closely at the condition of Judea relatively to the Roman Empire at the time of our Lord's birth and death. It was owing, as we have already mentioned, to Herod's being nominally a sovereign but virtually a subject, that the order for registration came to be executed in Palestine which forced Mary from Nazareth to Bethlehem. Is there nothing impressive in seeing the power of Rome thus interposed to determine the Redeemer's birthplace; the pride and policy of the world's great monarchy employed as an instrument for doing what the hand and counsel of the Lord had determined beforehand to be done? But even that nominal kingdom which Herod enjoyed soon passed from his family. A few years after the birth of Christ, Archelaus, who reigned in Judea in the room of his father Herod, was deposed and banished. Judea had then a Roman governor placed over it. Still, however, whether through respect to its banished princes, or some latent reverence for its Temple and ancient laws, the old national and priestly authorities were suffered to continue and enjoy some part of their old power and privileges. It was an anomalous and short-lived state of things; a Jewish law and Jewish officers, under a Roman law and Roman officers: the two fitted into each other by certain limits being assigned to the inferior or Jewish judicatories which they were not permitted to overpass. To no Jewish court, not even to the highest, the Sanhedrim, was the power of inflicting capital punishment intrusted; and it was wholly owing to that peculiar and temporary adjustment, that all the formality of an orderly trial, and all the publicity of a legal execution was stamped upon the closing scenes of the Saviour's life. Had Jesus Christ appeared one half-century earlier, or one half-century later than he did; had he appeared when the Jewish authorities had unchecked power, how quickly, how secretly had their deadly malice discharged itself upon his head? No cross had been raised on Calvary. Had he come a few years later, when the Jews were stripped even of that measure of power they for a short season enjoyed, would the Roman authorities, then the only ones in the land, of their own motion have condemned and crucified him? Even as it was, it was impossible to persuade Pilate that Jesus was either a rival whom Cæsar had any reason to fear, or a rebel whom it became him to punish. Why then was the rule over Judea at this time in the hands of Rome? and why was that power induced to treat Judea for a time so differently from her other subject provinces? Why, but that she might be standing there ready, when Christ fell into the hands of his exasperated countrymen, to extricate him from that grasp under which in darkness he might have perished; and, though she too denied him justice, yet by her weak and vacillating governor, that hers might be the voice proclaiming aloud his innocence;

hers the hand to erect the cross, and lift it up so high that the eyes of all the nations and all the ages might behold it.

But let us now turn to the narrative of our Redeemer's birth. When Mary was at first informed that Joseph and she must go to Bethlehem, perhaps she shrunk from so long a journey, lingered to the last ere she entered on it, and took it slowly. She was late at least in her arrival at the village. The inn, we may well suppose the single one that so small a place afforded for the entertainment of strangers,[1] was crowded. She had to take the only accommodation that the place afforded. Adopting here the early tradition of the Church, as reported by Justin Martyr, who was born about a century afterwards, and within fifty miles from Bethlehem, let us say, she had to go into one of the caves or grottos in the rock common in the neighbour-

[1] The inn or khan was frequently in the earliest times the house of the sheikh or chief man of the place. A very interesting *résumé* of all the historical notices of the inn or khan of Bethlehem is given in the *Athenæum* for December 26, 1863, which makes it more than probable that the place of Christ's birth was close to, if not within, the very house to which Boaz conducted Ruth, and in which Samuel anointed David king.

hood, connected with the inn. There, where the camels and the asses had their stalls; there, far away from home and friends, among strangers all too busy to care for her; amid all the rude exposures and confusion of the place, Mary brought forth her first-born son, and when her hour was over, having swathed him with her own weak hands, laid him in a manger.

A very lowly mode of entering upon human life: nothing whatever to dignify, everything to degrade. Yet the night of that wonderful birth was not to pass by without bearing upon its bosom a bright and signal witness of the greatness of the event. Sloping down from the rocky ridge on which Bethlehem stood, there lay some grassy fields, where all that night long some shepherds watched their flocks; humble, faithful, industrious men; men, too, of whom we are persuaded that, Simeon-like, they were waiting for the Consolation of Israel; who had simpler and more spiritual notions of their Messiah than most of the well-taught scribes of the metropolis. They would not have understood the angel's message so well; they would not have believed it so readily; they would not have hastened so quickly to Bethlehem; they would not have bent with such reverence over so humble a cradle; they would not have made known abroad what had been told them concerning this child,—made it known as a thing in which they themselves most heartily believed,—had they not been devout, believing men. Under the starry heavens, along the lonely hill-sides, these shepherds are keeping their watch, thinking perhaps of the time when these very sheep-walks were trodden by the young son of Jesse, or remembering some ancient prophecy that told of the coming of one who was to be David's son and David's Lord. Suddenly the angel of the Lord comes upon them, the glory of the Lord encompasses them with a girdle of light brighter than the mid-day sun could have thrown around them. They fear as they see that form, and as they are encircled by that glory, but their alarm is instantly dispelled. "Fear not," says the angel, "for, behold, I bring you good tidings of great joy, which shall be to all people. For unto you is born this day, in the city of David, a

Saviour, which is Christ the Lord." Mary had been told that her child was to be called Jesus, that he was to be great, to be son of the Highest, the heir to his father David's throne, the head of an everlasting monarchy. Joseph had been told that he was to call the child born of Mary, Jesus, for he was to save his people from their sins,—a simpler and less Jewish description of his office. The angel speaks of him to these shepherds in still broader and sublimer terms. Unto them and unto all people this child was to be born, and unto them and unto all he was to be a Saviour, Christ the Lord, the only instance in which the double epithet, Christ the Lord, is given in this form to him. A universal, a divine Messiahship was to be his.

The shepherds ask no sign as Zacharias and Mary had done; yet they got one: "And this," said the angel, "shall be a sign unto you; Ye shall find the babe wrapped in swaddling clothes, lying in a manger." But one such child, born that night, wrapped up in such a way, lying in such a place, could so small a village as Bethlehem supply. That village lay but a mile or so from the spot they stood on; the sign could speedily be verified. But they have something more to see and hear ere their visit to the village is paid. The voice of that single angel has scarce died away in the silence of the night—lost in wonder they are still gazing on his radiant form—when suddenly a whole multitude of the heavenly host bursts upon their astonished vision, lining the illuminated heavens. Human eyes never saw before or since so large a company of the celestial inhabitants hovering in our earthly skies; and human ears never heard before or since such a glorious burst of heavenly praise as those angels then poured forth,—couching it in Hebrew speech, their native tongue for the time foregone, that these listening shepherds may catch up at once the cradle-hymn that heaven now chants over the new-born Saviour; that these shepherds may repeat it to the men of their own generation; that from age to age it may be handed down, and age after age may take it up as supplying the fittest terms in which to celebrate the Redeemer's birth,—" Glory to God in the highest on earth peace, goodwill towards men."

At the moment when these words first saluted human ears, what a contrast did they open up between earth and heaven! As that babe was born in Bethlehem, this world lay around him in silence, in darkness, in ignorant unconcern. But all heaven was moved; for, large as that company of angels was which the shepherds saw, what were they to the thousands that encircle the throne of the Eternal! And the song of praise the shepherds heard, what was it to the voice, as of many waters, which rose triumphant around that throne! That little dropping of its praise committed for human use to human keeping, Heaven hastily veiled itself again from human vision. The whole angelic manifestation passed rapidly away. The shepherds are startled in their midnight rounds; a flood of glory pours upon them; their eyes are dazzled with those forms of light; their ears are full of that thrilling song of praise: suddenly the glory is gone; the shining forms have vanished; the stars look down as before through the darkness; they are left to a silent, unspeakable wonder and awe. They soon, however, collect their thoughts, and promptly resolve to go at once into the village. They go in haste; the sign is verified; they find Mary and Joseph, and the babe lying in the manger. They justify their intrusion by telling all that they had just seen and heard; and amid the sorrows and humiliations of that night, how cheering to Mary the strange tidings that they bring! Having told these, they bend with rude yet holy reverence over the place where the infant Saviour lies, and go their way to finish their night-watch among the hills, and then for all their life long afterwards to repeat to wondering listeners the story of that birth. With those shepherds let us bend for a moment or two over the place where the infant Redeemer lay, to meditate on one or two of the lessons which it is fitted to suggest.

By the manner of his entrance into this world, Christ hath dignified the estate of infancy, has hallowed the bond which binds the mother to her new-born child. He, the great Son of God, stooped to assume our humanity. He might have done so at once; taken it on him in its manhood form. The second Adam might have stood forth like the first, no childhood passed through. Why did he become an infant before he was a man? Was it not, among other reasons which may suggest themselves, that he might consecrate that first of human ties, that earliest estate of human life? The grave, we say, has been hallowed,—has not the cradle also,—by Christ's having lain in it?

By the humiliation of his birth, he stripped the estate of poverty of all reproach. Of all who have ever been born into this world, he was the only one with whom it was a matter of choice in what condition he should appear. The difference, indeed, between our highest and our lowest,—between a chamber in a palace, and a manger in a stable,—could have been but slight to him; yet he chose to be born in the stable, and to be laid in the manger. And that first stage of his earthly life was in keeping with all that followed. For thirty years he depended on his own or others' labour for his daily bread: for three years more, he was a houseless, homeless man, with no provision but that which the generosity of others supplied: " The foxes had holes, and the birds of the air had nests; but he had not where to lay his head." And has not that life of his redeemed poverty from all disgrace; has it not lifted it to honour?

As we bend in wonder over the infant Saviour, we learn the difference between the inferior and higher forms of an earthly greatness. On that night when Christ was born, what a difference was there in all outward marks of distinction, between that child of the Hebrew mother as he lay in his lowly cradle, and the Augustus Cæsar whose edict brought Mary to Bethlehem, as he reposed in his imperial palace! And throughout the lifetimes of the two there was but little to lessen that distinction. The name of the one was known and honoured over the whole civilized globe: the name of the other scarce heard of beyond the narrow bounds of Judea. And when repeated there, it was too often as a byword and a reproach. How stands it now? The throne of the Cæsars, the throne of mere human authority and power, has perished. That name, at which nations trembled, carries no power over the spirits of men. But the empire of Jesus, the empire of pure, undying, self-sacrificing love, will never perish ; its sway over the conscience and hearts of men, as the world grows older becomes ever wider and stronger. His name shall be honoured while sun and moon endure ;—men shall be blessed in him ; all nations shall call him blessed. This world owes an infinite debt to him, were it for nothing else than this, that he has so exalted the spiritual above the material ; the empire of love above the empire of power.

Again we bend over this infant as he lies in that manger at Bethlehem, and as we do so, strange scenes in his after life rise upon our memory. Those little, tender feet, unable to sustain the infant frame, are yet to tread upon the roughened waters of a stormy lake, as men tread the solid earth ! At the touch of that little, feeble hand, the blind eye is to open, and the tied tongue to be unloosed, and diseases of all kinds are to take wings and flee away ! That soft, weak voice, whose gentle breathings in his infant slumbers can scarce be heard, is to speak to the winds and the waves, and they shall obey it ; is to summon the dead from the sepulchre, and they shall come forth ! Who then, and what was he, whose birth the angels celebrated in such high strains? None other than he of whom Isaiah, anticipating the angels, had declared: "Unto us a child is born, unto us a son is given; and the government shall be upon his shoulder: and his name shall be called Wonderful, Counsellor, The mighty God, The everlasting Father, The Prince of Peace." It was He, the Word, who was from the beginning with God, and who was God; who was thus made flesh, and came to dwell among us. This is, in truth, the central fact or doctrine of our religion; the mystery of mysteries; the one great miracle of divine, everlasting love. Admit it, and all the other wonders of the Saviour's life become not only easy of belief,—they appear but the natural and suitable incidents of such a history as his. Deny it, and the whole gospel narrative becomes an inexplicable enigma. The very heart of its meaning taken out of it, you may try to turn it into a myth or fable if you please; but a credible story it no longer is. No; not credible even in that part of it into which nothing of the supernatural enters. Christ was either what he claimed to be, and what all those miraculous attestations conspire to establish that he was; he was either one with the Father, knowing the Father as the Father knew him, doing whatever the Father did,—so direct and full a revelation of the Father that it could be truly said that he who had seen him had seen the Father likewise;—or his character for simplicity and honesty and truthfulness stands impeached, and the whole fabric of Christianity is overturned.

Let those angels teach us in what light we should regard the birth of Christ, the advent of the Redeemer. They counted it as glad tidings of great joy that they give forth when they announced that birth; they broke forth together in exulting praises over it, as glorifying to God in the highest, as proclaiming peace on earth, as indicating goodwill toward men. In that goodwill of God to us in Christ let us heartily believe; into that peace with God secured to us in Christ let us humbly yet gratefully enter. Those glad tidings of great joy, let us so receive as that they shall make us joyful, that so Christ may be glorified in us on earth, and we be glorified with him throughout eternity!

III.

THE PRESENTATION IN THE TEMPLE.[1]

On the eighth day after his birth Christ was circumcised : the visible token of his being one of the seed of Abraham according to the flesh was thus imposed. In his case, indeed, this rite could not have that typical or spiritual meaning which in all other cases it bore. It could point to no spiritual defilement needing to be removed. But though on that ground exemption might have been claimed for him, on other grounds it became him in this as in other respects to fulfil the requirements of the Jewish law. From the earliest period, from the first institution of the rite, it had been the Jewish custom to give its name to the child on the occasion of its circumcision, as it is the Christian custom, borrowed from the Jewish, to give its name to the child on the

[1] Luke ii. 21-38.

occasion of its baptism. The angel, indeed, who had appeared to Zacharias and to Mary, had in each instance announced beforehand what the names of the two children were to be. These however were not formally imposed till the day of their circumcision. In the Baptist's case there was a large assemblage of relations and friends upon that day; and springing out of the peculiar condition of the father, the naming of John was attended with such striking circumstances, that the fame of them was noised abroad throughout all the hill country of Judea. At Bethlehem Joseph and Mary were too far away from all their kindred to call any assemblage of them together. In their humbler position they might not have done it, even had they been resident at the time in Nazareth. Quietly, privately, obscurely, they circumcised their child, and gave to him the name of *Jesus*, that name so rich in meaning, so full of promise.

Forty days after the birth of Jesus, Joseph and Mary carried the infant up to Jerusalem. There was a double object in this visit. Mary had to present the offering which the Jewish law required at the hands of every mother when the days of her purification were accomplished. This offering, in the case of all whose circumstances enabled them to present it, was to consist of a lamb of the first year for a burnt-offering, and a young pigeon or a turtle-dove for a sin-offering. With that consideration for the poor which marks so many of the Mosaic ordinances, it was provided that if the mother were not able to furnish a lamb, a pair of turtle-doves or two young pigeons were to be accepted, the one for the burnt-offering, and the other for the sin-offering. That such was the offering which Joseph and Mary presented to the priest, carried with it an unmistakable evidence of the poverty of their estate. Besides discharging this duty, Mary had at the same time to dedicate her infant son as being a first-born child to the Lord, and to pay the small sum fixed as the price of his redemption.

There were few more common, few less noticeable sights than the one witnessed that forenoon within the Temple when Christ's presentation as a first-born child took place. It happened every day that mothers brought their children to be in this way dedicated and redeemed. It was part of the daily routine work of the priest-in-waiting to take their payments, to hold up the children before the altar, to enrol their names in the register of the first-born, and so to complete the dedication; a work which from its commonness he went through without giving much attention either to parents or to child, unless indeed there was something special in their rank, or their appearance, or their offerings. But here there was nothing of this kind. A poor man and woman, in humblest guise, with humblest offerings, present themselves before him. The woman holds out her first-born babe; he takes, presents, enrols, and hands it back to her; all seems over, and what is there in so common, plain, and simple an old Jewish custom worthy of any particular notice? We shall be able to answer that question better, by considering for a moment what this rite of the dedication of the first-born among the Israelites really meant, especially as applied to this first-born, to this child Jesus.

When Moses first got his commission from the Lord in Midian, and was told to go and work out the great deliverance of his people from their Egyptian bondage, the last instruction he received was this: "And thou shalt say unto Pharaoh, Thus saith the Lord, Israel is my son, even my first-born. And I say unto thee, Let my son go, that he may serve me: and if thou refuse to let him go, behold, I will slay thy son, even thy first-born" (Exodus iv. 22, 23). As a mother reclaims her infant from the hands of a cruel nurse, as a father reclaims his son from the hands of a severe and capricious schoolmaster, so the Lord reclaimed his son, his first-born Israel, from the hands of Pharaoh. But the king's haughty answer to the demand was: "Who is the Lord, that I should obey his voice to let Israel go?" Sign after sign was shown, wonder after wonder wrought, woe after woe inflicted, but the spirit of the proud king remained unbroken. At last, all lesser instruments having failed, the sword was put into the hands of the destroying angel, and he was sent forth to execute that foretold doom, which,—meant to strike at the very heart of the entire community of Egypt,—fell actually only upon the first-born in every family. The nation was taken as represented by these its first and best. In their simultaneous death on that terrible night, Egypt throughout all its borders was smitten. But the first-born of Israel was saved, and through them, as representatives of the whole body of the people, all Israel was saved; saved, yet not without blood, not without the sacrifice of the lamb, for every household had the sprinkling of its shed blood upon the lintel and door-post. It was to preserve and perpetuate the memory of this judgment and this mercy, this smiting and this shielding, this doom and this deliverance, that the Lord spake unto Moses, saying, "Sanctify unto me all the first-born, both of man and beast; it is mine: for on the day that I smote all the first-born in the land of Egypt, I hallowed unto me all the first-born in Israel; mine they shall be: I am the Lord. And it shall be, when thy son asketh thee in time to come, saying, What is this? that thou shalt say unto him, By strength of hand the Lord brought us out from Egypt, from the house of bondage: and it came to pass, when Pharaoh would hardly let us go, that the Lord slew all the first-born in the land of Egypt, both the first-born of man, and the first-born of beast: therefore I sacrifice to the Lord all that openeth the matrix, being males; but all the first-born of my children I redeem."[1] During the earlier and simpler patriarchal economy, the first-born in every family was also its priest. Had that rule been followed when the twelve tribes were organized into the Theocracy, the first-born invested with a double sacredness, as peculiarly the redeemed of the Lord, would have been consecrated to the office of the priesthood. Instead of this, the tribe of Levi was set apart, that it might supply all the priests required for the services of the sanctuary; and the first-born for whom they were thus substituted were redeemed or released from that service by the payment each, on the day of their presentation in the Temple, of a merely nominal gratuity; by that payment, the original right and title, as it were, of the first-born to the office of the priesthood being still preserved.

This rite, then, of the presentation of the first-

[1] Exod. xiii. 1; Numb. iii. 13; Exod. xiii. 14, 15.

born in the Temple, had a double character and office. It was a standing memorial or remembrancer of a past fact in the history of the Jewish people,—the deliverance of their forefathers from the bondage of Egypt, and especially of the shielding of their first-born from the stroke which fell on all the first-born of the Egyptians; but the deliverance from Egyptian bondage was itself a type and prophecy of another higher and wider deliverance, and especially of the manner in which that deliverance was to be wrought out.

In the light of this explanation, let us look yet once again at our Lord's presentation in the Temple as a first-born child, and see whether— as the eye of faith looks through the outward actions to that which the actions symbolize, looks through the outward form and discerns the spiritual significance—the whole scene does not become, as it were, transfigured before us. You mount the steps, and come up into this Temple at Jerusalem. It is neither a feast-day nor a Sabbath-day, nor is it the fixed hour for prayer. A few priests, or Levites, or other hangers-on of the Holy Place, are loitering in the outer courts.

A man and woman in Galilean dress, the woman bearing an infant in her arms, cross the court and go forward to where the priest is standing, whose duty it is to present whatever individual sacrifices or oblations may that day be offered. They tell the priest their errand, hand to him or to one of his attendants, the two young turtle-doves, and the five shekels of the Sanctuary. He, in his turn, goes through with his part of the prescribed ceremonial, and gives the child back again to his parents as a first-born child that had been duly devoted to the Lord. The father, the mother, the priest, whatever onlookers there are, all imagine, that nothing more has been done in all this than is so often done when first-born children are consecrated. But was it so? Who is this child that lies so passive on its mother's breast, and all unconscious of what is being done with him, is handled by the officiating priest? He is, as his birth had proclaimed him to be, one of the seed of Abraham, and yet he afterwards said of himself, "Before Abraham was, I am." He is, as the angel had proclaimed him to be, David's son and David's heir; but as he said afterwards of himself, the root as well as the branch of David : David's Lord as well as David's son. He is the first-born of Mary, but he is also the first-born of every creature, the beginning of the creation of God. He is the infant of a few weeks old, but also the Ancient of Days, whose goings forth were from of old, from everlasting. Here then at last is the Lord, the Jehovah, whom so many of the Jews were seeking, brought suddenly, almost, as one might say, unconsciously into his own Temple. Here is the Lamb of God, of old provided, now publicly designated and set apart,—of which the paschal one, the sight of whose blood warded off the stroke of the destroying angel, was but the imperfect type. Here is the one and only true High Priest over the house of God, consecrated to his office, of whose all-prevailing, everlasting, and unchangeable priesthood, the Aaronic priesthood, the priesthood of the first-born, was but the dim shadow. Here is the Son presented to the Father, within the Holy Place on earth, as he enters upon that life of service, suffering, sacrifice, the glorious issue of which was to be his entering not by the blood of bulls and goats, but by his own blood, into that Holy Place not made with hands, having obtained eternal redemption for us, there for ever to present himself before the Father, as the living head of the great community of the redeemed, the general assembly and church of the first-born which are written in heaven.

How little did that Jewish priest, who took the infant Saviour and held him up before the altar, imagine that a greater than Moses, one greater than the Temple, was in his arms! How little did he imagine as he inscribed the new name of Jesus in the roll of the first-born of Israel, that he was signing the death-warrant of the Mosaic economy now waxing old and ready to vanish away; that he was ushering in that better, brighter day, when neither of the Temple upon Mount Zion, nor of that upon Gerizim, it should be said that there only was the true worship of Jehovah celebrated; but when, taught by this very Jesus to know God as Our Father in Heaven, unfettered and redeemed humanity in every land should worship him who is a Spirit in spirit and in truth. Yet even so it was; Christ's first entrance into the Temple, his dedication there unto the Lord, was no such common ceremonial as we might fancy it to be. Simple in form, there lay in it a depth and sublimity of meaning. It was nothing else than the first formal earthly presentation to the Father of the incarnate Son of God, his first formal earthly dedication to that great work given him to do. And was it not meet when the Father and the Son were brought visibly together in this relationship, that the presence of the Holy Spirit should be manifested; that by that Spirit Simeon and Anna should be called in, and by that Spirit their lips should be made to speak the infant Saviour's praise; that so within the Temple, Father, Son, and Holy Spirit might all appear, dignifying with their presence our Lord's first entrance into the Holy Place; his consecration to his earthly mediatorial work?

Two fitter channels through which the Spirit's testimony might thus be given could scarcely have been chosen. Simeon and Anna both belonged to that limited number, who in the midst of all the crude and carnal conceptions of the Messiah prevalent among their countrymen, were waiting for Christ and longing for his coming, not so much for the temporal as for the spiritual benefits which his coming and kingdom were to convey. Both were well stricken in years, fit representatives of the closing age of Judaism; both were full of faith and hope, fit representatives of that new age whose earliest dawn they were among the first to notice and to welcome.

So ardent as his years ran on had Simeon's faith and hope become, that this one thing had he desired of the Lord, that before his eyes closed in death they might rest upon his Saviour. And he was heard as to that for which he had so longed. It was revealed to him that the desire of his heart should be granted, but how and when he knew not. That forenoon, however, a strong desire to go up into the Temple seizes him. He was not accustomed to go there at that hour, but he obeys that inward impulse, which perhaps he recognised as the work of the Divine Spirit, by whom the gracious revelation had been made to him. He enters the Temple courts; he notices a little family group approach; he sees an infant dedicated to the Lord. That infant, an inward voice proclaims to him is the Messiah he had been waiting for, the Consolation of Israel come at last in the flesh. Then comes into his heart a joy beyond all bounds. It kindles in his radiant looks; it beats in his swelling veins; the strength of youth is back again into his feeble limbs. He hastens up to Mary, takes from the wondering yet consenting mother's hands the consecrated babe, and clasping it to his beating bosom, with eyes uplifted to heaven, he says, "Lord, now lettest thou thy servant depart in peace, according to thy word; for mine eyes have seen thy salvation, which thou hast prepared before the face of all people; a light to lighten the Gentiles, and the glory of thy people Israel." Joseph and Mary stand lost in wonder. How has this stranger come to see aught uncommon in this child; how come to see in him the salvation of Israel? Have some stray tidings of his birth come into the holy city from the hill country of Judea, or has the wondrous tale the shepherds of Bethlehem "made known abroad," been repeated in this old man's hearing? What he says is in curious harmony with all the angel had announced to Mary and to the shepherds about the child, and yet there is a difference; for now, for the first time, is it distinctly declared that this child shall be a light to lighten the Gentiles; nay, his being such a light is placed even before his being the glory of Israel. Has Simeon had a separate revelation made to him from heaven, and is this an independent and fuller testimony borne to the Messiahship of Jesus?

Simeon sees the wonder that shines out in their astonished looks; and, the spirit of prophecy imparted — that spirit which had been mute in Israel since the days of Malachi, but which now, once more, lifts up its voice within the Temple — he goes on, after a gentle blessing bestowed upon both parents, to address himself particularly to Mary, furnishing in his words to her fresh material for wonder, while opening a new future to her eye. "Behold," he said to her, "this child of thine is set for the fall and rising again of many in Israel." He may have meant, in saying so, that the purpose and effect of the Lord's showing unto Israel would be the casting down of many in order to the raising of them up again; the casting of them down from their earlier, worldlier thoughts and expectations, in order to the lifting them to higher, worthier, more spiritual conceptions of his character and office. Or, perhaps it was to different and not to the same persons that he referred, the truth revealed being this: that while some were to rise, others were to fall; that the stone which to some was to be a foundation-stone elect and precious, was to others to be a stone of stumbling and rock of offence; that Jesus was to come for judgment into the world, that those who saw not might see, that those who saw might be made blind; his name to be the savour of life unto life to the one, the savour of death unto death to the other.

From all Mary had yet heard she might have imagined that her child would be welcomed by all Israel (so soon as the day for his revelation came) as its long-looked for deliverer; and that a career of unsuffering triumph would lie before him,—a career in whose honours and bliss she could scarcely help at times imagining that she should have a share. But now, for the first time, the indication is clearly given that all Israel was not to hail her child, and welcome him as its Messiah; that hostility was to spring up even within the ranks of the chosen people; that he was to be a "sign which should be spoken against," or rather, for such is the more literal rendering of the words, a butt or mark at which many shafts or javelins should be launched. Nor was Mary herself to escape. Among the many swords or darts levelled at his breast, one was to reach hers: "Yea, a sword shall pierce through thine own soul also." Strange that in the very centre of so broad and comprehensive a prophecy concerning Christ, such a minute and personal allusion to Mary should come in; a high honour put upon the mother of our Lord that her individual sorrows should be foretold in this way in connexion with the deeper sorrows of her Son; and a singular token of the tender sympathy of Him by whom it was prompted, that now when her heart was filling with strange, bright hopes; now, while her child was yet an infant; now, ere the evil days drew on, when she should have to see him become the object of reproach and persecution, and stand herself to look at him upon that cross of shame and agony on which they hung him up to die,—that now to temper her firstborn joy, to prepare and fortify her for the bitter trials in store for her, this prophecy should have been thus early spoken.

"That the thoughts of many hearts may be revealed." No such revealer of the thoughts of men's hearts has the world ever seen as Jesus Christ. His presence, his character, his ministry, brought out to light the hidden things of many a human spirit. He walked abroad applying upon all sides the infallible test which tried the temper of the soul: "If I had not come," he said, "they had not had sin, but now they have no cloak for their sin." In its uncloaked nakedness he made the sin be seen. "I know you," said he to the Jews, "that ye have not the love of God in you," and the reason that he gave for this was, that they had rejected him. Coming into contact with them all in turn, he revealed the hypocrisy of the Pharisees, the worldliness of the young ruler, the faith of the Syro-Phenician woman, the malice of the Sanhedrim, the weaknesses of Pilate, the treachery of Judas, the rashness of Peter, the tender care and sympathy of Mary. Throughout the whole of his earthly life the description given here by Simeon was continually being verified. That description itself throughout reveals its divine origin and character. It proves itself to have been no bold conjecture of human wisdom, but a revelation of the future made by God.

Simeon's prophetic portraiture of the intention and effect of the advent of the Redeemer had been scarcely completed when another testimony was added; that of the aged Anna, the daughter of Phanuel, who like her venerable compeer appears but this once in the sacred page, and then is hidden for ever from our eyes. It is not said that any special impulse drew her to the temple. It was her daily haunt. Instantly serving God day and night, her life was one of fastings and prayers. When it was also made known to her that the infant whom she met in the Temple was no other than the Christ of God, her song of praise was added to that of Simeon, but the words of it are lost. It would, we may be assured, be a suitable accompaniment, a fit response to his.

He, as may be believed, retired from the Temple to close his eyes in peace, but she was moved to go about and speak of the Lord whom she had found to all that looked for redemption in Jerusalem,—the first preacher of the gospel, the first female evangelist in the holy city.

In the briefest terms let one or two practical reflections be now suggested.

Simeon did not wish to die till he had seen the Lord his Saviour; as soon as he saw him he was ready and willing to depart. Till our spiritual eyes be opened to see Him who is the way, the truth, and the life, which of us is ready to meet our Maker, is prepared to behold his face in peace? But when once our eyes have seen and our hearts embraced him, which of us should fear to die? Simeon desired to depart. It was not that like Job he wished to die because life had become burdensome. His wish to depart was not the product of hours of bitter sorrow, but of a moment of exceeding joy. It was not that like Paul he desired to depart in order to be with Christ. It was the fulness of that gratitude which he felt for the great gift of God in allowing him to see Christ in the flesh; it was the depth of that satisfaction and delight which filled his heart as his arms enfolded Jesus, which, leaving nothing more, nothing higher that he could hope for in this world, drew forth, as by a natural impulse, the expression, "Lord, now lettest thou thy servant depart in peace, for mine eyes have seen thy salvation." Though nothing is said about his age in the evangelical narrative, we may believe that the length of years which he had already reached, making the thought of approaching departure from this world familiar, conspired, if not to beget, yet to give emphasis to this expression of his desire. But it may be well, even though we be not in his exact position, to put to ourselves the question whether any desire or any willingness we have ever had to die was the fruit of hours of earthly disappointments, or of moments of spiritual elation and joy.

Christ was set for the fall and rising again of many in Israel; he is set for the fall and rising again of many still. His gospel never leaves us as it finds us. It softens or it hardens, it kills or it makes alive. That stone which the Jewish builders rejected, is rejected by many builders still, and yet it is the headstone of the corner. Blessed is he who grounds thereon his humble yet undoubting trust. "But many among them," saith the prophet, "shall stumble and fall, and be broken" upon this stone. May our feet be shielded from such a fate!

The sufferings of Mary were linked with the sufferings of her Son. It was his being wounded that wounded her. It was the stroke which descended on him that sent the sword into her heart. The same kind of tie should bind every believer to Christ. He is so sensitive as to all that affects his people's welfare and happiness, that whatever hurts the least of these his little ones, touches the apple of his eye. And they in turn should be so sensitive as to all that affects his honour, his cause, his kingdom on the earth, that whatever damages or injures them should send a thrill of answering sorrow through their heart.

Finally, Christ is the great Revealer of the thoughts and intents of the heart. Are we proud, are we covetous, are we worldly, are we self-willed? Nothing will more bring out the sway and empire of these or any kindred passions over us, than the bringing closer home to us the holy character and unmitigable claims of Jesus Christ. Keep them at a distance, and the strong man armed keeps the palace of the soul, and all comparatively is at peace. Bring them near, force them home upon the conscience and the heart; then it is that the inward struggle begins, and in that struggle the spirit unconsciously revealeth its true condition before God.

IV.

THE VISIT OF THE MAGI.[1]

THREE striking incidents marked the birth and infancy of our Lord: *first*, the midnight appearance of the angelic host to the shepherds on the plains of Bethlehem, and their visit to the village in which the great birth had that night occurred; *second*, the presentation of Jesus as a first-born child in the Temple, and the testimony there given to him in the prophetic utterances of Simeon and Anna; and *third*, the visit of the wise men from the East, and the worship and offerings which they presented to the new-born child. Each of these had its special wonders; in each a supernatural attestation to the greatness of the event was given; and woven together, they form the wreath of heavenly glory hung by the divine hand around the infancy of the son of Mary.

[1] Matthew ii. 1-12.

It is impossible to determine the date of the visit of the wise men. It must have occurred not long after the birth, while Joseph and Mary still lingered in Bethlehem, and it is of little moment whether we place it before or after the presentation in the Temple at Jerusalem. The epithet by which Matthew describes to us these Eastern strangers is not so vague and indefinite as it seems in our translation. He calls them Magi from the East. The birthplace and natural home of the magian worship was in Persia. And there the Magi had a place and power such as the Chaldæans had in Babylon, the Hierophants in Egypt, the Druids in Gaul, and the Brahmins still have in India. They formed a tribe or caste, priestly in office, princely in rank. They were the depositaries of nearly all the knowledge or science existing in the country where they lived; they were the first professors and practisers of astrology, worshippers of the sun and the other heavenly bodies, from whose appearance and movements they drew their divination as to earthly events,—all illustrious births below, being indicated, as they deemed, by certain peculiar conjunctions of the stars above. Both as priests and diviners they had great power. They formed in fact the most influential section of the community. In political affairs their influence was predominant. The education of royalty was in their hands; they filled all the chief offices of state; they constituted the supreme counsel of the realm. As originally applied to this Median priest-caste, the term Magi was one of dignity and honour. Afterwards, when transferred to other countries, and employed to designate not that peculiar sacerdotal order, but all persons of whatever description who were professors of astrology and practisers of divination, as these astrologers and diviners sunk in character, and had recourse to all kinds of mean imposture, the name of magian or magician was turned into one of dishonour and reproach. There seems no reason, however, to doubt that it was in its earlier and honourable meaning that it is used in the Gospel narrative.

Remarkable passages, both from Roman and Jewish writers,[1] have been quoted which inform us that at the period of our Saviour's birth, there

---

[1] Suetonius, Tacitus, Josephus.

prevailed generally over the East, in regions remote from Palestine, a vague but strong belief that one born in Judea was to arise and rule the world. Popularly this expectation was confined to the appearance of some warrior chief who, by the might of his victorious arms, was to subdue the nations under him. But there were many then in every land, whose faith in their old hereditary religions had been undermined; who from those Jews now scattered everywhere abroad, had learned some of the chief elements of the pure Israelitish faith; and half embracing it, had risen to a desire and hope which took a higher ground, and who in this expected king that was to spring out of Judah, were ready to hail a spiritual guide and deliverer. Such, we believe, were the Magi of Matthew's narrative. Balaam, a man of their own or a kindred tribe, in their own or in a neighbouring country, had centuries before foretold that a star should come out of Jacob, and a sceptre rise out of Israel (Numb. xxiv. 17). This and other of those old Jewish prophecies which pointed to the same event may have in some form or other reached their ears, preparing them for the birth of one who in the first instance was to be the king of the Jews, but whose kingdom was to connect itself with other than mere earthly interests, to have intimate relationships with man's highest hopes and his eternal destiny. Sharing the general hope, but with that hope purified and exalted, let us believe that these Magi were earnestly, devoutly, waiting the coming of this new king of the Jews and of mankind. Their office and occupation led them to the nightly study of the starry heavens; but still as they gazed and speculated and divined, they felt that it was not from that glittering broad-spread page of wonders hung above their heads that any clear or satisfying information as to the divine character and purposes was to be derived. Much as they fancied they could glean from them as to man's earthly fortunes, what could the bright mute stars tell them of the eternal destinies of those unnumbered human spirits which beneath their light were, generation after generation, passing away into the world beyond the grave? How often may the deep sigh of disappointment have risen from the depths of these men's hearts, as to all their earnest interrogatories not a word of distinct response was given, and the heavens they gazed on kept the untold secret locked in their capacious bosom. But the sigh of the earnest seeker after truth, like the sigh of the lowly, penitent, and contrite heart, never rises to the throne of heaven in vain. Many errors may have mingled with those men's religious opinions, much superstition have been in their religious worship, but God met in mercy the truth-seeking spirit in the midst of its errors, and made its very superstition pave the way to faith.

One night, as those Magi stood watching their cloudless skies, their practised eye detected a new-come stranger among the stars. The appearance of new stars is no novelty to the astronomer. We have authentic records of stars of first magnitude, rivalling in their brilliance the brightest of our old familiar planets, shining out suddenly in places where no star had been seen before, and after a season vanishing away. Singular conjunctions of the planets have also been occasionally observed, some of which are known to have occurred about the time of the Redeemer's birth. It may possibly have been some such strange appearance in the heavens that attracted the eyes of the wise men. It is said, however, in the narrative, that the star went before them till it came and stood over where the young child was. Understanding this as implying an actual and visible movement of the star—that it went, lantern-like, before them on their way, and indicated in some way, as by a finger of pointing light, the very spot where they were to find the child—as no such function could be discharged by any of the ordinary inhabitants of the heavens, all about its appearance must be taken as supernatural, and we must regard it as some star-like meteor shining in our lower atmosphere. But be it what it might, however kindled, whatever curiosity its strange appearance might excite,—though the Magi, penetrated by the popular belief, might naturally enough have regarded it as an omen of the great expected birth,—the star could of itself tell nothing. However miraculous its appearance, if left without an interpreter, it was but a dumb witness after all. The conviction is almost forced upon us that, in addition to the external sign, there was some divine communication made to these Magi, informing them of the errand which the star was commissioned to discharge. But why the double indication of the birth,—the star without, the revelation made within? Why, but as an evidence and illustration of the care and gracious condescension of Him who not only to the spiritual communication added the external sign, to be a help to the weak, infant, staggering faith, but who, in the very shaping of that outward sign, was pleased to accommodate himself to these men's earthly calling; and while to Mary and to the shepherds—Jews living in a land where stories of angelic manifestations were current—angels were sent to make announcement of the Redeemer's birth, to those astrologers of the East he sends a star, meeting them in their own familiar walks, showing itself among the divinities of their erring worship, gently to lead them into His presence to whom the world's true worship was to be given.

But when this star appeared, and after they understood what its presence betokened, was it a spontaneous impulse on their part to go and do homage to the new-born King, or did He who revealed the birth enjoin the journey? Whatever the prompting—human or divine—on which they acted, it does not appear that in the first instance anything beyond the general information was communicated, that somewhere in Judea the birth had taken place. The star, it would appear, did not go before them all the way, for in that case they would not have needed to institute any further inquiry. Its first office discharged, the star disappeared, leaving them to have recourse to such common sources of information as lay open to them. It was at Jerusalem, in the capital of the country over which this new-born King was to reign; it was there, if anywhere, the needed intelligence was to be obtained. To Jerusalem, therefore, they repair. Entering the holy city, they put eagerly and expectantly the question, "Where is he that is born King of the Jews? for we have seen his star in the east, and are come to worship him."

The question takes the startled city by surprise. No one here has seen the star, no one here has heard about this king. The tidings of the arrival of those distinguished strangers, and of the question which they asked, are carried quickly to the palace, and circulate rapidly through the city. Herod is troubled. The usurper trembles on his throne. Has a new claimant, with better title to that throne, indeed been born? How comes it, if it be so, that he has never heard of such a birth? Has treachery been already busy at its work; have they been concealing from him this event? Have the enemies of himself and of his family been cloaking thus their projects, waiting only for the fit time to strike the blow, and hurl him from his seat? The blood he had already shed to reach that height begins to cry for vengeance, and spectres of the slaughtered dead shake their terrors in his face. Herod's trouble at the tidings we well can understand, but why was it that all Jerusalem was troubled along with him? Was it the simple fear of change, the terror of another revolution; the knowledge of Herod's jealous temper and bloodthirsty disposition; the alarm lest his vindictive spirit might prompt to some new deed of cruelty, in order to cut off this rival? If so, how low beneath the yoke of tyranny must the spirit of those citizens of Jerusalem have sunk; how completely, for the time, must the selfish have absorbed the patriotic sentiment in their breasts!

But whatever alarm he felt, whatever dark purposes were brooding in his heart, Herod at first concealed them. He must know more about this affair, get some information before he acts. He calls together the chief priests and the scribes, and at no loss, apparently, to identify the King of the Jews that the Magi asked about, with the Christ the Messiah of ancient prophecy, he demands of them where Christ should be born. As little at a loss, they lay their hand at once upon the prophecy of Micah, which pointed to Bethlehem as the birthplace. Furnished with this information, the king invites the Magi to a private interview, conveys to them the information he had himself received, and concealing his sinister designs, sends them off to Bethlehem to search diligently for the child, and when they had found him, to bring him word again, that he too, as he falsely said, might go and worship him.

Let us pause a moment here to reflect upon the impression which this visit to Jerusalem, and the state of things discovered there, was fitted to make upon these eastern visitors. It must surely have surprised them to come among the very people over whom this new-born King was to rule, to enter the capital of their country, the city of the chief priests and scribes by whom, if by any, an event so signal should have been known, and to find there no notice, no knowledge of the birth; to find instead, that they, coming from a strange land, professors of another faith, are the first to tell these Jews of the advent of their own king. It must have done more than surprise them; they too, in their turn, must have been troubled and perplexed, to see how the announcement, when it was made, was received; to see such jealousy, such alarm; and, at the last, so great incredulity or indifference, that near as Bethlehem was, and interesting as was the object of their visit to it, there were none among those inhabitants of Jerusalem who cared to accompany them. Was there nothing here to awaken doubt, for such faith as theirs to stagger at? Might they not have been deceived? Perhaps it was a delusion they had listened to; a deceitful appearance they had seen in their own land. Had these Magi been men of a weak faith or an infirm purpose, they might, instead of going on to Bethlehem, have gone forth despondingly and distrustfully from Jerusalem, and taken their way back to their own homes. But strange and perplexing as all this is, it neither shakes their faith nor affects their conduct. They had good reason to believe that the communication at first made to them came to them from God, and once satisfied of this, no conduct on the part of others, however unaccountable or inconsistent, moves them away from the beginning of their confidence. Though all the dwellers in Jerusalem be troubled at tidings which should have been to them tidings of great joy; though not a Jew be ready to join them, or to bid them God-speed ere they leave the city's gate, to Bethlehem they go.

But a new perplexity arises. Somewhere in that village the birth has taken place, but who shall tell them where? If the inhabitants of the capital knew and cared so little about the matter, what help will they get from the villagers at Bethlehem? They may require to search diligently, as Herod bade them, and yet, after all, the search may be vain. Just then, in the midst of their perplexity, the star which they had seen in the east once more shone out above their heads, to go before them till it stood over where the young child lay. No wonder that when they saw that star, they rejoiced with an exceeding great joy. It dispelled all doubt, it relieved from all perplexity. When first they saw it in the east, it wore the face of a stranger among old friends; now it wears the face of an old friend among strangers, and they hail it as we hail a friend we thought was lost, but who comes to us at the very time we need him most.

Let us note the contrast, as to the mode and measure of divine guidance given, between the Magi from the East and the shepherds of Bethlehem and the Chief Priests and Scribes of Jerusalem. The shepherds were as sincere, perhaps more devout than the wise men; understanding better who and what the Messiah was to be, and longing more ardently for his coming; but they were uneducated men, men at least whose position and occupation prevented them from instituting independent inquiries of their own. They were left to find out nothing; to them a full revelation was at once given. Such minute information was furnished as to the time and place and circumstances of the birth, that they were enabled, with little or no inquiry, to proceed directly to the place where the young child lay. The Magi, on the other hand, were men of intelligence, education, wealth. They had the leisure, and they possessed all the means for prosecuting an independent research. To them no such full and minute directory of conduct was supplied. What they could not learn otherwise than by a divine revelation, was in that way communicated, but what they could learn by the use of ordinary means, they were left in that way to find out. They repair to, and they exhaust all the common sources of knowledge which lie open to them. They go to Jerusalem as to the likeliest place; they get there the information as to the place of the Lord's birth; they act upon the information thus obtained up to the furthest limit to which it can carry them. They tarry not in the unbelieving city, as many might have done, till further light was given them. They turn not the incredulity of others into a ground of doubt, nor the incompleteness of the intelligence afforded into a ground of discouragement and delay. They know now that somewhere in Bethlehem the object of their search is to be found, and if they fail in finding him, it will be in Bethlehem that the failure shall take place. Nor is it till they are on their way to that village, that the star of heavenly guidance once more appears; but then it does appear, and sends gladness into their hearts.

And have we not all, as followers of the Crucified, another and higher journey to perform; a journey not to the place of the Saviour's earthly birth, but that of his heavenly dwelling? And if, on that journey, we act as those men did, God will deal with us as he dealt with them. The path before us may be often hidden in obscurity; our lights may go out by the way; we may know as little of what the next stage is to reveal, as those men knew at Jerusalem what awaited them in their path to Bethlehem; but if, like them, we hold on our course, unmoved by the example of others; if we follow the light given us to the farthest point to which that light can carry us, then on us too, when lights all fail, and we seem about to be left in utter darkness, some star of heavenly guidance will arise, at sight of which we shall rejoice with an exceeding joy. Unto those that are thus upright, there shall arise light in the darkness; and to him that ordereth thus his conversation aright, God shall show his salvation.

But look, now, at the Chief Priests and Scribes of the holy city, into whose hands the ancient oracles of God had been specially committed. They could tell at once, from the prophecies of Micah, the place of the Messiah's birth; and they could almost as readily and as accurately from the prophecies of Daniel have known the time of his advent. To them, as furnished already with sufficient means of information, no supernatural communication of any kind is made; to them no angel comes, no star appears, no sign is given.

Had they but used aright the means already in their hands, they should have been waiting for the coming of the Lord, with ears all open to catch the first faint rumours which must have reached Jerusalem from a village not more than six miles off, of what the shepherds saw and heard; they should have been out to Bethlehem before these Magi came, ready to welcome those visitors from a far country, and to conduct them into the presence of their new-born King. But they neglected, they abused the privileges they possessed; and now, as the proper fruit of their own doings, not only is the same kind of information supplied to others denied to them, but the very way in which they are first informed works disastrously, and excites hostile prejudices in their breast. "Where is he," these strangers say to them, "who is born King of the Jews?" Has an event like this occurred—occurred within a few miles of the metropolis,—and they, the heads and rulers of the Jewish people, not know of it! For their first knowledge of it must they be indebted to these foreigners, men ignorant of Judea, unread in their sacred books! A star, forsooth, these men said had appeared to them in the East; was it to be believed that for them in their land of heathen darkness and superstition such a fresh light should be kindled in the heavens, whilst to God's own appointed priesthood, no discovery of any kind had been made? We discern thus in its very earliest stage, that antipathy to the son of Mary which, beginning in incredulity, and fostered by pride, grew into malignant hatred, and issued in the nailing of Jesus to the cross. And even in the first stage of the course they followed, they appear before us, reaping the fruit of their former doings, and sowing the seeds of their after crimes; for it is thus that the husbandry of wickedness goes on, —the seed-time and the harvest, the sowing and the reaping going on together. What a singular spectacle does the proud and jealous priesthood of Judea thus present, learned in the letter of their own Scriptures, but wholly ignorant of their spirit; pointing the way to others, not taking a single step in it themselves; types of the nation they belonged to, of the function which the Jews have so largely since discharged,—the openers of the door to Gentile inquirers, the closers of that door upon themselves.

We rejoin now the Magi at Bethlehem. They enter the indicated house, and stand before a mother and her child: a mother of very humble appearance; a child clad in simplest attire. Can this, they think, as they look around, be the roof beneath which infant royalty lies cradled! Can that be the child they have come so far to see and worship! Had they known all about that infant which we now know; had they known that an angelic choir had already sung his birth, lading the midnight breezes with a richer freight of melody than they had ever wafted through the skies; had they known that in that little hand which lay folded there in feebleness, in the gentle breath which was heaving that infant bosom, the power of omnipotence lay slumbering,—that at the touch of the one, the blind eye was to open and the tied tongue to be unloosed,—that at the bidding of the other, the wildest elements of nature in their stormiest march were to stand still, devils were to be driven out from their usurped abodes, and the dead to come forth from the sepulchre; had they known that at the death of this Son of Mary, the sun was to be darkened, the rocks were to be rent, and the graves to give up their old inhabitants,—that he himself was to burst the barriers of the tomb, and rise in triumph, attended by angel escort, to take his place at the right hand of the Majesty in the heavens,—we should not have wondered at the ready homage which they rendered to him. But they knew nothing of all this. What they did know we cannot tell. We only know that instantly, in absence of all outward warrant for the act, in spite of the most unpromising appearances, they bow the knee before that undistinguished infant, lower than it bent before the haughty Herod at Jerusalem; bow in adoration such as they never rendered to any earthly sovereign. And that act of worship over, they open their treasures and present to him their gifts: the gold, the frankincense, and the myrrh, the rarest products of the East; an offering such as any monarch might have had presented to him by the ambassadors from any foreign prince. When we take the whole course of these men's conduct into account; when we remember that they had none of the advantages of a Jewish birth or education, of an early acquaintance with the Jewish Scriptures; when we think of their starting on their long and perilous journey with no other object than the making of this single obeisance to the infant Redeemer of mankind; when we look at them standing unmoved, amid all the discouragements of the Jewish metropolis; when we attend them on their solitary way to Bethlehem; when we stand by their side, as beneath that lowly roof they silently worship, and spread out their costly gifts,—we cannot but regard their faith as in many of its features unparalleled in the gospel narrative; we cannot but place them in the front rank of that goodly company in whose acts the power and the triumph of a simple faith shine forth.

That single act of homage rendered, they return to their own country, and we hear of them no more. They come like spirits casting no shadow before them; and like spirits they depart, passing away into that obscurity from which they had emerged. But our affection follows them to their native land,—would fain penetrate the secret of their after lives and deaths. Did these men see, and hear, and know no more of Jesus? Were they living, when—after thirty years of profoundest silence, not a rumour of his name going anywhere abroad—tidings came at last of the words he spake, the deeds he did, the death he died? We would fain believe, so far, the quaint old legend of the middle ages, that connects itself with the fancied resting-place of their relics in the Cathedral of Cologne; we would fain believe that they lived to converse with one of the apostles of the Lord, and to receive Christian baptism at his hands. However it may have been, we can scarce believe that He whose star carried them from their eastern homes to Bethlehem, and whose Spirit prompted the worship they then rendered, left them to die in heathen ignorance and unbelief. Let us cherish rather the belief that they who bowed so reverently before the earthly cradle, are now worshipping with a profounder reverence before the heavenly throne.

But what special significance has this incident

in the early life of our Redeemer? Why were these men summoned from their distant homes to come so far, to pay that single act of homage to the infant Jesus, and then retire for ever from our sight? Why, but that even with the first weak beginnings of the Saviour's earthly life, there might be a foretokening of the wide embrace of that kingdom he came to establish; a first fulfilling of those ancient prophecies which had foretold that the Gentiles should come to this light, and kings to the brightness of its rising; that all they from Sheba should come, bringing gold and incense. These eastern Magi were the earliest ambassadors from heathen lands, the first shadowy precursors of that great company to be gathered in from the east, and from the west, and from the north, and from the south, to sit down with Abraham in the kingdom of the just. In these persons, and in their act, the Gentile world, of which they formed a part, gave an early welcome to the Redeemer, and hastened to lay its tribute at his feet. They were in fact, —and this should bind them the closer to our hearts,—they were our representatives at Bethlehem, making for us Gentiles the first expression of our faith, the first offer of our allegiance. Let us rightly follow up what they did in our name. First, they worshipped, and then they gave the best and richest things they had. The gold, the frankincense, the myrrh, had been of little worth had the worship of the heart not gone before and sanctified the gift. But the gift most appropriately followed the worship. First, then, let us give ourselves to the Lord, our heart the first oblation that we proffer; for the heart once given, the hand will neither be empty nor idle, nor will it grudge the richest thing that it can hold, nor the best service it can render.

V.

THE MASSACRE OF THE INNOCENTS, AND THE FLIGHT INTO EGYPT.[1]

THERE are three Herods who appear prominently in the pages of the New Testament. *First*, Herod the Great, the son of a crafty and wealthy Idumean or Edomite, who, during the reign of the last of the Asmonean princes, attained to great political influence in Judea, securing for his eldest son Phasælus the governorship of Jerusalem; and for Herod, his younger son, the chief command in Galilee. Phasælus was cut off in one of those political commotions which the raising of a foreign family to such an elevated position engendered, but Herod escaped all the perils to which he was thus exposed, distinguished himself by his address and bravery, showed great political foresight in allying himself closely with

[1] Matthew ii. 13-23.

the power which he saw was to prevail in Judea as over all other lands, sought and won the personal friendship of Cassius and of Mark Antony, and, mainly by the influence of the latter, was proclaimed King of the Jews.

Second, Herod Antipas, a son of this first Herod, who, in that division of his father's kingdom which took place at his decease, became Tetrarch of Galilee and Perea. This was the Herod who so often appears in the narrative of our Lord's ministry, who at first heard John the Baptist gladly, but who afterwards gave the order for his execution; who happened to be in Jerusalem at the time of Christ's trial and condemnation, and who was brought then into such singular contact with Jesus.

Third, Herod Agrippa, a grandson of the first Herod, though not a son of Herod Antipas, who was invested by the Romans with the royal dignity, and ruled over all the country which had been subject to his grandfather. This was the Herod who appears in the history of the Acts of the Apostles; who stretched forth his hands to vex certain of the church; who killed James, the brother of John, with the sword; who, because he saw that it pleased the Jews, proceeded to take Peter also; and whose awful death so soon afterwards at Cæsarea, St. Luke has so impressively recorded.

Our Saviour, we know, was born near the end of the long reign of the first of these Herods, and the latest and most successful investigations of the chronology of Christ's life have taught us to believe that it was in the last year of Herod's reign, and close upon that monarch's last illness and death, that the birth at Bethlehem took place. The terrible malady which made his closing scene not less awful than that of his grandson Agrippa, had already begun its work, and given forewarning of the fatal issue. He was in a moody, suspicious, vengeful state of feeling. His reign had long been outwardly brilliant and prosperous. He had defeated all the schemes of his political opponents. With a firm and cruel hand he had kept down all attempts at intestine revolt. By a large remission of taxation, by extraordinary liberality in times of famine, by lavish expenditure on public works, the erection of new cities and the rebuilding of the Temple at Jerusalem, he had sought to dazzle the public eye and win the public favour. But nothing could quench the Jewish suspicion of him as an Edomite. This suspicion fed upon his attempts to introduce and encourage heathen games and pastimes, and grew intensely bitter as it watched with what unrelenting hate he persecuted and cut off all the members of that Maccabean family whose throne he had usurped, around whom Jewish gratitude and hope still fondly clung. This ill-concealed enmity preyed upon the proud, dark spirit of Herod. It taught him to see his deadliest foes in the bosom of his own family. Passionately attached to her, he had married the beautiful but ill-fated Mariamne, the daughter of Alexander, one of the Asmonean princes. She inherited the pride and ambition of her family; bitterly resenting, as well she might, the secret order which she discovered Herod had issued, that she should be cut off if he failed to secure the throne for himself in the embassage to Rome which he undertook after the defeat of Mark Antony, his first patron. Her resentment of this order had the worst interpretation put upon it, and in the transport of a jealousy in which both personal and political elements were combined, Herod ordered her to be beheaded. Then followed those transports of remorse, which, for a time, bereft the frantic prince of reason. Mariamne gone, the father's jealousy was directed to his two sons by her, in whose veins the hated Asmonean blood was flowing. He sent for Antipater, his son by the wife he had divorced in order to marry Mariamne, and set him up as their rival and his successor. But the popular favour clung to Alexander and Aristobulus, the sons of the murdered Mariamne. Herod's court and family became a constant gloomy scene of dissension and distrust. Charges of treasonable designs on the part of Alexander and Aristobulus against his person and government were secretly poured into the ear of Herod. Men of inferior rank, supposed to be implicated, were seized, tortured, and executed, till at last, by their father's own order, the two young princes, then in the flower of their early manhood, were strangled. Antipater had been the chief instrument in urging Herod on to this inhuman deed, and now in that very son whom he had done so much for, he found the last worst object of his jealous wrath. Antipater was proved to have conspired to poison his old, doting, diseased, and dying father. He was summoned to Jerusalem. Herod raised himself from his bed of suffering, and gave the order for his execution. His own death drew on. It maddened him to think that there would be none to mourn for him; that at his death there would be a general jubilee. The fiendish idea seized him, that if there were none who voluntarily would weep for him, there should at least be plenty of tears shed at his death; and so his last command—a command happily not executed—was, that the heads of all the chief families in Judea should be assembled in the Hippodrome, and that as soon as it was known that he had drawn his last breath, they should be mercilessly slaughtered; and thus, his body consumed by inward ulcers, and his spirit with tormenting passions, Herod died.

I have recited thus much of this king's history, that you may see in what harmony with his other doings was his massacre of the innocents at Bethlehem. When he heard of the coming of the Magi, and of the birth of this new King of the Jews, the sceptre was already dropping from his aged and trembling hands.[1] But as the dying hand of avarice clutches its gold the firmer as it feels the hour draw on when it must give it up, so did the dying hand of ambition clutch the sceptre, and he determined that if he could hold it no longer, he would at least try to cut off all who might claim to wield it at his death. A lifetime's practice had made him a proficient in craft. He inquired privily of the wise men as to the time at which the star appeared. Had he even then, when he made this inquiry, matured his bloody project; and did he wish by knowing the precise time of the star's appearance to assure himself of the exact age of the child he intended to destroy; or was the inquiry made for the purpose of ascertaining whether any like star had been seen anywhere in Judea, seeking thus to confirm or invalidate what the wise men said? This only we can say, that if it were but a few days after

---

[1] He was seventy years old when he died.

the birth of Jesus that the Magi visited Jerusalem, and if the order that Herod afterwards issued to his executioners was founded on the information given him as to the time of the star's appearance, then the first appearance of the star must have been coincident, not with the birth of Jesus, but with the annunciation of that birth to Mary. Herod may have fancied from what he learned from the Magi that the child must now be about a year old, and, giving a broad margin that no chance of escape might be given, his order ran that all under two years of age should be destroyed.

Perhaps, however, Herod's only object in his first private interview with the Magi was to extract from them all the information he could, with no precise or definite purpose as to how he should act upon the information so obtained. When he told them to go and search diligently for the child, and when they had found him, to come and bring him word, it was not with any purpose on his part to go and worship him — in saying that he meant to do so, we may well believe him to have been playing the hypocrite, — but neither may it have been with an already fixed resolution to act as he afterwards did. But the wise men did not return; he ascertained that they had been in Bethlehem, that they had left that place, that without coming to see him and report as to the result of their search, they were already beyond his reach on their way back to their distant home. The birth was by this very circumstance made all the surer in his eyes, and to his natural alarm at such a birth, there was now added bitter chagrin at being mocked in this way by these strangers. Had they seen through the mask which he imagined he had fashioned so artfully and worn so well? Nothing galls the crafty more than when their craft is discovered, and the discovery is turned against themselves. Angry with the men who had treated him thus, Herod is angry, too, with himself for having given them the opportunity to outwit him. Why had he not sent some of his own trusty servants with them to Bethlehem? Why had he been so foolish as to trust these foreigners? Irritated at them, irritated at himself, determined that this child shall not escape, he sends his bandits out upon their bloody errand.

That errand was to be quickly and stealthily executed. In so small village as Bethlehem, and in the thinly scattered population which lay around it, there could be but a few male infants under two years old. It is but one of the dreams of the middle-age imagination which has swelled the numbers of the slaughtered to thousands; one or two dozens would be nearer to the mark. A few practised hands such as Herod could easily secure would have little difficulty in finishing their work in the course of one forenoon. It was spring-time of the year,[1] the parents were busy in the fields; the unprotected homes lay open. Before any concerted resistance could be offered, half the children might be slain. Every precaution, we may believe, was taken by Herod, that it should not be known at whose instance the deed was done. He was too wily a politician to make any such public manifestation of his vindictive alarm, as his sending forth a company of executioners, clothed visibly with the royal authority would have made. But secretly, promptly, vigorously

---

[1] It has been accurately ascertained that Herod must have died between the 13th March and the 4th April 750 A.U.C.

as his measures were taken, they came too late. When told that not a child of the specified age had been permitted to escape, he may have secretly congratulated himself on that peril to his government being thus summarily set aside. But an eye more vigilant than his was watching over the safety of the infant Jesus. In a dream of the night the angel of the Lord had appeared to Joseph; told him of the impending peril, and specially directed him as to the manner of escape. Without an hour's delay the warning given was acted on. The journey from Bethlehem to the nearest part of Egypt was soon performed, and secured from the stroke of Herod's bandits, and placed beyond the after reach of Herod's wrath, the child was safe. The flight was hasty, and the sojourn in Egypt was but short.[1] The way for the return was open, and in fulfilment of his promise the angel came to Joseph to tell him that they were dead who sought the young child's life. Struck by all the circumstances

---

[1] Accepting either the close of the year 749 A.U.C. or the beginning of 750 A.U.C. as the most probable date of the birth of Christ, and assuming that the visit of the Magi succeeded the presentation in the Temple, the stay in Egypt could have been but short.

which had accompanied the birth there, Joseph and Mary had perhaps resolved to take up their residence in Bethlehem. But on entering Judea they heard that though Herod was dead, his son Archelaus ruled in his stead; a prince who early proved that the spirit of his father had descended on him, one of the first acts of his reign being the slaughter of three thousand of his countrymen in Jerusalem. The apprehensions of Joseph were verified by the angel once more appearing to him in a dream, and directing him to pass on through Judea, and take up his abode again in Nazareth, a hamlet in the province of Galilee.

In the narrative of this passage of our Lord's infant life as given by St. Matthew, two things strike us.

1. The prominent part assigned to, and assumed by Joseph as the earthly guardian of the child; the frequency, the minuteness, and the manner in which these divine intimations were made to him on which he acted. In every instance it was in a dream of the night that the heavenly warning came. Nor was the warning in any instance vague, but remarkably definite and satisfactory.

He was told at first not simply that danger was at hand; he was told specifically what that danger was: "Herod will seek the young child to destroy him." He was told not simply to escape from Bethlehem, but to flee into Egypt; of Herod's death he got timely information, and while hesitating as to what he should do on his return into Judea, he had his doubts removed, and his fears allayed by another divine direction. Are we wrong in interpreting the heavenly messenger's manner of acting towards the foster-parent of our Saviour as indicative of a very watchful and tender solicitude on Joseph's part for the safety of that strange child to whom he was united by so strange a tie? He appears as the heaven-appointed, heaven-instructed sentinel, set to watch over the infant days of the Son of the Highest, chosen for this office, and aided in its discharge, not without such regard to his personal qualifications as is ordinarily shown under the divine government in the selection of fit agents for each part of the earthly work. We are led thus to think of him as taking an almost more than paternal interest in the babe committed to his care, thinking about him so much and so anxiously by day that his dreams by night are of him, and that it is in these dreams the angel comes to give the needed guidance, and to seal, as it were, by the divine approval the watchful care by which the dreams had been begotten. And we are the more disposed to think thus favourably of Joseph as we reflect upon the peculiar relationship in which he stood to Jesus, and remember that this is the only glimpse we get of the manner in which the duties of that relationship were discharged. In the record of our Lord's ministry he never appears. The conclusion seems natural that he had died before that ministry began. It is only in his connexion with the birth and infancy and childhood of Jesus that any sight of Joseph is obtained, and it pleases us to think that he who was honoured to be the guardian of that sacred life in the first great peril to which it was exposed, was one not unworthy of the trust, but who lovingly, faithfully, tenderly executed it.

2. In reading this portion of the Gospel of St. Matthew, we are struck with the frequent references to the history and prophecies of the Old

Testament. Such references are peculiar to St. Matthew, and they are due to the character of those to whom his Gospel was especially addressed, and to the object he had especially in view. His Gospel was written for converted Jews, and his great aim was to present to such Jesus Christ as the Messiah promised to their fathers. Continually, therefore, throughout his narrative, as almost nowhere in the narratives of the other Evangelists, he quotes from the Old Testament Scriptures with the view of showing how accurately and completely they were fulfilled in the life and death of Jesus of Nazareth. The very formula, "that it might be fulfilled," is peculiar to the first Gospel. The method thus followed by St. Matthew was admirably fitted to soothe the prejudices of Jewish converts, and establish them in a true faith in Christ. Thus it is that in the passage now before us, he attempts to obviate objections that might naturally arise in Jewish minds, on their being told of such events—to them so untoward and unlooked-for—in the life of the infant Messiah as his being forced to find a temporary retreat in the land of Egypt, the slaughter of so many infants on his account, and the fixing of his abode in a remote hamlet of Galilee. Nothing could be more calculated to allay any prejudice created by the recital of such incidents than to point to parallel or analogous ones in the history of ancient Israel. The three citations of this kind which St. Matthew makes differ somewhat in their character. Of only one of them is it certain that there was a literal fulfilment of a prophecy uttered with immediate and direct reference to Christ. He came and dwelt, it is said, in Nazareth, "that it might be fulfilled which was spoken by the prophets, He shall be called a Nazarene." Yet it is singular that this prophecy, which was obviously one spoken directly of the Messiah, is nowhere to be found in the Old Testament Scriptures as they now are in our hands. But this hinders not our belief that by some one or other of the ancient prophecies the words that St. Matthew quotes had been spoken. As Jude recites and verifies a prophecy of Enoch of which otherwise we should have been ignorant, as St. Paul reports a saying of our Lord which otherwise should not have been preserved, so St.

Matthew here records a prophecy which but for his citation of it would have perished.

It is different, however, with the other two citations from ancient prophecy. These we can readily lay our hands upon, and in doing so become convinced that St. Matthew did not and could not mean to assert that in the events which he related they had directly and literally been verified. His object was rather to declare—and that was sufficient—that the incidents to which those old prophecies did in the first instance refer, were not only kindred in character, but were typical or symbolically prophetic of those which he was describing in the life of Jesus. He quotes thus a part of that verse in the 11th chapter of Hosea which runs thus: " When Israel was a child, then I loved him, and called my son out of Egypt." If that ancient Israel of which the Lord had said, 'He is my son,' 'He is my first-born,' while yet he was as it were but an infant, was carried down into and thereafter brought safe out of Egypt, was it a strange thing that He who was Jehovah's own and only Son, the first-born among many brethren, of whom and of whose Church that Israel was a type, should in his infancy have passed through a like ordeal of persecution and of deliverance? The point of the fulfilment of the prophecy here alleged does not lie in Hosea's having Christ actually and personally in his eye when he penned the words quoted by St. Matthew, but in the fact related by Hosea having a typical reference to a like fact in that after history which stands shadowed forth throughout in the outward history of ancient Israel.

It is in the same way that we are to understand the quotation from the 31st chapter of the prophecies of Jeremiah. It is in direct connexion with his statement of the fact that Herod sent forth and slew all the children that were in Bethlehem, from two years old and under, that St. Matthew says, "Then was fulfilled that which was spoken by Jeremy the prophet." "But Matthew," says Calvin, "does not mean that the prophet had predicted what Herod should do, but that at the advent of Christ that mourning was renewed which many ages before the women of Benjamin had made." Primarily the words of the prophet referred to the carrying away of a large portion of the tribes of Benjamin and Judah captives to Babylon. In describing the bitter grief with which the heart of the country was then smitten, Jeremiah, by a figure as bold as it is picturesque and impressive, summons the long-buried Rachel, the mother of Benjamin, from her grave, representing her as roused from the sleep of ages to bewail the captivity of her children. But Rachel's grave lay near to Bethlehem, and now another bitter woe had come upon the land in the murder of those innocents in that village, and what more natural than that St. Matthew should revive, re-appropriate, and re-apply that image of Jeremiah, representing Rachel as anew issuing from her tomb to weep over these her slaughtered children.

But there was something more here than a mere apposite application to a scene of recent sorrow of a poetical image that originally referred to the grief caused by the captivity. That very grief which filled the land of Judah may have been intended to prefigure the lamentation that now filled Bethlehem and all its borders. Rachel rising from her tomb, and filling the air then with her lamentations, may have been meant to stand as a type or representative of these mothers of Bethlehem, all torn in heart by the snatching of their little ones from their struggling arms, and the killing of them before their eyes. If it be so, then that passage in Jeremiah speaks of something more than of the mere suffering inflicted and the sorrow it produced. The weeping Rachel is not suffered to weep on, to weep out her grief. There are words of comfort for her in her tears. There is a message from the Lord to her that speaks in no ambiguous terms of the after-destiny, the future restoration of those children so rudely torn from their maternal embrace. For what are the words which immediately follow those which St. Matthew has quoted :—" Thus saith the Lord, Refrain thy voice from weeping, and thine eyes from tears : for thy work shall be rewarded, saith the Lord ; and they shall come again from the land of the enemy. And there is hope in thine end, saith the Lord, that thy children shall come again to their own border." If we have any right to apply this part of the prophecy to this incident of the evangelic history, then may we take the words that I have now quoted as carrying with them the assurance that those children who perished under the stroke of Herod's hirelings died not spiritually; that they shall come again from the land of the last enemy, come again with Him whose birth was so mysteriously connected with their death. We know that those infants, whose ghastly remains the weeping mothers gathered up to lay in their untimely graves, shall rise again in the resurrection at the last day. To them that resurrection, itself a fruit of the Saviour's advent, must come as a boon, a benefit, not as a bane or curse. Let it be what it may to others, who have had full opportunity to receive or reject the Saviour, to them it can be nothing else than a resurrection into everlasting life. To believe otherwise of them, and of all who die in infancy, would be to believe that those who are called away from this world while yet the first dew-drops of life are on them, are placed thereby in a worse condition than that in which it is the declared purpose of the gospel to place all mankind. It is a belief which we cannot adopt. Our assurance is clear, and, as we think, well grounded —though these grounds we cannot now pause to unfold—that all who die in infancy are saved. Distinguished among them all, let us believe this of those slaughtered babes of Bethlehem. Their fate was singularly wrapped up with that of the infant Saviour. The stroke that fell on them was meant for him; the sword of persecution which swept so mercilessly in many an after age through the ranks of Christ's little ones was first reddened in their blood. The earliest victims to hatred of the Nazarene—if not consciously and willingly, yet actually dying for him—let us count them as the first martyrs for Jesus, and let us believe that in them the truth of the martyr's motto was first made good, "Near to the sword, near to God." "O blessed infants!" exclaims Augustine; "He who at his birth had angels to proclaim him, the heavens to testify, and Magi to worship him, could surely have prevented that these should have died for him, had he not known that they died not in that death, but rather lived in higher bliss."

VI.

THE THIRTY YEARS AT NAZARETH—CHRIST AMONG THE DOCTORS.[1]

Up among the hills of Galilee, in a basin surrounded by swelling eminences, which shut it in on every side, lies the little village of Nazareth. Its name does not occur in Old Testament history. Josephus never mentions it, though he speaks of places lying all round it. Its inhabitants were not worse than their neighbours, nor exposed on account of their character to any particular contempt, yet Nathanael, himself a Galilean, could say, Can there any good thing come out of Nazareth? so small and insignificant was the place. It was here, as in a fit retreat, that the childhood, youth, and early manhood of our Lord passed quietly and unnoticed away. Those thirty years of the life of the Son of God

[1] Luke ii. 40-52.

upon this earth, how deeply hidden from us do they lie! how profound the silence regarding them which the sacred writers preserve! a silence all the more remarkable when we consider how natural and strong is our desire to know something, to be told something of the earlier days of any one who, at some after period of his life, has risen to distinction. But all that here is told us of the first twelve years of our Saviour's life is that the child grew, waxed strong in spirit, was filled with wisdom, and that the grace of God was upon him. Had any of these wonders which attended his birth been renewed, had anything supernatural occurred in the course of those years, we may presume it would have been related or alluded to. Nothing of that kind we may infer did happen. Outwardly and inwardly the growth of Jesus under Mary's care at Nazareth, obeyed the common laws under which human infancy and childhood are developed. Beyond that gentle patience which nothing could ruffle, that simple truthfulness which nothing could turn aside; beyond that love which was always ready to give back smile for smile to Mary and the rest around, and to go forth rejoicingly on its little errands of kindness within the home of the carpenter; beyond that wisdom which, wonderful as it was, was childlike wisdom still, growing as his years grew, and deriving its increase from all the common sources which lay open to it; beyond the charm of all the graces of childhood in their full beauty and in their unsullied perfection,—there was nothing externally to distinguish his first twelve years. So we conclude from the absence of all notices of them in the gospel narrative. Of the void thus left, however, the Christian Church became early impatient. Many attempts were made to fill it up. In the course of the first four centuries numerous pseudo-gospels were in circulation, a long list of which has been made up out of the references to them which occur in the preserved writings of that period.[1] Some of these apocryphal gospels are still extant, two of them entitled the Gospel of the Infancy; and it is very curious to notice how those succeeded who tried to lift the veil which covers the earlier years of Christ. One almost feels grate-

[1] See Jones on the Canon.

ful that such early attempts were made to fill up the blank which the four Evangelists have left.[1] They enable us to contrast the simplicity, the naturalness and consistency of all that the Evangelists have recorded of Christ, with such empty and unmeaning tales. They do more. These apocryphal gospels were written by Christians, by men who wished to honour Christ in all they said about him; by men who had that por-

[1] These Gospels of the infancy of our Lord are full of miracles of the most frivolous description, miracles represented as wrought first by the simple presence of the infant, by the clothes he wore, the water in which he was washed, wrought afterwards by the Son of Mary himself as he grew up at Nazareth, many alleged incidents of his boyhood there being gravely related, as when we are told that he and the other children of the village went out to play together, busying themselves in making clay into the shapes of various birds and beasts, whereupon Jesus commanded his beasts to walk, his birds to fly, and so excelled them all; or again, when we are told that passing by a dyer's shop he saw many pieces of cloth laid out to be dyed, all of which he took and flung into a neighbouring furnace, throwing the poor owner of the shop into an agony of consternation and grief, and then pleasantly relieving him by drawing all the pieces out of the furnace each one now of the very colour which had been desired. Such are the specimens, chosen chiefly because they are the least absurd of the many which are recorded in these Gospels. It was thus, as these writers would exhibit it, that the early boyhood of our Lord was spent; it was by miracles such as those which I have recited, that he even then distinguished himself.

traiture of his character before them which the four Gospels supply; and yet we find them narrating, as being in what seemed to them entire harmony with that character, that when boys interrupted Jesus in his play, or ran against him in the street of the village, he looked upon them and denounced them, and they fell down and died. It was said, I believe by Rousseau, that the conception and delineation of such a character as that of the man Christ Jesus, by such men as the fishermen of Galilee, would have been a greater miracle than the actual existence of such a man. In these apocryphal gospels we have a singular confirmation of that saying; we have the proof that men better taught, many of them, than the Apostles, even when they had the full delineation of the manhood of Jesus in their hands, could not attempt a fancy sketch of his childhood without not only violating our sense of propriety, by attributing to him the most puerile and unmeaning displays of divine power, but shocking our moral sense, and falsifying the very picture they had before their eyes, by attributing to him acts of vengeance.

CHRIST AMONG THE DOCTORS.

Joseph and Mary "went to Jerusalem every year at the feast of the Passover." The Mosaic law required that all the male inhabitants of Judea should go up three times yearly to the capital, to keep the three great festivals of the Passover, Pentecost, and Tabernacles. A later Rabbinical authority had laid an injunction upon women to attend the feast of the Passover. Living as they did in so remote a part of the country, it is probable that the parents of our Lord satisfied themselves with going up together once yearly to Jerusalem; Joseph thus doing less, and Mary more than the old law enjoined. When Jesus was twelve years old, Joseph and Mary took him up with them to Jerusalem. He had then reached that age, when, according to Jewish reckoning, he crossed the line which divides childhood from youth, got the new name of a son of the Lord, and had he been destined to any public office, would have passed into the hands of the Rabbis, for the higher instructions which their schools supplied. Jesus, however, had received no other instruction than the village school, attached to the synagogue at Nazareth, had supplied, and was destined to no higher employment than that of the trade his father followed. The purpose of Joseph and Mary in taking him up with them to Jerusalem was not that he might be placed at the feet of Gamaliel, or any other of the great distinguished teachers of the metropolis, but simply that he might see the holy city, and take part with them in the sacred services of the Passover.

There a new world opened to the boy's wondering eyes. With what interest must he have looked around, when first he trod the courts of the Temple, and gazed upon the ministering priests, the altar with its bleeding sacrifice and rising incense, the holy place, and the secret shrine that lay behind the veil! The places, too, of which we shall have to speak immediately, where youths of his own age were to be found, would not be left unvisited. What thoughts were stirred within his breast by all these sights, it becomes us not even to attempt to imagine. The key is not in our hands with which we might unlock the mysteries of his humanity at this stage of its development. He has himself so far unveiled his thoughts and feelings as to teach us how natural it was that he should linger in the holy city, and under the power of a new attraction feel for a day or two as if the ties that bound him to Nazareth and to his home there were broken.

The seven days of the feast went by. It had been a crowded procession from Galilee, which Joseph and Mary had joined. Galilee was then, as Josephus informs us, very thickly populated, studded with no less than two hundred and forty towns, containing each fifteen thousand inhabitants or more, sending forth in the war with the Romans an army of no less than one hundred thousand men. The separate companies which this crowded population sent up at the Passover time to Jerusalem would each be large, and as the youths of the company consorted and slept near one another in the course of the journey, it is the less surprising that, on leaving Jerusalem to return to Nazareth, Joseph and Mary should not during the day have missed their son, who had stayed behind, nor have become aware of his absence till they sought for him among his companions when they rested for the night. The discovery was a peculiarly distressing one. What if some oversight had been committed by them? if they had failed to tell their son of the time of the departure, if they had failed to notice whether he was among the other youths before they left the city? They had such confidence in that child, who never before in a single instance had done anything to create anxiety or distrust; they were so sure that he would be where, as they thought, he ought to be, that they had scarcely felt perhaps an ordinary degree of parental solicitude. And where could he now be; what could have happened to him? Their eager inquiries would probably soon satisfy them that he had not fallen aside by the way, that he had never joined the returning travellers, that he must have remained behind in Jerusalem. But with whom? for what? He knew no friends there with whom to stay. Had some accident befallen him? was he detained against his will? Did any one at Jerusalem know the secrets of his birth; were there any there who still sought the young child's life? Herod was dead; Archelaus was banished; the parents themselves had not been in Jerusalem since the time they had presented the infant in the Temple. It was not likely they should be recognised; none of their friends at Nazareth knew about the mysteries of the conception and the birth. They had thought there was no risk in taking Jesus with them, but now their hearts are full of dark forebodings; some one may have known, may have told; some secret design may still have been cherished. Where was their child, and what had happened to him?

You may imagine what a night of sleepless anxiety followed their discovery at the first nightly resting-place of the caravan. Mid-day saw them back in the city. It is said to have been after three days' search they found him; if we count the day of their return as one of these three, there would still be one entire day's fruitless search. There may have been two such days,—days of eager inquiry everywhere throughout the city, in the house where they had lived, among all those with whom they had had any converse or connexion. At last they find the lost one, not in the courts of the Temple, not in any of those parts of the edifice consecrated to public worship, but in one of those apartments in the outer buildings used as a school of the Rabbis. Among the Jews at this period, each synagogue had a schoolroom attached to it, in which the rudiments of an ordinary education were taught. Besides, however, these schools for primary instruction, wherever there were ten men in a position to devote their whole time to this purpose, a room was built for them, in which they carried on their pupils in all the higher walks of the sacred learning of the Jews. These constituted the schools of the Rabbis, and formed an important instrument in the support and extension of that system of Rabbinism which, as Milman tells us, "became, after the ruin of the Temple, and the extinction of the public worship, a new bond of national union, and the great distinctive feature in the character of modern Judaism." There were three apartments employed in this way attached to the Temple. It was in one of these that Joseph and Mary found their son. He was sitting in the ordinary attitude, and engaged in the ordinary exercises of a pupil in the middle of the doctors, hearing them and asking them questions,—the Jewish method of education being chiefly catechetical,—the pupil himself sometimes answering the questions put, and astonishing his hearers with his wisdom. When this strange, rude-looking, bright-looking, solemn-looking Galilean boy first came in among them, was it the wisdom he then showed which drew the hearts of some of these Rabbis to him, and led them, as if anxious to gain a scholar who might turn out to be the chief ornament of their school, to take him in and treat him tenderly? Was it with them, in the room they occupied in the outer Temple buildings, that the two nights in which Jesus was separated from his parents were spent? The tie, whatever it was, between him and them, is now destined to be broken, never to be renewed.

Joseph and Mary find him in the midst of them. Joseph is too much astonished to say anything, nor is it likely that Mary spoke till he had gone with her apart; but now her burdened mother's heart finds utterance. "Son," she says to him, "why hast thou thus dealt with us?" words of reproach that were new to Mary's lips. Never before had she to chide that child. Never before had he done anything to require such chiding. But now, when it appears that no accident had happened, no restraint had been exercised, that it had been of his own free will that Jesus had parted from his parents, and was sitting so absorbed by other persons and with other things, she cannot account for such conduct on his part. It looks like neglect, and worse; like indifference to the pain which he must have known this separation would cost them. "Son," she says, "why hast thou thus dealt with us? Behold, thy father and I have sought thee sorrowing."

Innocently, artlessly, childishly, in words which, though not meant to meet the reproach with a rebuke, yet carried with them much of the meaning and effect of the words spoken afterwards at the marriage-feast at Cana, Jesus answers, "How is it that ye sought me?" 'could you, Mary, believe that I would act under other than heavenly guidance; could you allow the idea of my being liable to any risk or danger simply because I was not under your eye and care; do you not know, were you not told whose Son I truly am; and should not that knowledge have kept you from seeking and sorrowing as you have done: wist ye not, that wherever I was I must have been still beneath that Father's eye and care,—whatever I was about, I must have been about that Father's business? Mary, you have called me Son, and I acknowledge the relationship; you have called Joseph my father; that relationship I disown; my own, my only Father is He in whose house you have now found me, whose will I came on earth to do; about whose matters I must constantly, and shall now henceforth and for ever be engaged.'

It is in this consciousness of his peculiar relationship to God, now for the first time, perhaps, fully realized, that we catch the true meaning, and can discern something of the purpose of this early, only recorded incident in the history of our Lord's youth. Mary, we are told, understood not the answer of her son. With the knowledge that she possessed, we can scarcely imagine that she had any difficulty in at once perceiving that Jesus spake of his Father in heaven, and comprehending in so far at least the meaning of his words. But there may have been a special reason for

Mary's surprise here—the difficulty she felt of comprehension and belief. It cannot readily be imagined that she had herself told her child during the first twelve years of his life, or that any one else had told him, of the mystery of his birth. From the first dawning of conscious intelligence, he must have been taught to call Joseph father, nor had it outwardly been communicated to him that he was only his reputed father, that he had no earthly parent, that his true and only father was God. If that were the actual state of the connexion between Mary and Jesus up to the time of this incident in the Temple; if she had never breathed to him the great secret that he was none other than the Son of the Highest; if there had been nothing, as she knew there was not, in the quiet tenor of the life which for twelve years Jesus lived, to afford any outward indication or evidence, either to himself or others, of the nature of his Sonship to God,—then how surprised must Mary have been when in the Temple, and by that answer to her question, Jesus informed her that he knew all, knew whence he was, knew for what he came, knew that God was his

Father in such a sense that the discharge of his business carried with it an obligation which, if the time and the season required, overbore all obligation to real or reputed earthly parents.

But whether it came upon Mary by surprise or not, was there no object in letting us and all believers in the Saviour know, as the record of this incident does, that Jesus was thus early and fully alive to the singularity of his relationship to God? Conceive that it had been otherwise; that these thirty years had been veiled in an impenetrable obscurity; that not one single glimpse had been given of how they passed away; that our first sight of the man Christ Jesus had been when he stood before John to be baptized in the waters of the Jordan, and to receive the Holy Ghost descending upon him. How natural in that case had been the impression that it was then for the first time, when the voice from heaven declared it, that he knew himself to be the Son of God; that it was then, when the Spirit first descended, that the Divine associated itself in close and ineffable union with the human. Then had those thirty years appeared in a quite different light to us; then had we conceived of him as living throughout their course the simple common life of a Galilean villager and craftsman. But now we know, and we have to thank this narrative of St. Luke for the information, that if not earlier, yet certainly at his twelfth year, the knowledge that he and the Father were one, that the Father was in him, and that he was in the Father, had visited and filled his spirit, had animated and regulated his life. With what a new sacredness and dignity do the eighteen years that intervened between this incident and that of his public manifestation to Israel become invested, and what new lessons of instruction do they bring us! At the bidding of a new impulse, excited within his youthful breast by this first visit to the Temple, he breaks for a day or two all earthly bonds, and seems lost amid the shadows of the Sanctuary, absorbed with the higher things of Him who was worshipped there. But at the call of duty, his hour for public service, for speaking acting suffering dying, before all and for all, not yet come, he yields at once to the desire of Joseph and Mary, and returns with them to Nazareth; becoming subject to them, burying, as it were, this great secret in his breast; consenting to wait, submitting to all the restraints of an ordinary household, putting himself once more under the yoke of parental authority, taking upon him all the common obligations of a son, a brother, a neighbour, a friend, a Galilean villager, a Jewish citizen; discharging all without a taint of sin; travelling not an inch beyond the routine of service expected in these relationships; doing absolutely nothing to betray the divinity that lay within, nothing to distinguish himself above others, or proclaim his heavenly birth; living so naturally, unostentatiously, undemonstratively, that neither did his brethren, the inmates of his home, his own nearest relatives believe in him, discerning not in all those years any marks of his divine prophetic character; his name so little known in the immediate neighbourhood that Nathanael, who lived in Cana, a few miles off, had never heard of him, and was quite unprepared to believe Philip, when he told him, that in one Jesus of Nazareth he had found him of whom Moses in the law, and the prophets, did write.

From the bosom of that thick darkness which covers the first thirty years of our Lord's earthly life, there thus shines forth the light which irradiates the whole period, and sheds over it a lustre brighter than ever graced the life of any other of the children of men. You may have wondered at this one event of his childhood being redeemed from oblivion, so insignificant does it seem, and at first sight so little correspondent with our preconceived conceptions of the great Messiah's character and work. Looking at Jesus as nothing more than the son of Joseph and Mary, there might be some difficulty in explaining his desertion of them at Jerusalem. But when you reflect on his self-recognition at this time as the Son of God; on his declaration of it to Mary; on his thenceforth acting on it in life; on his words in the Temple, followed by eighteen years of self-denial, and gentle, cheerful, prompt obedience; on his growing consciousness of his divine lineage, and his earthly work and heavenly heritage; on the evils he came on earth to expose and remedy; on the selfishness, the worldliness, the formalism, the hypocrisy, he detected all around him at

Nazareth;—when you reflect further on his divine reticence, on his sublime and patient self-restraint, on his refraining from all interference in public matters, and all exposure to public notice, on his devoting himself instead to the tasks of daily duty in a very humble sphere of life; when you reflect fixedly and thoughtfully on these things, do you not feel that there rests on this portion of the life of Jesus, and upon its introductory and explanatory incident, an interest different indeed in kind, yet in full and perfect harmony with that belonging to the period when he stood forth as the Saviour of the world? If he came to empty himself of that glory which he had with the Father before the world was, to take upon him the form of a servant, to seek not his own glory, to do not his own will, not to be ministered unto but to minister, then assuredly it was not only during the three years of his public ministry, but during all the three-and-thirty years of his life on earth, that the ends of his mission were accomplished.

We think, I apprehend, too little of these quiet domestic years of secluded unpretending piety at Nazareth. Our eyes are dazzled by the outward glory which surrounded his path when he burst at last from his long concealment, and showed himself as the Son of the Highest; and yet there is a sense in which we should have more interest in the earlier than in the later period of his life. It is liker the life we have ourselves to lead. The Jesus of Nazareth is more of a pattern to us than the Jesus of Gethsemane and the Cross. He was not less the Son of God in the one case than in the other; not less in the one character than in the other has he left us an example that we should follow his steps. It was thus the great lesson of his life at Nazareth, as interpreted by his sayings in the Temple, that we should be doing our Father's business in the counting-house, in the workshop, at the desk, as much as in any of the higher or more public walks of Christian or philanthropic effort; that a life confined and devoted to the faithful execution of the simple, humble offices of daily domestic duty, if it be a life of faith and love, may be one as full of God, as truly divine and holy, as Christ-like and as honouring to Christ, as a life devoted to the most important public services that can be rendered to the Church on earth. In the quiet and deep-lying valleys of life, all hidden from human eye, who may tell us how many there are, who, built up in a humble trust in Jesus, and animated by their hope in him, are performing cheerfully their daily tasks because a Father's wisdom has allotted them, and bearing patiently their daily burdens because they have been imposed by a Father's love? Content to live and labour, and endure and die, unnoticed and unknown, earthly fame hanging no wreath upon their tomb, earthly eloquence dumb over their dust, these are they, the last among men, who shall be among the first in the kingdom of the just.

VII.

THE FORERUNNER.[1]

THE same angel who announced to Mary at Nazareth the birth of Jesus, had six months previously announced the birth of John to the aged priest Zacharias, as he ministered before the altar, within the Temple at Jerusalem. Zacharias was informed that his wife Elisabeth should have a son, whose name was to be John, who was to be "great in the sight of the Lord," going before him "in the spirit and power of Elias, to make ready a people prepared for the Lord." Zacharias doubted what the angel said. At once as a punishment of his incredulity, and as a new token of the truth of the angelic message, he was struck with a temporary dumbness. When he came forth he could not tell his brother priests or the assembled people anything about what he

[1] Luke i. 1-18; Matt. iii. 1-12; Mark i. 1-8.

had seen or heard within. From the signs he made, and the strange awe-struck expression of his countenance, they fancied he had seen a vision; but it is not likely that he took any means of correcting whatever false ideas they entertained. His one wish, was to get home and reveal the secret to his wife Elisabeth. His days of ministration lasted but a week, and as soon as they were over, he hastened to his residence in the hill country of Judea. In due time what Gabriel had foretold took place. The child was born. The eighth day, the day for its circumcision, and the bestowing of its name arrived. A large circle of relatives assembled. They proposed that the child should be called Zacharias, after his father. Foreseeing that some such proposal might be made, Zacharias had provided against any other name than that assigned by the angel being given to his son. Acting upon his instructions, Elisabeth interposed, and declared that the child's name should be John. The relatives remonstrated. None of her kindred, they reminded her, had ever borne that name. The dumb father was now by signs appealed to.

He called for a writing-table, and wrote the few decisive words, "His name is John." They were all wondering at the prompt and peremptory settlement of this question, when another and greater ground of wonder was supplied: the tongue of the dumb was loosed, and, in rapt, rhythmical, prophetic strains that remind us forcibly of those in which, three months before, and in the same dwelling, Mary and Elisabeth had exchanged their greetings, he poured out fervent thanks to God for having visited and redeemed his people, and foretold the high office which his own new-born son was to execute as Forerunner of the Messiah.

With that scene of the circumcision day the curtain drops upon the household of Zacharias and Elisabeth, nor is it lifted till many years are gone, and then it is the child only, now grown to manhood, who appears. His parents had been well stricken in years at the date of his birth, and as no mention of them is made afterwards, we may presume that like Joseph they were dead before anything remarkable in the life of their son had happened. Little as we know of the first thirty years of the life of

Jesus, we know still less of the like period in the life of John. All that we are told is that till the time of his showing unto Israel he was in the desert, in those wild and lonely regions which lay near his birthplace, skirting the north-western shores of the Dead Sea. True to the angelic designation, accepting the vow that marked him as a Nazarite from his birth, John separated himself early from home and kindred, retired from the haunts of men, buried himself in the rocky solitudes of the wilderness, letting his hair grow till it fell loose and dishevelled over his shoulders, denying himself to all ordinary indulgences whether of food or dress, clothing himself with the roughest kind of garment he could get, a robe of hair-cloth, bound around him with a leathern girdle, satisfying himself by feeding on the locusts and wild honey of the desert. But it was not in a morose or ascetic spirit that he did so. He had not fled to those solitudes in chagrin, to nurse upon the lap of indolence regrets over bygone disappointments; nor had he sought there to shroud his spirit in a religious gloom deep as that of Engedi and Adullam, which may have been among his haunts. His whole appearance and bearing, words and actions, when at last he stood forth before the people, satisfy us that there was little in him of the mystic, the misanthrope, or the monk. Though dwelling apart from others, avoiding observation, and shunning promiscuous intercourse, he was not wasting those years in idleness, heedless of the task for the performance of which the life he led was intended, as we presume he must have been informed by his parents, to prepare him to execute. Through the loop-holes of retreat we can well imagine the Baptist as busily scanning the state of that community upon which he was to act. When he stepped forth from his retirement, and men of all kinds and classes gathered round him, he did not need any one to tell him who the Pharisees, or the Sadducees, or the publicans were, or what were their peculiar and distinctive faults. He appears from the first to have been well informed as to the state of things outside the desert. It may, in truth, in no small measure have served to fit him for his peculiar work that— removed from all the influences which must have served, had he lived among them, to blunt his sense of surrounding evils, and to mould his character and habits according to the prevailing forms and fashions of Jewish life—he was carried by the Spirit into the desert to be trained and educated there, thence, as from a watch-tower, to look down upon those strange sights which his country was presenting, undistractedly to watch, profoundly to muse and meditate, the fervour of a true prophet of the Lord kindling and glowing into an intenser fire of holy zeal; till at last, when the hour for action came, he launched forth upon his brief earthly work, with a swift impetuosity like the rush of those short-lived cataracts, yet with a firmness of unbending will and purpose, like the stability of those rocky heights among which for thirty years he had been living.

But what had those thirty years in the current of Jewish history presented? At their beginning those intestine wars which previously had somewhat weakened the Roman power, had closed in the peaceful establishment of the Empire under Augustus Cæsar. The dangers to Jewish liberty grew all the greater, and the impatience of the people under the Roman yoke became the more intense; the extreme patriot party, who were in favour with the people generally, became fanatic in their zeal. After the death of Herod the Great, while yet it remained uncertain whether Augustus would recognise the accession of Archelaus to the throne, an insurrection broke out in Jerusalem, which was only quelled by the slaughter of three thousand of the insurgents, and by the ill-omened stoppage of the great Passover festival. Augustus, unwilling to lay any heavier yoke on those who were already fretting beneath the one they bore, confirmed the will of Herod by which he divided his kingdom among his sons, suffered the Jews still to have nominally a government of their own, and recognised Archelaus as king over Judea and Samaria. His reign was a short and troubled one, and at its close Judea and Samaria were attached to Syria, made part of a Roman province, and had procurators or governors from Rome set over them, of whom the sixth in order was Pontius Pilate, who entered upon his office about the very time when the Baptist began his ministry. The lingering shadows of royalty and independence were thus removed. Not content with removing them, the usurper intermeddled with the ecclesiastical as well as the civil government of Judea. In the Mosaic Institute, the High Priest, the most important public functionary of the Jews, attained his office hereditarily, and held it for life. The Emperor now claimed and exercised the right of investiture, and appointed and deposed as he pleased. During the period between the death of Herod and the destruction of Jerusalem, we read of twenty-eight High Priests holding the office in succession, only one of whom retained it till his death. This dependence on Rome, not only for the appointment but for continuance in it, necessarily generated great servility on the part of aspirants to the office, and great abuses in the manner in which its duties were discharged. A supple, sagacious, venal man, like Annas, though not able to establish himself permanently in the chair, was able to secure it in turn for five of his sons, for his son-in-law Caiaphas, with whom he was associated at the time of the crucifixion, and afterwards for his grandson. Such a state of things among the governing authorities fomented the popular animosity to the foreign rule. The whole country was in a ferment. Popular outbreaks were constantly occurring. The public mind was in such an inflammable condition that any adventurer daring enough, and strong enough to raise the standard of revolt, was followed by multitudes. Among those insurrectionary chiefs, some of whom were of the lowest condition and the most worthless character, Judas of Galilee distinguished himself by his open proclamation of the principle that it was not lawful to pay tribute to Cæsar, and his political creed was adopted by thousands who had not the courage, as he had, to pay the penalty of their lives in acting it out. It can easily be imagined what a fresh hold their faith and hopes as to the foretold Messiah would take upon the hearts of a people thus galled and fretted to the uttermost by political discontent. The higher views of his character would naturally be swallowed up and lost in the conception of him as the great deliverer who was to break those hated bonds which bound them, restore the old Theocracy, and make Jerusalem, not Rome, the seat and centre of a universal monarchy.

Such was the state of public affairs and of the public feeling, when a voice, loud and thrilling like the voice of a trumpet, issues from the desert, saying, "Repent ye, for the kingdom of heaven is at hand." Crowds come forth to listen; they look at the strange man, true son of the desert, from whose lips this voice cometh. He has all the aspect, he wears the dress, of one of their old prophets. They ask about him; he is of the priestly order. Some old men begin now to remember about his father in the Temple, and the strange "sayings that were noised abroad through all the hill country of Judea" soon after his birth. They listen to his words; it is true he does not directly claim divine authority; the old prophetic formula, "Thus saith the Lord," he does not employ; he points to no sign, he works no miracle; he trusts to the simple power of the summons he makes, the prophecy he utters; yet there is something in the very manner of his utterance so prophet-like, that a prophet they cannot help believing him to be. There is nothing particularly ingratiating in his call to repent, but the announcement that the kingdom of heaven is at the door, and that they must all at once arise and prepare for it, meets the deepest, warmest wishes of their hearts. It is at hand at last, this strange man says,—the kingdom for which they have so long been waiting; and shall they not go forth to welcome its approach, and rejoice in its triumphs? The spell of the Baptist's preaching, in whatever it lay, was one that operated with a speed and a power, and to an extent of which we have the parallel only in times of the greatest excitement, like those of the Crusades, or of the Reformation. "Then went out to him," we are told, "all Judea, and they of Jerusalem, and all the region round about Jordan, and were baptized of him in Jordan, confessing their sins." It would seem as if with one consent the entire population of the southern part of Palestine had gathered around the Baptist, and for the time were pliant in his hands. It may have facilitated their assemblage, if, as has been conjectured, it was a Sabbatic year when John began his work, and the people, set free from their ordinary labours, were ready to follow him, as he led them to the banks of the Jordan to be baptized.

This baptism in the river was so marked a feature in the ministry of John, that it gave him his distinctive title, The Baptist. It was a new and peculiar rite; of Divine appointment, as appears not only from the question which our Lord put to the Jewish rulers, "The baptism of John, was it from heaven, or of men?" but also from the declaration of John himself, "He that sent me to baptize with water." It may have been suggested by, as it was in some respects similar to, the various ablutions or washings with water prescribed in the Mosaic ritual; yet from all of these baptisms, if baptisms they could be called, it differed in many respects. They were all intended simply as instruments of purification from ceremonial defilement; it had another character and object. With a few exceptional cases, they were all performed by the person's own hands, who went through the process of purification; it was performed by another, by the hands of John himself, or some of his disciples. They were repeated as often as the defilement was renewed; it was administered only once. There was indeed one Jewish custom which, if then in use, presents a clear analogy to the baptism of John. When proselytes from heathenism were admitted into the pale of the Jewish commonwealth, after circumcision they were baptized. "They bring the proselyte," says an old Jewish authority,[1] "to baptism, and being placed in the water, they again instruct him in some weightier and in some lighter commands of the law, which being heard, he plunges himself and comes up, and behold he is an Israelite in all things." It would look as if the baptism of John was borrowed from this proselyte baptism of the Jews; but though it were, it will at once appear to you that the former rite had marked peculiarities of its own. And as it stood thus distinguished from all Jewish, so also did it stand distinguished from the Christian rite ordained by our Lord himself, which involved a fuller faith, symbolized a higher privilege, and was always administered in the name of Christ. The one rite might be regarded indeed as running into and being superseded by the other, but of the great difference between them we have proof in the fact that those who

[1] Maimonides.

had received the baptism of John were nevertheless re-baptized on their admission into the Christian Church.[1] John's baptism, like everything about his ministry, was imperfect, preparatory, temporary, and transient, involving simply a confession of unworthiness, and a faith in one to come, through whom the remission of sins was to be conveyed.

The people who flocked around John readily submitted to his baptism, whether regarding it as altogether new, or the modified form of some of their own old observances. The accompaniment of his teaching with the administration of such an ordinance may have helped to reconcile the Pharisees, who were such lovers of the ritualistic, to a preaching which had little in itself to recommend it to them, as the absence on the other hand of all doctrinal instruction, all references to the unseen world, to angels and spirits, and the resurrection, may have helped to conciliate the prejudices of the Sadducees. At any rate, we learn that, borne along with the flowing tide, Pharisees and Sadducees did actually pre-

[1] See Acts xix.

sent themselves before John to claim baptism at his hands. His quick, keen, spiritual insight at once detected the veiled deceit that lay in their doing so, and in the very spirit which his great Master afterwards displayed, he proceeded to denounce their hypocrisy, giving them indeed the very title which Jesus bestowed on them. John's whole ministry, his teaching and baptizing, if it meant anything, meant this, that without an inward spiritual change, without penitence, without reformation, no Israelite was prepared to enter into that kingdom whose advent he announced. His preaching was the preaching of repentance, his baptism the baptism of repentance; the one great lesson the whole involved, was that all Israel had become spiritually unfit for welcoming the Messiah, and sharing the blessings of his reign. But here were some, the Pharisees and Sadducees who now stood before him, of whom he knew, that so far from their entertaining the least idea that they required to go through any such process, regarded themselves as pre-eminently the very ones to whom from their position in Israel this kingdom was at once to bring its blessings. Penetrating their secret thoughts, the Baptist said to them, "Think not to say within yourselves, We have Abraham to our father," and therefore are, simply as his descendants, entitled to all the benefits of that kingdom which is to be set up in Judea; "I say unto you, that God is able of these stones to raise up children unto Abraham;"—a dim, yet not uncertain pre-intimation of the spiritual character and wide extension of the new kingdom of God; the possibility even of the outcast and down-trodden Gentile being admitted into it.

John's bold and honest treatment of the Pharisees and Sadducees only made him look the more prophet-like in the eyes of the common people. It encouraged them to ask, What shall we do then? In a form of precept like to that which Christ frequently employed, John said to them, "He that hath two coats, let him impart to him that hath none. He that hath meat, let him do likewise." There is no better sign morally of a community than when such kindly links of brotherly sympathy so bind together all classes, as that those who have are ever ready to help those who want; as, on the other hand, there is no clearer proof of a community morally disorganized than the absence of this benevolent disposition. Judea was at this time, both as to its religious and political condition, thoroughly disorganized, and in inculcating in this direct and emphatic way, the great duty of a universal charity, John was at once laying bare one of the sorest of existing evils, and pointing to the method of its cure.

Then came to him the Publicans also, those Jews who for gain's sake had farmed the taxes imposed by the Romans; a class odious and despised, looked upon by their countrymen generally as traitors, who, by extortion, drew large profits out of the national degradation. They, too, get the answer exactly suited to them: "Exact no more than what is appointed to you." Then came to him soldiers, Jews we may believe who had enlisted under the Roman standard, and who not satisfied with the soldier's common pay abused their power as the military police of the country, and by force, or threat of accusation before the higher authorities, sought to improve their condition. They, too, get the answer suited to their case: "Do violence to no man: neither accuse any falsely, and be content with your wages." These are but a few stray specimens of the manner in which the Baptist dealt with those who came to him: one quite new, yet so much needed. What power must have been exerted over a people so long accustomed to the inculcation of a mere ceremonial pietism, by this thoroughly intrepid, downright, plain, practical, unaccommodating and uncompromising kind of teaching! The great secret of its success lay here, that unsupported by any confirming signs from heaven, —in a certain sense not needing them,—he inculcated the duties of justice, truthfulness, forbearance, charity, by a direct appeal to the simple, naked sense of right and wrong that dwells in every human bosom. And the world has seldom seen a more striking proof of the power of conscience, and of the response which, when taken suddenly and before it has time to get warped and biassed, conscience will give to all direct, sincere, and vigorous addresses to it, than when those multitudes from Judea and Jerusalem, and all the land, gathered round the Baptist on the banks of the Jordan.

What an animating spectacle must these banks have then exhibited; a spectacle which has ever since been annually renewed by the resort of thousands of pilgrims thither. Our last and best describer of Palestine[1] brings it thus before our eyes: "No common spring or tank would meet the necessities of the multitudes. The Jordan now seemed to have met with its fit purpose. It was the one river of Palestine sacred in its recollections, abundant in its waters; and yet at the same time the river not of cities but of the wilderness, the scene of the preaching of those who dwelt not in king's palaces, nor wore soft clothing. On the banks of the rushing stream the multitudes gathered;—the priests and scribes from Jerusalem, down the pass of Adummim; the publicans from Jericho on the south, and the Lake of Gennesareth on the north; the soldiers on their way from Damascus to Petra, through the Ghor, in the war with the Arab chief Hareth; the peasants from Galilee, with One from Nazareth,

[1] Stanley.

through the opening of the plain of Esdraelon. The tall reeds or canes in the jungle waved, shaken by the wind; the pebbles of the bare clay hills lay around, to which the Baptist pointed as capable of being transformed into the children of Abraham; at their feet rushed the refreshing stream of the never-failing river."

This description, indeed, applies to a period in the narrative a little further on than the one which is now immediately before us. The "One from Nazareth" may have left his village home, and been already on the way, but as yet he was buried in obscurity, deep hidden among the people. All the people were musing in their hearts whether John were not himself the Christ. He knew what was in their hearts; he knew how ready they were to hail him as their promised deliverer. No man of his degree has ever had a fairer opportunity of lifting himself to high repute upon the shoulders of an acclaiming multitude. Did the tempting thought for a moment flit across his mind that he should seize upon the occasion so presented? If it did, he was in haste to expel the intruder, and prevent the multitude by at once proclaiming that he was not the great prophet they were ready to believe he was; that another was at hand much greater than he to whom he was not worthy to discharge the lowest and most menial office of a slave, the carrying of his sandal, the unloosing of his shoe-latchet. He, John, baptized with water unto repentance, an incomplete and altogether preparatory affair, but the greater than he would baptize with the Holy Ghost and with fire.

Such was the prompt and decisive manner in which he disowned all high pretensions. And when, shortly afterwards, posterior to our Lord's baptism, of which they may have heard nothing, a deputation from Jerusalem came down to ask him, Who art thou? he met the question with the emphatic negative, I am not the Christ. Art thou Elias then? they said. John knew that the men who put this query to him were caring only about his person, and careless about his office,— in the true spirit of all religious formalists, wanting so much to know who the teacher was, and but little heeding what his teaching meant; he knew that their idea was that the heavens were to give back Elijah to the earth, and that he was to appear in person to announce and anoint the Messiah, and that many of them believed that besides Elias another of the old prophets was to arise from the dead, to dignify by his presence the great era of the Messiah's inauguration. Answering their questions according to the meaning of the questioners when they said, Art thou Elias? he said, I am not; when they asked him, Art thou that prophet? he answered, No. And when still further they inquired, Who art thou then, that we may give an answer to them that sent us? he said, that he was but a voice and nothing more, "the voice of one crying in the wilderness, Make straight the way of the Lord, as said the prophet Esaias." Pressing him still further by the interrogation, why it was that he baptized if he were neither Christ, nor Elias, nor that prophet; he speaks again of his own baptism as if it were too insignificant a matter for any question about his right to administer it being raised or answered, and of the greater than he already revealed to him by the sign from heaven: "I baptize with water, but there standeth one among you whom ye know not. He it is who coming after me is preferred before me, whose shoe-latchet I am not worthy to unloose."

It is this prompt acknowledgment of his own infinite inferiority to Christ, his thorough appreciation of the relative position in which he stood to Jesus, the readiness with which he undertook the honourable but humble task of being but his herald, the unimpeachable fidelity and unfaltering steadiness with which he fulfilled the special course marked out for him by God, and above all the entire and apparently unconscious self-abnegation which in doing so he displayed, that shine forth as the prominent features in the personal character of the Baptist.

To these, particularly to the last, we shall have occasion hereafter to allude. Meanwhile, let us dwell a moment on the place and office which the ministry of John occupied midway between the old and the new economy. "The law and the prophets were until John." In him and with him they expired. He was a prophet, the only one among them all whose coming and whose office were themselves of old the subject of prophecy, honoured above them all by the nearness of his standing to Jesus, by his being the friend of the Bridegroom, to whom it was given to hear the Bridegroom's living voice. But he was more than a prophet. Of the greatest of his predecessors, of Moses, of Elijah, of Daniel, it was true that they filled but a limited space in the great dispensation with which they were connected; their days but an handbreadth in the broad cycle of events with which their lives and labours were wrapped up, the individuality of each, if not lost among, yet linked with that of a multitude of compeers. But John presents himself alone. The prophet of the desert, the forerunner of the Lord, appears without a coadjutor, a whole distinct economy in himself. To announce Christ's advent, to break up the way before him, to make ready a people prepared for the Lord, this was the specific object of that economy which began and ended in John's ministry.

The kind, and amount of the service which the Baptist thus rendered, as well as the need of it, it is difficult for us now thoroughly to understand and appreciate. In what respect

Christ would have been placed at a disadvantage had not John preceded him; in what respects the Baptist did open up the way before the Lord; in what respects John's ministry told upon the condition of the Jewish people, morally and spiritually, so as to make it different from what it otherwise would have been,—so as to make the soil all the better prepared to receive the seed which the hand of the Divine sower scattered,—it is not very easy for us to estimate. One thing is clear enough, that it was John's hand which struck the first bold stroke at the root of the strong national prejudice which narrowed and carnalized the expected kingdom of their Messiah. It is quite possible, that, as to the true nature and extent of the coming kingdom, John may have been as much in the dark as the twelve apostles were till the day of Pentecost. One thing, however, was revealed to him in clearest light, and it was upon his knowledge of this that he spoke with such authority and power, that whatever the future kingdom was to be, it should be one in which force and fraud, and selfishness and insincerity, and all sham piety, were to be denied a place; for which those would stand best prepared who were readiest to confess and give up their sins, and to act justly and benevolently towards their fellow-men, humbly and sincerely towards their God. You have but the rudiments, indeed, of the true doctrine of repentance in the teaching of the Baptist—the Christian doctrine but in germ; but it is not difficult to see in it the same great lesson broached as to the inner and spiritual qualifications required of all the members of the kingdom of Christ, which was afterwards, with so much greater depth and fulness, unfolded privately to Nicodemus at the very beginning of our Lord's ministry in Judea, when he said to him: "Except a man be born again, he cannot see, he cannot enter into the kingdom of God;" and publicly to the multitudes on the hill-side of Galilee, when the Lord said to them: "Blessed are the poor in spirit, for theirs is the kingdom of heaven."

It would be quite wrong, it would indicate an ignorance of the peculiar service which the Baptist was called upon to render, were we to imagine that there must be a preparatory process of repentance and reformation gone through by each of us before we believe in Jesus, and by faith enter the kingdom. Our position is so different from that occupied by the multitude to whom John preached, that what was most suitable for them is not so suitable for us.

And yet not without some broad and general lessons for the Church, at all times and in all ages, was it ordered so that the gentle preacher of peace should be preceded by the stern preacher of repentance; that John should be seen in the desert in advance of Jesus,—in his appearance, his haunts, his habits, his words, his ordinance, proclaiming and symbolizing the duty and discipline of penitence. It was only thus, by the ministry of the one running into the ministry of the other, that the Christian life, in its acts of penitence, as well as in its acts of faith and love, could stand before us in vivid relief, embodied in a full-orbed and personal portraiture. Jesus had no sin of his own to mourn over, no evil dispositions to subdue, no evil habits to relinquish. In the person, character, and life of Jesus, the great and needful duty of mortifying the body of sin and death could receive no visible illustration. He could supply to us no model or exemplar here. Was it not then wisely ordered that moving before, and for a time beside him, there should be seen that severer figure of the Baptist, as if to tell us that the proud spirit that is in us must be bowed, and the mountain-heights of pride in us be laid low, and the crooked things be made straight, and the rough places plain, to make way for the coming in of the Prince of Peace, and the setting up of his kingdom in our hearts; that we must go with the Baptist into the solitudes of the desert, as well as with the Saviour into the happy homes and villages of Galilee? Would you see, in its full, finished, and perfect form, the character and course of conduct, which, as followers of the Crucified, we are to aim at and to realize, go study it in the life of Jesus. But would you see it in its formation as well as in its finish, go study it in the life of the Baptist; put the two together, John and Jesus, and the portraiture is complete.

VIII.

THE BAPTISM.[1]

WE have no definite information as to the date of the commencement of John's ministry, or his own age at that time. As we know, however, that he was six months older than Jesus, as we are told that Jesus was about thirty years of age when he began his public ministry, and as that was the age fixed in the Jewish law for the priests entering on the duties of their office, it seems reasonable to conclude that the ministry of John had already lasted for six months when Jesus presented himself before the Baptist on the banks of the Jordan. This would allow full time for intelligence of a movement which so rapidly pervaded the entire population of the southern districts of the country, penetrating Galilee, and

[1] Matt. iii. 13-17; Mark i. 9-11; Luke iii. 21-23; John i. 30-33.

reaching even to Nazareth. Moved by this intelligence, other Galileans of that district as well as Jesus may have followed the wake of the multitude, and directed their steps to the place where John was baptizing. In these circumstances Christ's departure from his home may not have created the surprise which it otherwise would have done. When Mary saw her son, who had hitherto so quietly and exclusively devoted himself to their discharge, throw up all his household duties and depart; when she learned whither it was that his footsteps were tending, and gathered, as she may have done, from the tidings which were then afloat, that it was none other than the son of her relative Elisabeth who was shaking the entire community of the south by his summons to repent, and his proclamation of the nearness of the kingdom, she could scarcely have let Jesus go, for the first time that he had ever so parted from her, without following him with many wistful, wondering anxieties, and hopes. But she did not know that he now left that home in Nazareth never but for a few days to return to it. Had she known it, could she have let him go alone? It was alone, however, and externally undistinguished among the crowd, that Jesus stood before John, and craved baptism at his hands. He did this in the simplest, least ostentatious way, allowing the great mass of the baptisms to be over, mingling with the people, and offering himself as one of the last to whom the rite was to be administered. "It came to pass," Luke tells, that "when all the people were baptized," Jesus was baptized also. But his baptism did not go past as the others did. So soon as John's eye fell upon this new candidate for the ordinance, he saw in him one altogether different in person and character from any who had hitherto been baptized. He felt at once as if this administration of his baptism would be altogether out of place; that for Jesus to be baptized by him would be to invert the relationship in which he knew and felt that they stood to one another. By earnest speech or expressive gesture he intimated his unwillingness to comply with the request. The word which St. Matthew uses in telling us that John forbade him, is one indicative of a very strenuous refusal on his part. This refusal he accompanied with the words: "I have need to be baptized of thee, and comest thou to me?"

These words, you will particularly remark, were spoken at the commencement of their interview, before the baptism of our Lord, before that sign from heaven was given of which he had been forewarned, and for which he was to wait before pronouncing of any individual that he was the greater One who was to come, who was to baptize with the Holy Ghost and with fire. Till he saw the Spirit descending and remaining, John could not know certainly, and had no warrant authoritatively to say that this was He of whom he spake. From the Baptist saying twice afterwards, "I knew him not," it has been imagined that up to this meeting John had never seen Jesus, had no personal acquaintance with his relative the son of Mary; and the distance at which they lived from one another, with the entire length of the land between them, the retired life of the one at Nazareth, and the dwelling of the other in the desert, have been referred to as explaining the absence of all acquaintance and intercourse. That there could have been but little intercourse is clear; that they may never have seen each other till now is possible. But if so, how are we to explain John's meeting the proposal of Jesus with so instant and earnest a declaration, and saying to him, I have need to be baptized of thee, and comest thou to me? Jesus must either before these words were spoken have told John who he was, and the Baptist must have known from ordinary sources what a sinless and holy life he had been leading for these thirty years at Nazareth, or this knowledge must have been supernaturally communicated; for knowledge of Jesus to this extent at least, that he was no fit subject for a baptism which was for sinners, was obviously implied in this address.

Is it, however, so certain, or even so probable, that John and Jesus had never met till now? Zacharias and Elisabeth had to instruct their son as to his earthly work, his heavenly calling, and in doing so must have told him of the visit of Mary, and the birth of Jesus. He must have learned from them enough to direct his eye longingly and expectantly to his Galilean relative as no other than the Messiah, for whose coming he was to prepare the people. True, he retired early

THE BAPTISM.   171

to the desert, which was his place of ordinary residence till the time of his showing unto Israel, but did that imply that he never was at Jerusalem, never went up to the great yearly festivals? Jesus was once, at least, in Jerusalem in his youth, and may have been often there before his thirtieth year. So, too, may it have been with John, and if so, they must have met there, and become acquainted with one another. Much, however, as there may have been to lead John to the belief that Jesus was he that was to come after him, the lapse of those thirty years, during which the two had been almost totally separated, and the absence of all sign or token of the Messiahship during Christ's secluded life at Nazareth, may have led him to doubt. Even after he had received his great commission he might continue in the same state of uncertainty, waiting, as he had been instructed, till the sign from heaven was given. Whatever John's inward surmises or convictions may have been, he must have felt that it became him neither to speak of them nor to act on them, till the promised and visible token of the Messiahship lighted on him whom he was then to hold forth to the people as the Lamb of God, who was to take away the sin of the world. Such we conceive to have been the state of John's mind and feelings towards Jesus when he presented himself before him for baptism. From previous acquaintance he may instantly have recognised him as the son of Mary, to whom his thoughts and hopes had for so many years been pointing. He certainly did at once recognise him as his superior, as one at least so much holier than himself that he shrunk from baptizing him. But he did not certainly know him as the Christ the Son of God; did not so know him at least as to be entitled to point him out as such to the people. When, some weeks afterwards, he actually did so, he was at pains to tell those whom he addressed that it was not upon the ground of any previous personal knowledge, or individual connexion, that he spake of him as he did. "I knew him not," he said; "but he that sent me to baptize with water, the same said unto me, Upon whom thou shalt see the Spirit descending, and remaining on him, the same is he which baptizeth with the Holy Ghost. And I saw, and bear record that this is the Son of God."

We now know more of Jesus than perhaps John did when Christ stood before him to be baptized; we know that he was the Holy One of God, who had no sin of his own to confess, no pollution to wash away; and we too, like John, may wonder that the sinless Son of God should have submitted to such a baptism as his, a baptism accompanied with the acknowledgment of sin, and the profession of repentance, and which was the symbol of the removal of the polluting stains of guilt. But our Lord's words fall upon our ears as they did on those of John. "Suffer it to be so now, for thus it becometh us to fulfil all righteousness." Firmly yet gently, authoritatively yet courteously, clothing the command in the form of a request, he carries it over the reluctance and remonstrance of the Baptist. "Suffer it to be so now," for this once, so long as the present transient earthly relationship between us subsists. Suffer it, "for so it becometh us to fulfil all righteousness." It is not then as a violator but as a fulfiller of the law that Jesus comes to be baptized; not as one who confesses to the want of such a perfect righteousness as might be presented for acceptance to

God, but as one prepared to meet every requirement of his Father, and to render to it an exact and complete obedience. Who could speak thus, as if it were such an easy, as well as such a becoming thing in him to fulfil all righteousness, but the only begotten of the Father, he who, in coming into this world could say, Lo! I come to do thy will, O God.

And here in subjecting himself to the baptism of John, you have the first instance of Christ's acting in his public official character as the Messiah. He steps forth at last from his long retirement, his deep seclusion at Nazareth, to appear how? to do what?—to appear as an inferior before the Baptist, to ask a service at his hands, to enrol himself as one of his disciples; for this was the primary purpose of this ordinance. It was the initiatory rite by which repentant Israelites enrolled themselves as the hopeful expectants of the coming kingdom; and He, the head of that kingdom, stoops to enrol himself in this way among them. "By one spirit," says the apostle, "we are all baptized into one body;" the outward baptism the sign or symbol of our incorporation into that one body the Church.

In the same way the Lord himself enters into that body, honours the ordinance which God had sent John to administer, conforms even to that preparatory and temporary economy through which his infant Church was called to pass, putting himself under the law, making himself in all things like unto his brethren.

Still, however, the difficulty returns upon us, as to what meaning such a rite as that of John's baptism could have in the case of Jesus; sin he had none to confess, nor penitence to feel, nor reformation to effect, nor a faith in the One to come to cherish. Yet his baptism in the Jordan was not without meaning; nay, its singular significance reveals itself as we contemplate the sinlessness of his character. We rightly regard the baptism of Jesus as the first act of his public ministry; and does he not present himself at the very outset in that peculiar character and office which he sustains throughout his mediatorial work, identifying himself with his people as their representative and their head; taking on him their sins, numbering himself with transgressors,—doing now, enduring afterwards what it became them as sinners to do, as sinners to suffer? In himself he was pure and undefiled, having no stain whose removal this outward baptism with water might symbolize; but even as an Israelite of old, though personally pure, might become ceremonially unclean by simple contact with the dead, and as such had to go through the required ablution, so by his close contact with our spiritually dead humanity, might the Son of Man be considered as defiled, and thus require to pass through the waters of baptism under the hand of John. And even as the high priest of old, though not a stain was on his body, had to wash it all over with pure water before he put on those holy and beautiful garments, clad with which he entered within the veil into the Holy of Holies; even so did the holy Jesus, whilst here without the camp, a bearer of our reproach, consent to pass through those baptismal waters, as a step in his preparation for entering into the true Holy of Holies, and putting on there those holy and beautiful garments, the garments of that glory with which his consecrated, exalted, enthroned humanity is invested.

But let us now fix our eye on what happened immediately after the baptism of Christ. He came up straightway out of the water. He did not wait, as the Jews asked the proselyte to do, to listen to still further instruction out of the law ;—instruction likely to be the more deeply impressed by the time and circumstances under which it was given. He did not wait, as we are led, from the very expression employed here, to believe that many of those did who received the baptism from John. In him there was no need for such delay or any such instruction. The law of his God, was it not written wholly, deeply, indelibly, in his heart? Straightway, therefore, he goes forth from under the Baptist's hands. John's wondering eye is on him as he ascends the river banks. There he throws himself into the attitude, engages in the exercise of prayer, and then it is, as with uplifted hands he gazes into the heavens, that he sees them opened above his head, the Spirit of God descending like a dove, and lighting on him, and a voice from heaven saying to him, "Thou art my beloved Son, in whom I am well pleased."

The requirements of the narrative, as given by St. Matthew, St. Mark, and St. Luke, do not involve us in the belief that the bystanders generally, if present in any numbers, saw these sights and heard that voice. Its being so distinctly specified by each of the Evangelists that it was He who saw and heard, would rather lead us to the inference that the sight and the hearing were confined to our Lord alone. John, indeed, tells us that he saw the vision, and we may believe therefore that he also heard the voice, but beyond the two, who may have been standing apart and by themselves, it would not seem that the wonders of this incident were at the time revealed. Other instances of like manifestations had this feature attached to them, that they were revealed to those whose organs were opened, and allowed to take them in, and were hidden from those around. Stephen saw the heavens opened, and the Son of man standing on the right hand of God. The clamorous crowd about him did not see as he did. Had the vision burst upon their eyes, it would have awed their tumultuous rage to rest. When Saul was struck down on his way to

Damascus, his companions saw indeed a light and heard some sounds, but they neither saw the person of the Saviour nor distinguished the words he spoke, though, in one sense, in a much fitter condition to do so than Saul was. It is said of the disciples on the day of Pentecost, that there appeared unto them tongues as of fire which rested on the head of each; it is not likely that these were seen by those who mocked.

But be it as it may as to the other spectators and auditors, it is evident that these supernatural appearances gave to the baptism of Jesus a new character in the Baptist's eyes, as they should do in ours. In the descending dove, outward emblem of the descending Spirit, he not only saw the pre-appointed token that the greater than he who was to baptize with the Holy Ghost was before him, but in the whole incident he beheld the first great step in our Lord's public and official life: the setting of him openly apart as the Lamb for the sacrifice; his consecration to, and his qualification for, the great office of the one and only High Priest over the House of God. The Levitical law required that the priesthood should be inaugurated with washing and anointing. Eight days were occupied (as we read in the 8th chapter of Leviticus) in the various imposing services of that original ceremonial, by which the family of Aaron was for ever set apart to the priestly office. It was now on the banks of the Jordan that a greater than Aaron was set apart for a higher than earthly priesthood. There was little about this consecration externally imposing, but the want was well supplied. No gorgeous temple, no brazen laver, but in their stead the pure waters of the running stream below, and the vast blue vault of heaven above; no holy and beautiful garments, the raiment of rich material, and fine needlework, but in their stead the spotless robe with which the fulfiller of all righteousness was clad; no chrysm, no costly sacred oil to pour upon the new priest's head, but in its stead the anointing with the Holy Ghost.

As Jesus stepped forth after the baptism on the banks of the river, he stood severed from the past, connected with a new future; Nazareth, its quiet home, its happy days, its peaceful occupations, lay behind; trials and toils, and suffering and death, lay before him. He would not have been the Son of man had he not felt the significance and solemnity of the hour; he would not have been the full partaker of our human nature had the weight of his new position, new duties, new trials, not pressed heavily upon his heart. He turns, in the pure, true instinct of his sinless humanity to seek support and strength in God, to throw himself and all his future upon his Father in prayer. But who may tell us how he felt, and what he prayed; what desires, what hopes, what solicitudes went up from the heart, at least, if not from the lips, of this extraordinary suppliant! Never before had the throne of the heavenly Grace been thus approached, and never before was such answer given. The prayer ascends direct from earth to heaven, and brings the immediate answer down. It is as he prays, that the Spirit comes, bringing light, and strength, and comfort to the Saviour, sustaining him under that consciousness of his Sonship to God, which now fills, expands, exalts his weak humanity. And does not our great Head and Representative stand before us here a type and pattern of every true believer in the Lord as to the duty, the privilege, the power of prayer? Of him, and of him only of the sons of men, might it be said that he prayed without ceasing; that his life was one of constant and sustained communion with his Father; and yet you find him on all the great occasions of his life having recourse to separate, solitary, sometimes to prolonged acts of devotion. His baptism, his appointment of the twelve apostles, his escape from the attempt to make him a king, his transfiguration, his agony in the garden, his death upon the cross, were all hallowed by prayer. The first and the last acts of his ministry were acts of prayer: from the lowest depth, from the highest elevation of that ministry, he poured out his spirit in prayer. For his mission on earth, for all his heaviest trials, he prepared himself by prayer. And should we not prepare for our poor earthly service, and fortify ourselves against temptations and trials, by following that great example? The heavens above are not shut up against us, the Spirit who descended like a dove has not taken wings and flown away for ever from this earth. There is a power by which these heavens can still be penetrated, which can still bring down upon us that gentle messenger of rest,—the power that lies in simple, humble, earnest, continued believing prayer.

The Holy Spirit as he descended upon Jesus was pleased to assume the form and gentle motion of a dove gliding down from the skies. He came not now as a rushing mighty wind. He sat not on Jesus as a cloven tongue of fire. It was right that when he came to do the work of quick and strong conviction, necessary in converting the souls of men, to bestow those gifts by which the first missionaries of the cross should be qualified for prosecuting that work, the rush as of a whirlwind should sweep through the room in which the disciples were assembled, and the cloven tongues of fire should come down and rest upon their heads. But the visitation of the Spirit to the Saviour was for an altogether different purpose, and it could not be more fitly represented than by the meek-eyed dove, the chosen symbol of gentleness and affection. The eagle with its wing of power, its eye of fire, its beak of terror, was the bird of Jove. The dove the bird of Jesus. To him the Spirit came not, as in dealing with the souls of men, to bring light out of darkness, order out of confusion; but to point out as the Saviour of the world, the meek and the lowly, the gentle and the loving Jesus.

But was no ulterior purpose served by the descent of the Spirit on this occasion? We touch a mystery here we cannot solve, and need not try to penetrate. The sinless humanity of Jesus was brought into intimate and everlasting union with the divine nature of the Son of God, doubly secured as we should say from sin, and fully qualified for all the Messianic service, and yet we are taught that that humanity was impregnated and fitted for its work by the indwelling of the Holy Spirit. He was born of the Holy Ghost. He was led by the Spirit into the wilderness. In the synagogue of Nazareth, where he had first opened his lips as a public teacher, there was given to him the book of the prophet Isaiah: he read the words, The Spirit of the Lord is upon me; and having read the passage out, he closed the book, and said, This day is this Scripture fulfilled in your ears. John testified of him saying: "He whom God hath sent speaketh the words of God, for God giveth not the Spirit by measure unto him." Jesus said of himself: "If I cast out devils by the Spirit of God, then is the kingdom of God come unto you." God sent Peter to Cornelius in opening the kingdom to the Gentiles. "God anointed Jesus of Nazareth with the Holy Ghost and with power." It was through the eternal Spirit that he offered himself without spot to God (Heb. ix. 14). He was declared to be the Son of God with power, according to the Spirit of holiness, by the resurrection from the dead (Rom. i. 4). It was through the Holy Ghost that he gave commandments to the apostles whom he had chosen, until the day in which he was taken up (Acts i. 2). So it is that through every stage of his career the Spirit is with him, qualifying him for every work, why or how, he alone could tell us who could lift that veil which shrouds the innermost recesses of the Spirit of the Incarnate Son of God.

As the Spirit lighted upon Jesus, there came to him a voice from heaven. This voice was twice heard again;—on the Mount of Transfiguration, and within the Temple. It was the voice of the Father. No man, since the fall of our first parent, had ever heard that voice before, as no man has ever heard it since. The fall sealed the Father's lips in silence; all divine communications afterwards with man were made through the Son. It was he who appeared and spake to the patriarchs; it was he who spake from the summit of Sinai, and was the giver of the law; but now for the first time the Father's lips are opened, the long-kept silence is broken, that this testimony of the Father to the Sonship of Jesus, this expression of his entire good pleasure with him as he enters upon his ministry, may be given. That testimony and expression of approval were repeated afterwards in the very same words at the transfiguration; the words indeed on that occasion were spoken not to, but of Jesus, and addressed to the disciples; and so with a latent reference perhaps to Moses and Elias, the Father said to them: "This is my beloved Son, in whom I am well pleased: hear ye him." But at the baptism St. Mark and St. Luke agree in stating that the words were spoken not of, but directly to Christ himself. Primarily and eminently it it may have been for Christ's own sake that the words were upon this occasion spoken; and as we contemplate them in this light, we feel that no thought can fathom their import, nor gauge what fulness of joy and strength they may have carried into the bosom of our Lord. But here too there is a veil which we must not try to lift. Instead of thinking then what meaning or power this assurance of his Sonship, and of the Father's full complacency in him, may have had for Christ, let us take it as opening to our view the one and only way of our adoption and acceptance by the Father, even by our being so well pleased in all things with Christ, our having such simple, implicit faith in him that the Father looking upon us as one with him, becomes also well pleased with us.

IX.

THE TEMPTATION.[1]

SATAN was suffered to succeed in his temptation of our first parents. His success may for the moment have seemed to him complete, secure; for did not the sentence run, "In the day that thou eatest thereof, thou shalt surely die"? And did not that sentence come from One whose steadfast truthfulness,—dispute it as he might in words with Eve,— none knew better than himself? Having once then got man to sin, he might have fancied that he had broken for ever the tie that bound earth to heaven, that he had armed against the first inhabitants of our globe the same resistless might, and the same unyielding justice, by which he and the partners of the first revolt in heaven had been driven away into their dark and ignominious prison-house. But if such a hope

---
[1] Matthew iv. 1-11; Mark i. 12, 13; Luke iv. 1-13.

had place for a season in the tempter's breast, it must surely have given way when, summoned together with his victims into the divine presence, the Lord God said to him: "I will put enmity between thee and the woman, and between thy seed and her seed; it shall bruise thy head, and thou shalt bruise his heel." Obscure as these words may at the time have seemed, yet must they have taught Satan to know that his empire over this new-formed world was neither to be an undisputed nor an undivided one. An enmity of some kind between his seed and the woman's seed was to arise; no mere temporary irritation and insubordination on the part of his new subjects, but an enmity which would prove fatal to himself and to his kingdom, the final advantage in the predicted warfare being all against him, for while he was to bruise the heel of his enemy, that enemy was to bruise his head, to crush his power.

It could not therefore have been with a sense of security free from uneasy anticipations, that from the days of the first Adam down to the birth of the second, the God of this world held his empire over our earth. His dominion was the dominion of sin and death, and his triumph might seem complete, none of all our race being found who could keep himself from sin; whilst every one that sinned had died. But were there no checks to the exercise of his power, nothing to inspire him with alarm? Had not Enoch and Elijah passed away from the world without tasting death? And must it not have appeared to him an inscrutable mystery that so many human spirits escaped at death altogether from beneath his sway? There were those prophecies, besides, delivered in Judea, of which he could not be ignorant, getting clearer and clearer as they grew in number, speaking of the advent of a great deliverer of the race; there were those Jewish ceremonies prefiguring some great event disastrous to his reign; there was the whole history and government of that wonderful people, the seed of Israel, guided by another hand than his, and regulated with a hostile purpose.

All this must have awakened dark forebodings within Satan's breast; forebodings stirred into a heightened terror when one of the woman's seed at last appeared, who, for thirty years, with perfect ease, apparently without a struggle, resisted all the seductions by which his brethren of mankind had been led into sin. The visit of Gabriel to Nazareth, the angelic salutations, the angels that appeared and the hymns that floated over the hills of Bethlehem, the adoration of the shepherds, the worship of the wise men, the prophecies of the Temple,—all these, let us believe, were known to the great adversary of our race; but not one nor all of them together excited in him such wonder or alarm as this simple fact, that here at last was one who stood absolutely stainless in the midst of the world's manifold pollutions. So long, however, as Jesus lived quietly and obscurely at Nazareth he might be permitted to enjoy his solitary triumph undisturbed, but his baptism in the Jordan brings him out from his retreat. This voice from heaven, a voice that neither man nor devil had ever heard before, resounding through the opened skies, proclaims Him to be more than a son of man—to be, in very deed, the Son of God. Who can this mysterious being be?—an alien and an enemy, Satan has counted him from his youth. But his Sonship to God! What can that imply; how is it to be manifested? The time has come for putting him to extreme trial, and, if he may not be personally overcome, for forcing him to disclose his character at the commencement of his career.

The opportunity for making the attempt is given. "Then was Jesus led up of the Spirit into the wilderness to be tempted of the devil." It was not, we may believe, under anything like compulsion, outward or inward, that Jesus acted when immediately after his baptism he retired to the desert. Between the promptings of the Spirit of God and the movements of Christ there ever must have been the most entire consent and harmony. Why, then, so instantly after his public inauguration to his earthly work, is there this voluntary retirement of our Lord, this hiding of himself in lonely solitudes? Accepting here the statement of the Evangelist, that it was to furnish the Prince of Darkness with the fit opportunity of assaulting him, may we not believe that these forty days in the wilderness without food served some other ends besides,—did for our Lord in his higher vocation what the forty days of fasting did for Moses and Elijah in their lesser prophetic office; that they were days of preparation, meditation, prayer,—a brief season interposed between the peaceful private life of Nazareth, and the public troubled life on which he was about to enter, for the purpose of girding him up for the great task assigned to him,—a season of such close, absorbing, elevating, spiritual exercises that the spirit triumphed over the body, and for a time felt not even the need of daily food? It was not till these forty days were over that he was anhungered, nor was it till hunger was felt that the tempter came in person to assault. The expressions used indeed by St. Mark and St. Luke appear to imply that the temptation ran through all the forty days; but if so, it must, in the first instance, have been of an inward and purely spiritual character, such as we can well conceive mingling with and shadowing those other exercises to which the days and nights of that long solitude and fasting were devoted.

And yet, though the holy spirit of our Lord prompted him to follow with willing footstep the leadings of the Holy Ghost, his true humanity may well have shrunk from what awaited him in the desert. He knew that he was there to come into close contact with, to meet in personal encounter the Head of that kingdom he was commissioned to overthrow; and, even as in the Garden human weakness sank tremblingly under the burden of immeasurable woe, so here it may have shrunk from such an interview and such a conflict, needing as it were to be urged by Divine compulsion, and thus authorizing the strong expression which St. Mark employs, "Immediately the Spirit driveth him into the wilderness." It may in fact have been no small part of that trial which ran through the forty days that he had continually before him, the approach and the encounter with the Prince of Darkness.

Whatever that state of his spirit was which rendered him insensible to the cravings of hunger, it terminates with the close of the forty days. The inward supports that had borne him up during that rapt ecstatic condition are removed. He sinks back into a natural condition. The common bodily sensations begin to be experienced; a strong craving for food is felt. Now, then, is the moment for the tempter to make his first assault upon the Holy One, as weak, famished, the hunger of his long fast gnawing at his heart, he wanders with the wild beasts as his sole companions over the frightful solitudes. Coming upon him abruptly, he says to Jesus, "If thou be the Son of God, command that these stones be made bread." The words of the recent baptismal scene at the Jordan are yet ringing in Satan's ears. He knows not what to make of them. He would fain believe them false; or better still, he would fain prove them false by prevailing upon Christ himself to doubt their truth. For, for him to doubt his Father's word would be virtually to renounce, disprove his Sonship. Even then, as by his artful insidious speech to the woman in the garden— Yea, has God said, In the day thou eatest thou shalt die?—he sought to insinuate a secret doubt of the divine truthfulness and divine goodness, so here, into the bosom of Jesus in the wilderness, he seeks to infuse a kindred doubt.

'If thou be really the Son of God, as I have so lately heard thee called. But canst thou be? can it be here, and thus—alone in these desert places, foodless, companionless, comfortless, for so many days—that God would leave or trust his Son? But if thou wilt not doubt that thou art his Son, surely God could never mean nor wish that his Son should continue in such a state as this? If thou be truly what thou hast been called, then all power must be thine; whatsoever things the Father doeth, thou too must be able to do. Show, then, thy Sonship, exert thy power, relieve thyself from this pressing hunger; "command that these stones be made bread."' The temptation here is twofold : to shake if possible Christ's confidence in Him who had brought him into such a condition of extreme need, and to induce him, under the influence of that distrust, to exert at once his own power to deliver himself, to work a miracle to provide himself with food. The temptation is at once repelled, not by any assertion of his Sonship, or of his abiding trust in God, in opposition to the insidious doubt suggested,—for that doubt the Saviour never cherished; the shaft that carried this doubt in it, though artfully contrived and skilfully directed, glanced innocuous from the mind of that confiding Son, who was ever as well pleased with the Father, as the Father had declared himself to be with him.

Nor was the temptation repelled by any such counter argument as that it was inadmissible to exert his Divine power merely for his own benefit; but by a simple quotation from the book of Deuteronomy: "It is written, Man shall not live by bread alone, but by every word that proceedeth out of the mouth of God." Jesus waives thus all question about his being the Son of God, or how it behoved him in that character to act. He takes his place as a son of man, and lays his hand upon an incident in the history of the children of Israel, who, led out into the wilderness, and continuing as destitute of common food for forty years as he had been for forty days, received in due time the manna provided for them by God, who said to them afterwards, by the lips of Moses: "The Lord thy God humbled thee, and suffered thee to hunger, and fed thee with manna, that he might make thee know that man doth not live by bread alone, but by every word that proceedeth out of the mouth of God." It was by the word of the

Lord's creative power that for those hungry Israelites the manna was provided; that word went forth at the Lord's own time, and to meet his people's wants in the Lord's own way; and upon that word, that is, upon Him whose word it was, Jesus, when now like the Israelites an-hungered in the wilderness, will rely. It is not necessary for him to turn stones into bread in order to sustain his life; other kind of food his Father, if he so pleased, could provide, and he will leave him to do as he pleases. From that entire dependence on his Father, to which in his present circumstances, and under that Father's guidance, he had been shut up, he had no desire to be relieved— would certainly do nothing prematurely to relieve himself, and least of all at Satan's bidding would use the higher, the divine faculty that was in him, as a mere instrument of self-gratification. It was in the same spirit of self-denial, that ever afterwards he acted. Those who taunted him on the cross, by saying, "It thou be the Son of God, come down from the cross," knew not how exact an echo their speech at Calvary was of Satan's speech in the wilderness,—how thoroughly they were proving their parentage, as being of their father the Devil. But Jesus would do neither as Satan nor these his children bade him. His power divine was given him to execute the great office of our spiritual deliverer: his way to the execution of his office lay through trial, suffering, and death, and he would not call that power in to save him from any part of the required endurance; neither from the hunger of the wilderness, nor from any of the far heavier loads he had afterwards to bear.

Foiled in his first attempt, accepting but profiting by his defeat, the artful adversary at once reverses his method, and assaults the Saviour precisely on the other side. He has tried to shake Christ's trust in his Father; he has failed; that trust seems only to gather strength the more severely it is proved; he will work now upon that very trust, and try to press it into presumption. "Then the Devil taketh him up into the holy city, and setteth him on a pinnacle of the Temple, and saith unto him, If thou be the Son of God, cast thyself down." 'I acknowledge that you have been right in the wilderness, that you have acted as a true Son of the Father. You have given, in fact, no mean proof of your entire confidence in him as your Father, in standing there in the extremity of hunger, and virtually saying, I am here by the will of God, here he can and he will provide, I leave all to him. But come, I ask you now to make another and still more striking display of your dependence in all possible conjunctures on the Divine aid. Show me, and all those worshippers in the court below, how far this faith of yours in your Father will carry you. Do now, what in the sight of all will prove you to be the very one the Jews are looking for. If thou be the Son of God, then, as we shall presume thou art, cast thyself down; the God who sustained thy body without food in the wilderness, can surely sustain it as you fling yourself into the yielding air; the people who are longing to see some wonder done by their expected Messiah, will hail you as such at once, when they see you, instead of being dashed to pieces, floating down at their feet as gently as a dove, and alighting in the midst of them. Give to me and them this proof of the greatness of your faith, the reality of your Sonship to God; and if you want a warrant for the act in those Scriptures which you have already quoted, remember what is written in one of those ancient Psalms, a psalm that the wise men say relates to you: "He shall give his angels charge concerning thee, and in their hands shall they bear thee up, lest at any time thou dash thy foot against a stone.'"

As promptly as before the Lord replies: "It is written again, Thou shalt not tempt the Lord thy God." Here again, there is no attempt at argument, no correction of the quotation which the tempter had made, no reminding him that, in quoting, he had omitted one essential clause, "He shall keep thee in all thy ways," the ways of his appointment, not of thine own fashioning. The one Scripture is simply met by the other, and left to be interpreted thereby. "Thou shalt not tempt the Lord thy God." To trust was one thing, to tempt another. Jesus would rely to the very uttermost upon the Divine faithfulness, upon God's promised care and help; but he would not put that faithfulness to a needless trial. If put by the Devil in a position of difficulty and danger, he will cherish an unbounded trust in God, and if extrication from that position be desirable, and no other way of effecting it be left, he will even believe that God will miraculously interpose in his behalf. But he will not of his own accord, without any proper call or invitation, for no other purpose than to make an experiment of the Father's willingness to aid him, to make a show of the kind of heavenly protection he could claim; he will not voluntarily place himself in such a position. He was here on the pinnacle of the Temple, from that pinnacle there was another open, easy, safe method of descent; why should he refuse to take it if he desired to descend; why fling himself into open space? If he did so unasked, unordered by God himself, what warrant could he have that the Divine power would be put forth to bear him up? God had indeed promised to bear him up, but he had not bidden him cast himself down, for no other purpose than to see whether he would be borne up or no; to do what Satan wished him to do, would be to show not the strength of his faith, but the extent of his presumption. Thus once again by that sword of the Spirit, which is the Word of God, is the second thrust of the adversary turned aside.

These first two temptations, whilst opposite in character, have yet much that is common to both. The preface to each of them is the same: "If thou be the Son of God,"—a preface obviously suggested by the recent testimony at the baptism. They have also the common object of probing to the bottom, and thus trying to ascertain, the powers and privileges which this Sonship to God conferred. There was curiosity as well as malice in the double effort to do so, and the subtlety of their method lay in this, that they were so constructed that had Christ yielded to either, in the very disclosure of his Godhead, there had been an abuse of its power. Had Jesus taken the Devil's way of proving his strength, he would have taken the very way to have broken it. In those first two temptations, Satan had spoken nothing of himself, had revealed nothing of his purposes: but balked in them he now drops the mask, appears in his own person, and boldly claims homage from Christ: "Again, the Devil taketh him up into an exceeding high mountain, and showeth him all the kingdoms of the world, and the glory of them; and saith unto him, All these things will I give thee, if thou wilt fall down and worship me." Had it been upon the actual summit of the Temple at Jerusalem that Jesus previously had been placed, and if so, how was his conveyance thither effected? was it upon the actual summit of some earthly mountain that the feet of our Saviour were now planted, and if so, how was it, how could it be that all the kingdoms of the world and the glory of them were brought before his eye?. We have no answer to give to those questions; we care not to speculate as to the outward mode in which each temptation was managed. We are willing to believe anything as to the accessories of this narrative which leave untouched its truthfulness as a historic record of an actual and personal encounter between the Prince of Darkness and the Prince of Light. That the gospel narrative is such a record, we undoubtingly believe, and are strengthened in our faith as we perceive not only the suitableness and the subtlety of each individual temptation, as addressed to the humanity of our Lord, assaulting it in the only quarters in which it lay open to assault; but the comprehensiveness of the whole temptation, as exemplifying those classes of temptations by which humanity at large, by which each of us, individually, is seduced from the path of true obedience unto God. The body, soul, and spirit of our Lord were each in turn invaded; by the lust of the flesh, by the lust of the eyes, by the pride of life, it was attempted to draw him away from his allegiance. The first temptation was built upon bodily appetite, the hunger of the long fast; the second, upon the love of ostentation, the desire we all have to show to the uttermost in what favour we stand with God or men; the third, upon ambition, the love of earthly, outward power and glory.

The third had, however, a special adaptation to Christ's personal character and position at the time, and this very adaptation lent to it peculiar strength, making it, as it was the last, so also the most insidious, the most alluring of the three. Jesus knew the ancient prophecies about a universal monarchy that was to be set up in the days of Messiah the Prince. From the days of his childhood, when in the Temple he had sat among the doctors, hearing them and asking them questions, the sacred volume which contained these prophecies had been in his hands. Who shall tell us with what interest, with what wonder, with what self-application these prophecies were pondered by him in the days of his youth, during which he grew in wisdom as he grew in years? Who shall tell us how soon or how fully he attained the sublime consciousness, that he was himself the Messiah of whom that volume spake? Whatever may have been his earlier experience, at the time at least when the attestation at his baptism was given, that consciousness filled and pervaded his spirit. But he fell not into the general delusion which, in its desire for a conquering and victorious prince, lost sight of a suffering, dying Redeemer. He knew full well that the path marked out for him as the Saviour of mankind lay through profoundest sorrow, and would end in an agonizing death. How much of all this Satan knew, it would be presumptuous to conjecture. This, however, we are assured that he knew,—for he had heard and could quote the ancient prophecies which pointed to it,—he knew about a monarchy that in the last days the God of heaven was to set up, which was to overturn his own, which was to embrace all the kingdoms of the world, and into which all the glory of these kingdoms was to be brought. And he may, we might almost say, he must have known beforehand of the toil, and strife, and hard endurance through which the throne of that monarchy was to be reached by his great rival.

And now that rival is before him, just entering upon his career. Upon that rival he will make a bold attempt. He will show him all those kingdoms that have been so long under his dominion as the God of this world. He will offer them all to him at once, without a single blow being struck, a single peril encountered, a single suffering endured. He will save him all that conflict which, if not doubtful in the issue, was to be so painful in its progress. He will lay down his sceptre, and suffer Jesus to take it up. In one great gift he will make over his whole right of empire over these kingdoms of the world to Christ, suffer him at once to enter upon possession of them, and clothe himself with all their glory. This is his glittering bribe, and all he asks in return is that Jesus shall do him homage, as the superior by whom the splendid fief was given, and under whom it is held.

A bold and blasphemous attempt, for who gave him those kingdoms thus to give away? And how could he imagine that Jesus was open to a bribe, or would ever bow the knee to him? Let us remember, however, that we all judge others by ourselves; that there are those who think that every man has his price; that, make the bribe but large enough, and any man may be bought. And at the head of such thinkers is Satan. He judged Jesus by himself. And even as through lust of government he, archangel though he was, had not hesitated to withdraw his worship from the Supreme, so may he have thought that, taken unawares, even the Son of God himself might have fallen before the dazzling temptation. Had he done so, Satan would indeed have triumphed; for putting wholly out of the question the violated relationship to the Father, Jesus would thus have renounced all the purely moral and religious purposes of his mission—would have ceased to be regarded as the author of a spiritual revolution, and the founder of a spiritual kingdom, affecting myriads of human spirits from the beginning to the end of time, and would thenceforth have taken up the character of a mere vulgar earthly monarch.

But Satan knew not with whom he had to do. The eye of Jesus may for a moment have been dazzled by the offer made, and this implied neither imperfection nor sin, but it refused to rest upon the seducing spectacle. It turned quickly and resolutely away. No sooner is the bribe offered than it is repelled. In haste, as if that magnificent panorama was not one on which even his pure eye should be suffered to repose; as if this temptation were one which even he could not afford to dally with; in anger too at the base condition coupled with the bribe, and as if he who offered it could no longer be suffered to remain in his presence, he calls the Devil by his name, and says: " Get thee hence, Satan; for it is written, Thou shalt worship the Lord thy God, and him only shalt thou serve." Satan had wanted Jesus to give him some proof of his Divine power, and now he gets it; gets it as that command is given which he must instantly obey. At once all that glittering illusion that he had conjured up vanishes from the view. At once his hateful presence is withdrawn, the conflict is over, the victory is complete. Jesus stands once more alone in the wilderness, but he is not left alone. Angels come and minister unto him, gazing with wonder on that mysterious man who has entered into this solitary conflict with the head of the principalities and powers of darkness, and foiled him at every point.

But how are we to look upon this mysterious passage in the life of Christ? Are we to read the record of it as we would the story of a duel between two great chiefs, under neither of whom we shall ever have to serve, in the mode and tactics of whose warfare we have consequently but little interest? The very reverse. He who appeared that day in the wilderness before Jesus, and by so many wily acts strove to rob him of his integrity as a Son of the Father, goeth about still as the arch-enemy of our souls, seeking whom he may devour. His power over us is not weakened, though it failed on Christ. His malice against us is not lessened, though it was impotent when tried on him. The time, the person, the circumstances, all bestowed an undoubted peculiarity upon these temptations of the wilderness, the Temple, and the mountain-top. We may be very sure that by temptations the same in outward form no other human being shall ever be assailed. But setting aside all that was special in them, let us lay our hand on the radical and essential principle of each of these three temptations, that we may see whether each of us is not still personally exposed to it.

In the first instance, Christ, when under the pressure of one of the most urgent appetites of our nature, is tempted to use a power that he got for other purposes, to minister to his own gratification. He is tempted, in fact, to use unlawful means to procure food. Is that a rare temptation? Not to speak here of those poor unfortunates who, under a like pressure, are tempted to put forth their hands to what is not their own, what shall we say of the merchant whom, in the brightest season of his prosperity, some sore and unexpected calamity overtakes? Through some reckless speculation, he sees the gay vision of his hopes give way, and utter ruin stand before him but a few days off. The dismal picture of a family accustomed to wealth plunged into poverty already haunts his eye and rends his heart. But a short respite still is given. Those around him are ignorant how he stands, his credit still is good, confidence in him is still unbroken. He can use that credit, he can employ the facilities which that confidence still gives. He dishonourably does so; with stealthy hand he places a portion of his fortune beyond the reach of his future creditors to keep it for his family's use. That man meets and falls under the very same temptation with which our Lord and Master was assailed. Distrusting God, he uses the powers and opportunities given him, unrighteously and for selfish ends. He forgets that man liveth not by bread alone, but by every word which proceedeth out of the mouth of God.

Or what again shall we say of him who, fairly committed to the faith of Christ, and embarked in the great effort of overcoming all that is evil in his evil nature, plunges, with scarce a thought, into scenes and amid temptations such that it would need a miracle to bring him forth unscathed? That man meets and falls under the very same temptation with which our Saviour was assailed, when the Devil said, Cast thyself down, and quoted the promise of Divine support. Many and most precious indeed are the promises of Divine protection and support given us in the Word of God, but they are not for us to rest on if recklessly and needlessly we rush into danger, crossing any of the common laws of nature, or trampling the dictates of ordinary prudence and the lesson of universal experience beneath our feet. It is not faith, it is presumption which does so.

It might seem that we could find no actual parallel to the last temptation of our Lord, but in truth it is the one of all the three that is most frequently presented. Thrones and kingdoms, and all their glory, are not held out to us, but the wealth and the distinctions, the honours and the pleasures of life,—these in different forms, in different degrees, ply with their solicitations all of us in every rank from the highest to the lowest, tempting us away from God to worship and serve the creature more than the Creator, who is blessed for evermore. A spectacle not so wide, less gorgeous in its colouring, but as sensuous, as illusive as that presented to Jesus on the mountain-top, the arch-deceiver spreads out before our eyes, whispering to our hearts, "All this will I give you;" all this money, all that ease, all that pleasure, all that rank, all that power, but in saying so he deals with us more treacherously than he dealt with Christ of old. With him he boldly and broadly laid it down as the condition of the grant, that Christ should fall down and worship him. He asks from us no bending of the knee, no act of outward worship; all he asks is, that we believe his false promises, and turn away from God and Christ to give ourselves up to worldliness of heart and habit and pursuit. If we do so he is indifferent how we now think or act toward himself personally, for this is one of the worst peculiarities of that kingdom of darkness over which he presides, that its ruler knows no better subjects than those who deny his very being, and disown his rule.

But if it be to the very same temptations as those which beset our divine Lord and Master, that we are still exposed, let us be grateful to him for teaching us how to overcome them. He used throughout a single weapon. He had the whole armory of heaven at his command; but he chose only one instrument of defence, the Word, the written Word, that sword of the Spirit. It was it that he so successfully employed. Why this exclusive use of an old weapon? He did not need to have recourse to it. A word of his own spoken would have had as much power as a written one quoted; but then the lesson of his example had been lost to us,—the evidence that he himself has left behind of the power over temptation that lies in the written Word. Knowing, then, that you wrestle not with flesh and blood alone, but with angels, and principalities, and powers, and with him the head of all, of whose devices it becomes you not to be ignorant, take unto you the whole armour of God, for all is needed; but remember, of all the pieces of which that panoply is composed, the last that is put into the hand of the Christian soldier by the great Captain of his salvation,—put into his hand as the one that he himself, on the great occasion of his conflict with the Devil, used,—put into his hand as the most effective and the only one that serves at once for defence and for assault,—is the sword of the Spirit, the Word of God. By it all other parts of the armour are guarded. The helmet might be shattered on the brow, the shield wrenched from the arm, did it not protect; for hope and faith, that helmet and that shield, on what do they rest, but upon the Word of the living God? When the tempter comes, then, and plies you with his manifold and strong solicitations, be ready to meet him, as Jesus met him in the wilderness, and you shall thus come to know how true is that saying of David : " By the words of thy lips I have kept me from the path of the destroyer."

X.

THE FIRST DISCIPLES.[1]

FROM the forty days in the desert, from the long fast, from the triple assault, from the great victory won, from the companionship of the ministering angels, Jesus returns to the banks of the Jordan, and mingles, unnoticed and unknown, among the disciples of the Baptist. On the day of his return, a deputation from the Sanhedrim in Jerusalem arrives, to institute a formal and authoritative inquiry into the character and claims of the great preacher of repentance. John's answers to the questions put by these deputies, are chiefly negative in their character. He is not the Christ; he is not Elijah risen from the dead; neither is he that prophet, by whom, as they imagined, Elijah was to be accompanied; who he is he would not say, however pointedly interro-

[1] John i. 29-51.

gated. But what he is, he so far informs them as to quote and apply to himself the passage from the prophecies of Isaiah, which spake of a voice crying in the wilderness, "Prepare ye the way of the Lord, make his paths straight." Challenged as to his right to baptize, if he is not that Christ, nor Elias, nor that prophet, John can now speak as he had not been able to do previously. Hitherto he had spoken indeterminately of one whom he knew not, the greater than he, who was to come after him; but now the sign from heaven had been given, the Spirit had been seen descending and abiding on Jesus. From the day of his baptism Jesus had withdrawn John knew not whither, but now he sees him in the crowd, and says: "I baptize with water: but there standeth one among you, whom ye know not; he it is, who, coming after me, is preferred before me, whose shoe's latchet I am not worthy to unloose."

Having got so little to satisfy them as to who the Baptist was, it does not seem that the deputies from Jerusalem troubled themselves to make any inquiries as to who this other and greater than John was. Nor was it otherwise with the multitude. Though the words of the Baptist, so publicly spoken, were such as might well awaken curiosity, the day passed, and Jesus remained unknown, assuming, saying, doing nothing by which he could be recognised. That John needed to point him out in order to recognition confirms our belief, derived in the first instance directly from the narrative itself, that at the baptism none but John and Jesus heard the voice from heaven, or saw the descending dove. Had the bystanders seen and heard these, among the disciples of John there would have been some ready at once to recognise Jesus on his return from the desert. But it is not so. Jesus remains hidden, and will not with his own hand lift the veil,—will not bear any witness of himself,—leaves it to another to do so.

But he must not continue thus unknown,— that were to frustrate the very end of all John's ministry. The next day, therefore, as John sees Jesus coming to him, whilst yet he is some way off, he points to him, and says: " Behold the Lamb of God, which taketh away the sin of the world! This is he of whom I said, After me cometh a man which is preferred before me; for he was before me. And I knew him not: but that he should be made manifest to Israel, therefore am I come baptizing with water." "I saw the Spirit descending from heaven like a dove, and it abode upon him. And I knew him not: but he that sent me to baptize with water, the same said unto me, Upon whom thou shalt see the Spirit descending, and remaining on him, the same is he which baptizeth with the Holy Ghost. And I saw, and bare record that this is the Son of God."

John's first public official testimony to Christ was, as it seems to me, particularly remarkable, as containing no reference whatever to that character or office in which the mass of the Jewish people might have been willing enough to recognise him, but confined to those two attributes of his person and work which they so resolutely rejected. There is no mention here of Jesus as Messiah, the Prince, the King of Israel. The record that John bears of him is, that he is the Son of God, the Lamb of God. He had lately heard the voice from heaven saying: "Thou art my beloved Son, in whom I am well pleased."

In giving him then this title, in calling him the Son of God, John was but re-echoing, as it were, the testimony of the Father. Taught thus to use and to apply it, it may be fairly questioned, whether the Baptist in his first employment of it entered into the full significance of the term, as declarative of Christ's unity of nature with the Father. That in its highest, its only true sense indeed, it did carry with it such a meaning, and was understood to do so by those who knew best how to interpret it, appears in many a striking passage of the life of Jesus, and most conspicuously of all, in his trial and condemnation before the Jewish Sanhedrim. It was a title whose assumption by Jesus involved, in the apprehension of those who regarded him but as a man, nothing short of blasphemy. Such is the title here given to him by the Baptist. Whether he fully understood it or not, we can trace its adoption and employment to an obvious and natural source.

But that other title, the Lamb of God, and the description annexed to it, " who taketh away the sin of the world," how came the Baptist to apply these to Christ, and what did he mean by doing so? Here we cannot doubt that the same inner and divine teaching, which taught him in a passage of Isaiah's prophecies to see himself, taught him in another to see the Saviour, and that it was from that passage in which the prophet speaks of the Messiah as a Lamb brought to the slaughter, as a sheep dumb before his shearers, that he borrowed the title now for the first time bestowed upon Jesus. From the same passage, too, he learned that the Anointed of the Lord was to be "wounded for our transgressions, to be bruised for our iniquities, the chastisement of our peace was to be upon him, and with his stripes we are to be healed." Here in Jesus, John sees the greater than himself whose way he was to prepare before him, but that way he sees to be one leading him to suffering and to death; his perhaps the only Jewish eye at that moment opened to discern the truth that it was through this suffering and this death that the spiritual victories of the great King were to be achieved, that it was upon them that his spiritual kingdom was to have its broad and deep foundations laid. John's baptism had hitherto been one of repentance for the remission of sins. This remission had been held out in prospect as the end to which repentance was to conduct; but all about its source, its fulness, its certainty had been obscure,—obscure perhaps to John's own eyes, obscure at least in the manner of his speaking about it; but now he sees the Lamb of God, the suffering, dying Jesus, taking away by bearing it the sin of the world,—not taking away by subduing it the sinfulness of the world, that John could not have meant, this Jesus has not done,— but taking the world's sin away by taking it on himself, and expiring beneath its load, making the great atoning sacrifice, fulfilling all the types of the Jewish ceremonial, all that the paschal lamb, all that the lamb of the morning and evening sacrifice had been typifying.

In the two declarations then of John, "This is the Son of God," "Behold the Lamb of God, who taketh away the sin of the world," you have in a form as distinct, as short and compendious as it is anywhere else to be found,—the gospel of the kingdom. The divine nature of the man Christ Jesus, the completeness and efficacy of the shedding of his blood, of the offering up of himself for the remission of sins, are they not here very simply and plainly set forth? We are not asked to believe that the Baptist himself understood his own testimony to Christ, as with the light thrown on it by the Epistles, and especially in this instance, by the Epistle to the Hebrews, we now understand it; but assuredly he understood so much of it as that he himself saw in Christ, and desired that others should see in him, the heaven-laid channel, opened up through his life and death, of that Divine mercy which covereth all the transgressions of every penitent believing soul.

How interesting to hear this gospel of the grace of God preached so early, so simply, so earnestly, so believingly by him whose office in all the earlier parts of his ministry was so purely moral, a call simply to repentance, to acts and deeds of justice, mercy, truth. But this was the issue to which all those preparatory instructions were to conduct. The law in the hands of John was to be a schoolmaster to guide at last to Christ; and when the time for that guidance came, was it not with a sensation of relief, a bounding throb of exulting satisfaction, that—conscious of how impotent in themselves all his efforts were to get men to repent and reform, while the pardon of their sins was anxiously toiled after in the midst of perplexity and doubt, instead of being gratefully and joyfully accepted as God's free gift in Christ—the Baptist proclaimed to all around, "Behold the Lamb of God, which taketh away the sin of the world."

Nor was he discouraged that his announcement met with no response that day from the crowd around, that still his voice was as the voice of one crying in a wilderness. The many who waited on his ministry, and partook of his baptism, came from curiosity, acted on a passing impulse, hoped that some new and better state of things socially and politically was to be ushered in by this strange child of the desert,—and had no deeper wants to be supplied, or spiritual longings to be satisfied. Quite strange—if not unmeaning, yet unwelcome—to their ears, this new utterance of the Baptist. It was not after the Lamb of God, not after one who was to take away their sins, that they were seeking. But there were others of a different mould, partakers of the spirit of Simeon and

Anna, waiting for the consolation of Israel, for the coming of one to whom, whatever outward kingdom he was to set up, they mainly looked as their spiritual Lord and King, in the days of whose kingdom peace was to enter troubled consciences, and there should be rest for wearied hearts. The eyes of these waiters for the morning saw the first streaks of dawn in the ministry of the Baptist, and some of them had already enrolled themselves as his disciples, attaching themselves permanently to his person.

The next day after he had given his first testimony to Christ's lamb-like and sacrificial character and office,—a testimony apparently so little heeded, attended at least with no outward and visible result,—John is standing with two of these disciples by his side. He will repeat to them the testimony of yesterday; they had heard it already, but he will try whether it will not have another and more powerful effect when given not promiscuously to a general audience, but specifically to these two. Looking upon Jesus as he walked, he directed their attention to him, by simply saying once again, " Behold the LAMB OF

God!"—leaving it to their memory to supply all about him which in the course of the two preceding days he had declared. Not now without effect. Neither of these two men may know as yet in what sense he is the Lamb of God, nor how by him their sin is to be taken away; but both have felt their need of some one willing and able to guide their agitated hearts to a secure haven of rest, and they hope to find in him thus pointed out the one they need. They follow him. John restrains them not; it is as he would wish. Willingly, gladly, he sees them part from him to follow this new Master. He knows that they are putting themselves under a better, higher guidance than any which he can give. But who are these two men? One of them is Andrew, better known to us by his brotherhood to Simon. The other reveals himself by the very manner in which he draws the veil over his own name. He would not name himself, and by that very modesty which he displays he stands revealed. It is no other than that disciple whom Jesus loved; no other than the writer of this Gospel, upon whose memory those days of his first acquaintance with Jesus had fixed themselves in the exact succession of their incidents so indelibly, that though he writes his narrative at least forty years after the death of Christ, he writes not only as an eye-witness, but as one who can tell day after day what happened, and no doubt the day was memorable to him, and the very hour of that day, on which he left the Baptist's side to join himself to Jesus.

John and Andrew follow Jesus. We wonder which of the two it was that made the first movement towards him. Let us believe it to have been John, that we may cherish the thought that he was the first to follow as he was the last to leave. He was one at least of the first two men who became followers of the Lamb; and that because of their having heard him described as the Lamb of God. When this first incident in his own connexion with Jesus is considered, need we wonder that this epithet "the Lamb" became so favourite a one with John; that it is in his writings, and in them alone of all the writings of the New Testament, that it is to be found, occurring nearly thirty times in the book of the Apocalypse.

The two disciples follow Jesus, silently, respectfully, admiringly—anxious to address him, yet unwilling to obtrude. He relieves them from their embarrassment. The instinct of that love which is already drawing them to him, tells him that he is being followed for the first time by human footsteps, answering to warm-beating, anxious human hearts. He turns and says to them, "What seek ye?" a vague and general question, which left it open to them to give any answer that they pleased, to connect their movement with him or not. But their true hearts speak out. It is not any short and hurried converse by the way that will satisfy their ardent longings. They would have hours with him, days with him, alone in the seclusion of his home. "Rabbi"— they say to him, the first time doubtless that Jesus was ever so addressed,—" where dwellest thou? He saith to them, Come and see; and they came and saw where he dwelt, and abode with him that day, for it was about the tenth hour." If, in his Gospel, John numbers the hours of the day according to the Jewish method of computation, then it must have been late in the afternoon, at four o'clock, having but two hours of that day to run, that Christ's invitation was given and accepted. We incline to believe, however, that John follows not the Jewish but the Roman method of counting, and if so, then it was in the forenoon, at ten o'clock, that the two disciples accompanied our Lord. And we are the rather induced to believe so, as it gives room for the other incident, the bringing of Simon to Jesus, to happen during the same day, which, from the specific and journal-like character of this part of John's narrative, we can scarcely help conceiving that it did.

But where and whose was the abode to which Jesus conducted John and Andrew, and how were their hours employed? It could only have been some house which the hospitality of strangers had opened for a few days' residence, to one whom they knew not, and over all the intercourse that took place beneath its roof the veil is drawn. It is the earliest instance this of that studied reserve as to all the minuter details of Christ's daily life and conversation upon which we may have afterwards to offer some remarks. John has not yet learned to lay his head on that Master's bosom, but already he is sitting at his feet. And there for all day long, and on into the quiet watches of the night, would he sit drinking in our Lord's first opening of his great message of mercy from the Father. Andrew has something of the restless active spirit of his brother in him, and so no sooner has he himself attained a sure conviction that this is indeed the Christ whom he has found, than he hurries out to seek his own brother Simon, and bring him to Jesus. We should have liked exceedingly to have been present at that interview, to have stood by as Jesus for the first time looked at Simon, and Simon for the first time fixed his eye on Jesus. The Lord looks upon Simon and sees all he is, and all that he is yet to be. His great confession, his three denials, his bitter repentance, his restoration, the great services rendered, the death like that of his Master, he is to die, all are present to the thoughts of Jesus as he looks. "Thou art Simon," he says at once to him, as if he had known him from his youth,—" Simon, the son of Jona." This word Jona, in Hebrew, means a dove, and it has been thought, fancifully perhaps, that it was with a sidelong reference to the place of the dove's usual resort that Jesus said: "Thou art Simon the son of the dove, which seeks shelter in the rock; thou shalt be called Cephas, shalt be the rock for the dove to shelter in." On an after occasion Jesus explained more fully why it was that this new name of Peter the Rock was bestowed. Here we have nothing but the simple fact before us, that it was at the first meeting of the two, and before any converse whatever took place between them, that the change of name was announced; with what effect on Peter we are left to guess,—his very silence, a silence rather strange to him, the only thing to tell us how deep was the impression made by this first interview with Christ.

The next day, the fifth from that on which this chronicling of the days begins, Jesus goes forth on his return to Galilee, finds Philip by the way, and saith to him, "Follow me." Philip was of Bethsaida. Bethsaida lay at the northern extremity of the Sea of Galilee, not on the line of Christ's route from Bethabara to Nazareth or Cana. We infer from this circumstance, that like John,

Andrew, and Peter, Philip had left his home to attend on the ministry of the Baptist. On the banks of the Jordan, or afterwards from one or other of his Galilean countrymen, who had already joined themselves to Christ, he had learned the particulars of his earlier earthly history. Any difficulty that he might himself have had in recognising the Messiahship of one so born and educated, was soon got over, the wonder at last enhancing the faith. Finding Nathanael, Philip said to him: " We have found him of whom Moses in the law and the prophets did write, Jesus of Nazareth, the son of Joseph." It was a very natural reply for one who lived so near to Nazareth, and knew how insignificant a place it was, to say: " Can there any good thing, any such good thing, come out of Nazareth ?" Come and see, was Philip's answer. It proved the very simplicity and docility of Nathanael's nature, that he did at once go to see. Perhaps, however, his recent exercises had prepared him for the movement. Before Philip called him, he had been under the fig-tree, the chosen place for meditation and prayer with the devout of Israel. There had he been pondering in his heart, wondering when the Hope of Israel was to come, and praying that it might be soon, when a friend comes and tells him that the very one he has been praying for has appeared. With willing spirit he accompanies his friend. Before, however, he gets close to him, Jesus says, Behold an Israelite indeed, in whom is no guile! How much of that very guileless spirit which we have learned to call by his name is there in Nathanael's answer! Without thinking that he is in fact accepting Christ's description of him as true, and so exposing himself to the charge of no small amount of arrogance,. disproving in fact that charge by the very blindness that he shows to the expression of it, he says, "Whence knowest thou me?" Our Lord's reply, "Before that Philip called thee, when thou wast under the fig-tree I saw thee," we may regard as carrying more with it to the conscience and heart of Nathanael than the mere proof that Christ's eye saw what no human eye, placed as he was at the time, could have seen, but that the secrets of all hearts lay open to him with whom he had now to do. Nathanael comes with doubting mind, but a guileless heart; and so now, without dealing with it intellectually, the doubt is scattered by our Lord's quick glance penetrating into his inner spirit, and an instant and sure faith is at once planted in Nathanael's breast.

I am apt to think from the very form of Nathanael's answer, from the occurrence in it of a phrase that does not seem to have been a Jewish synonym for the Messiah, that Nathanael too had been at the Jordan, and had heard there the testimony that John had borne to Jesus. Rabbi, he says, Thou art what I have lately heard thee called, and wondered at them calling thee,—" Thou art the Son of God, thou art the King of Israel." There was something so fresh, so fervent, so full-hearted in the words, they fell so pleasantly on the ear of Jesus, that a bright vision rose before his eye of the richer things that were yet in store for all that believed on him. First, he says to Nathanael individually, Because I said unto thee, I saw thee under the fig-tree, believest thou? thou shalt see greater things than these;—and then looking on the others, whilst still addressing himself to him, he adds :—Verily, verily, I say unto you, Hereafter, or rather from this time forward, ye shall see heaven open, and the angels of God ascending and descending upon the Son of Man. You have heard, that a few weeks ago, on the banks of the river, the heavens opened for a moment above my head, and the Spirit was seen coming down like a dove upon me. That was but a sign. Believe what that sign was meant to confirm; believe in me as the Lamb of God, the Saviour of the world, the baptizer with the Holy Ghost, and your eye of faith shall be quickened, and you shall see those heavens standing continually open above my head,—opened by me for you; and the angels of God,—all beings and things that carry on the blessed ministry of reconciliation between earth and heaven, between the souls of believers below and the heavenly Father above,—going up and bringing blessings innumerable down, ascending and descending upon the Son of Man. Son of God, —my Father called me so at my baptism, the devil tempted me as such in the desert, the Baptist gave me that name at Bethabara, and thou, Nathanael, hast bestowed it on me now once again; but the name that I now like best, and shall oftenest call myself, is that of the Son of Man; and yet I am both, and in being both truly and eternally fulfil the dream of Bethel. It was but in a dream that your father Jacob saw that ladder set up on earth, whose top reached to heaven, up and down which the angels were ever moving. It shall be in no dream of the night, but in the clearest vision of the day,—in the hours when the things of the unseen world shall stand most truly and vividly revealed,—you shall see in me that ladder of all gracious communication between earth and heaven, my humanity fixing firmly the one end of that ladder on earth, in my divinity the other end of that ladder lost amid the splendours of the throne.

At first sight the narrative of these five days after the temptation, which we have thus followed to its close, has but little to attract. It recounts what many might regard as the comparatively insignificant fact of the attachment of five men—all of them Galileans, none of them of any note or rank among the people—to Christ. But of these five men four afterwards became apostles (all of them, indeed, if, as is believed by many of our best critics, Nathanael and Bartholomew were the same person); and two of them, Peter and John, are linked together in the everlasting remembrance of that Church which they helped to found. Had the Baptist's ministry done nothing more than prepare those five men for the reception of the Messiah, and hand them over so prepared to Jesus, to become the first apostles of the faith, it had not been in vain. These five men were the first disciples of Jesus, and in the narrative of their becoming so we have the history of the infancy of the Church of the living God, that great community of the saints, that growing and goodly company, swelling out to a multitude that no man can number, out of every kindred, and tongue, and people, and nation. If there be any interest in tracing the great river that bears at last on its broad bosom the vessels of many lands, to some little bubbling fountain up among the hills; if there be any interest in tracing the great monarchy whose power overshadowed the earth, to the erection of a little organized community among the Sabine hills; if the traveller regards with wonder the little gushing stream, or the historian, the first weak beginnings of the Roman commonwealth; then may the same emotion be permitted to the Christian as he reads the page that tells of the first foundations being laid of a spiritual kingdom, which is to outlive all the kingdoms of this earth, and abide in its glory for ever.

Still another interest attaches to the narrative now before us. It tells us of the variety of agencies employed in bringing the first of his disciples to Christ. Two of these five men acted on the promptings of the Baptist, one of them on the direct call or summons of our Lord himself; one at the instance of a brother, one on the urgency of a friend. It would be foolish to take these cases of adherence to the Christian cause as typical or representative of the numbers brought respectively to Christ by the voice of the preacher, the word of Christ himself, and the agency of relative or acquaintance; but we cannot go wrong in regarding this variety of agency within so narrow limits, as warranting all means and methods by which any can be won to a true faith in

Christ. Whatever these means and methods may be, in order to be effectual they must finally resolve themselves into direct individual address. It was in this way the first five disciples were gathered in. By John speaking to two, Jesus to one, Andrew to one, Philip to one. It is the same species of agency similarly employed which God has always most richly blessed; the direct, earnest, loving appeal of one man to his acquaintance, relative, or friend. How many are there among us who have been engaged for years either in supporting by our liberality, or aiding by our actual service one or other of those societies whose object is to spread Christianity, but who may seldom if ever have endeavoured, by direct and personal address, to influence one human soul for its spiritual and eternal good! Not till more of the spirit of John and Jesus, of Andrew and Philip, as exhibited in this passage, descend upon us, shall we rightly acquit ourselves of our duty as followers of the Lamb.

But in my mind the chief interest of the passage lies in the conduct of our Lord himself. Those five days were not only the birth-time of the Church, they were the beginning of Christ's public ministry, and how does that ministry open? Silently, gently, unostentatiously; no public appearances, no great works done, no new instrumentality employed; by taking two men to live with him for a day, by asking another to follow him, by dealing wisely and tenderly and encouragingly with two others who are brought to him,—so enters the Lord upon the earthly task assigned to him. Would any one sitting down to devise a career for the Son of God descending upon our earth, to work out the salvation of our race, have assigned such an opening to his ministry, and yet could anything have been more appropriate to him who came not to be ministered unto but to minister, than this turning away from being ministered unto by the angels in the desert, to the rendering of those kindly and all-important services to John and Andrew and Peter, and Philip and Nathanael?

IX.

THE FIRST MIRACLE.[1]

"And the third day there was a marriage in Cana of Galilee." Looking back to the preceding narrative, you observe that from the time of the arrival at Bethabara of the deputation from Jerusalem sent to inquire into the Baptist's character and claims, an exact note of the time is kept in recording the incidents which followed. "The next day," *i.e.*, the first after that of the appearance of the deputation, John sees Jesus coming unto him, and points him out as the "Lamb of God, which taketh away the sin of the world." "Again the next day after," standing in company with two of his disciples, John repeats the testimony, and the two disciples followed Jesus; one of them, Andrew, going and bringing his own brother Simon; the other, John, sitting at his

[1] John ii. 1-12.

new Master's feet. "The day following," Jesus, setting out on his return to Galilee, findeth Philip. Philip findeth Nathanael, and so, accompanied by these five (Andrew, John, Peter, Philip, and Nathanael), Jesus proceeds upon his way back to his home. Occurring in a narrative like this, where the regular succession of events is so accurately chronicled, we naturally, in coming to the expression, "the third day," interpret it as meaning the third day after the one that had immediately before been spoken of, that is, the one of Christ's departure from the banks of the Jordan. Two days' easy travel carry him and his new attendants to Nazareth, but there is no one there to receive them. The mother of Jesus and his brethren are at Cana, a village lying a few miles farther to the north. Thither they follow them, and find that a marriage is being celebrated there, to the feast connected with which Jesus and his five disciples are invited. One of the five, Nathanael, belonged to Cana, and might have received the invitation on his own account as an acquaintance of the family in whose house the marriage-feast was held. But the others were strangers, only known to that family as having accompanied Jesus for the last few days,—their tie of discipleship to him quite a recent one, and as yet scarcely recognised by others. That on his account alone, and in consequence of a connexion with him of such a kind, they should have been at once asked to be present at an entertainment to which friends and relatives only were ordinarily invited, would seem to indicate some familiar bond between the family at Nazareth and the one in which this marriage occurs. The idea of some such relationship is supported by the freedom which Mary appears to exercise, speaking to the servants not like a stranger, but as one familiar in the dwelling. Besides, if Simon, called the Canaanite, was called so because of his connexion with the village of Cana, his father Alphæus or Cleophas, who was married to a sister of Christ's mother, may have resided there, and it may have been in his family that this marriage occurred. Could we but be sure of this,—which certainly is probable, and which early tradition affirms,—the circumstance that when Jesus seated himself at this marriage-feast he sat down at a table around which mother, and brothers and sisters, and uncle and aunt, and cousins of his own now gathered, it would give a peculiarly domestic character to the scene, and throw a new charm and interest around the miracle which was wrought at it. At any rate, we may assume that it was in a family connected by some close ties, whether of acquaintance or relationship with that of Jesus that the marriage-feast was kept.

"And when they wanted wine, the mother of Jesus saith to him, They have no wine." The wine, provided only for the original number of guests, began to fail. Mary, evidently watching with a kind and womanly interest the progress of the feast, and rightly ascribing the threatened exigency to the unexpected arrival of her son and his companions, becomes doubly anxious to shield a family in which she took such an interest from the painful feeling of having failed in the duties of hospitality. But why did Mary, seeing what she did, and feeling as she did, go to Jesus and say to him, "They have no wine"? That she expected him in some way to interfere is evident;

but what ground had she to expect that he would do so in any such manner as he did? She had never seen him work a miracle before. She had no reason, from past experience, to believe that he would or could make wine at will, or that by his word of power he would supply the deficiency. She had, however, been laying up in her heart, and for thirty years revolving all that had been told her at the beginning about her son. She had none at Nazareth but Joseph to speak to; none but he who would have believed her had she spoken. Joseph now is dead, and she is left to nurse the swelling hope in her solitary breast. At last the period comes, when rumours of the great preacher of repentance who has appeared in the wilderness of Judea, and to whom the whole country is rushing, spread over Galilee. Her son hears them, and rises from his work, and bids her adieu; the first time that he has parted from her since she had lost him in Jerusalem, now eighteen years ago. What can be his object in leaving her, his now widowed mother? She learns —perhaps he himself tells her—that he goes with other Galileans who want to see and hear the new teacher, it may be to enrol themselves by baptism as his disciples. She asks about this new teacher. Can it be that she discovers him to be no other than the son of her relative Elizabeth, whose birth was in so strange a manner linked with that of Jesus? If so, into what a tumult of expectation must she have been thrown!

But whether knowing aught of this or not, now at last, after a two months' absence, her son rejoins her, strangely altered in his bearing; attended, too, by those who, young as he is, hail him as their Master, and pay him all possible respect. She scarcely ventures to ask him what has happened in the interval of his absence; but them she fully questions; and as they tell her that John had publicly proclaimed her son to be no other than He whose coming it was his great object to announce; had pointed to him as the Lamb of God, the Son of God, the Baptizer with the Holy Ghost; as they tell that they had found in him the Messias, the Christ, of whom Moses in the law and the prophets did write, and that it was as such they were now following him,—to what a pitch of joyful expectation must she have been raised! Now at last the day so long looked for has come. Men have begun to see in him, her son, the Hope of Israel. Soon all Israel shall hail him as their Messiah. Meanwhile he is here among friends and relatives; has willingly accepted the invitation given to join this marriage-feast; has lost nothing, as it would seem, of all his early kindly feelings to those around him. What will he think, what will he do, if he be told that owing to his presence, and that of his disciples, a difficulty has arisen, and discredit is likely to be thrown upon this family, which has shown itself so ready to gratify him, by asking these strangers to share in the festivities of the occasion? She thinks, perhaps, of the cruse of oil, of the barley-loaves of the old prophets. Surely if her son be that great Prophet that is to appear, he might do something to provide for this unforeseen emergency; to meet this want; to keep the heart of this poor, perhaps, but generous household from being wounded. But what shall she ask him to do? what shall she suggest? She will leave that to himself. She knows how kind in heart, how wise in counsel he is, and believes

THE FIRST MIRACLE.   249

now that his power is equal to his will. She modestly contents herself with simply directing his attention to the fact, and saying to him, " They have no wine."

It is the very delicacy of this approach and address which renders so remarkable our Lord's reply, " Woman, what have I to do with thee?" —exactly the same form of expression which, on more than one occasion, the demons, whom he was about to dispossess, addressed to Jesus, when they said to him, What have we to do with thee? or, What hast thou to do with us, Jesus, thou Son of God? On their part, such language implied a repudiation of his interference; a denial of and a desire to resist his power and authority. And what can the same form of expression mean as addressed now by Jesus to his mother? Interpret it as we may; soften it to the uttermost so as to remove anything like harshness; still it is the language of resistance and reproof. There may have been some over-haste or impatience on Mary's part; some motherly vanity mingling with her desire to see her son exert his power, and reveal his character before these assembled guests, which required to be gently checked; but our Lord's main object in speaking to her as he did, was to teach Mary that the period of his subjection to her maternal authority had expired; that in the new character he had assumed, in that new sphere of action upon which he had entered, it was not for her, upon the ground simply of her relationship to him, to dictate or suggest what he should do. There was some danger of her forgetting this; of her cherishing and acting on the belief that he was still to be her son, as he had been throughout those thirty by-past years. It was right, it was even kind, that at the very outset she should be guarded against this danger, and saved the disappointment she might have felt had the limits of her influence and authority been left vague and undefined. Jesus would, therefore, have her to know definitely, and from the beginning of his ministry, that mother though she was as to his humanity, this gave her no right to interfere with him as the Son of the Highest, the Saviour of mankind. Thus gently but firmly does he repel the bringing of her maternal relationship to bear upon his Messianic work; thus gently but firmly does he assert and vindicate his perfect independence, disengaging himself from this the closest of earthly ties, that he may stand free in all things to do only the will of his Father in heaven. This manner of his conduct to the mother whom he so tenderly loved, may be regarded as the first of those repeated rebukes which Jesus gave by anticipation to that idolatrous reverence which has carried the human bond into the spiritual kingdom; carried it even into the heavenly places; exalting Mary as the Queen of heaven; seating the crowned mother on a throne sometimes on a level with, sometimes above that occupied by her Son, teaching us to pray to her as an equal intercessor with Christ.

"Woman, what have I to do with thee? Mine hour is not yet come." With him no impatience, no undue haste, no hurrying prematurely into action. He has waited quietly those thirty years, without a single trial of that superhuman strength which lay in him, content to bide till the set time came. And now he waits, even as to the performance of his first miracle, till the right and foreseen hour for its performance has arrived. As to this act of his power, and as to every act of it; as to this incident of his life, and as to every incident of it,—he could tell when the hour had not come, and when it had. He who at this marriage-feast could say to Mary, "Mine hour is not yet come," could say to the Omniscient in the upper chamber at Jerusalem, "Father, the hour is come, glorify thy Son." Mapped out before his foreseeing eye in all its times, places, events, issues, lay the whole of his earthly life and ministry. The perfect unbroken unity of design and action running throughout the whole proclaims a previous foresight, a premeditated, well-ordered plan. It has not been so with any of those men who have played the greatest and most prominent parts on the stage of human history. Their own confessions, the story of their lives, their earlier compared with their later acts, all tell us how little they knew or thought beforehand of what they finally were to be and do. Instead of one fixed, uniform, unchanging scheme and purpose running through and regulating the whole life, in all its lesser as well as its greater movements, there have been shiftings and changings of place to suit the shiftings and the changes of circumstance. Surprisals here, disappointments there; old instruments of action worn out and thrown away, new ones invented and employed; the life made up of a motley array of many-coloured incidents, out of which have come issues never dreamt of at the beginning. Was it so with the life that Jesus lived on earth? Had he been a mere man, committing himself to a great work under the guidance of a sublime, yet purely human, and therefore weak and blind impulse,—had he seen only so far into the future as the unaided human eye could carry, how much was there in the earlier period of his ministry to have excited false hopes, how much in the latter to have produced despondency! But the people came in multitudes around him, and you can trace no sign of extravagant expectation. The tide of popular favour ebbs away from him, and you see no token of his giving up his enterprise in despair. No wavering of purpose, no change of plan, no altering of his course to suit new and obviously unforeseen emergencies. There is progress: a steady advance onward to the final consummation of the cross and the burial, the resurrection and ascension; but all is consistent, all is harmonious. The attempt has been lately made, with all the resources of scholarship and all the skill of genius, to detect a discrepancy of design and expectation between the opening and closing stages of our Saviour's earthly course. It has failed. I cannot help thinking that all candid and intelligent readers of that life as we have it in the Gospels, whatever be their religious opinions or prepossessions, will acknowledge that M. Renan's failure is patent and complete. If so, it leaves that life of Jesus Christ distinguished from all others by a fixed, pre-established, unvarying design.[1]

---

[1] This feature in our Lord's character appears to have strongly impressed the mind of Napoleon I., as appears from the following extracts:—

"In every other life than that of Christ, what imperfections, what inconsistencies! Where is the character that no opposition is sufficient to overwhelm? Where is the individual whose conduct is never modified by event or circumstance, who never yields to the influences of the time, never accommodates himself to manners or passions that he cannot prevail to alter?

"I defy you to cite another life like that of Christ, exempt from the least vacillation of this kind, untainted by any such blots or

THE FIRST MIRACLE. 255

Our Lord's answer to Mary was ill fitted, we might imagine, to foster hope, postponing apparently to an indefinite period any interposition on his part. And yet she turns instantly to the servants, and says to them: " Whatsoever he saith unto you, do it." However surprised or perplexed she may have been, she appears as confident as ever that he would interpose. It

wavering purpose. From first to last he is the same; always the same, majestic and simple, infinitely severe and infinitely gentle; throughout a life that may be said to have been lived under the public eye, Jesus never gives occasion to find fault; the prudence of his conduct compels our admiration by its union of force and gentleness. Alike in speech and action, Jesus is enlightened, consistent, and calm. Sublimity is said to be an attribute of Divinity; what name then shall we give to him in whose character were united every attribute of the sublime?

"I know men; and I tell you that Jesus is not a man.

"In Lycurgus, Numa, Confucius, and Mahomet, I only see legislators who, having attained to the first place in the State, have sought the best solution of the social problem; I see nothing in them that reveals Divinity; they themselves have not pitched their claims so high.

"It is evident that it is only posterity that has deified the world's first despots,—heroes, the princes of the nations, and the founders of the earliest republics. For my part, I see in the heathen gods and those great men, beings of the same nature with myself. Their intelligence, after all, differs from mine only in form. They burst upon the world, played a great part in their day, as I have done in mine. Nothing in them proclaims divinity: on the contrary, I see numerous resemblances between them and may have been her strong and hopeful faith which, notwithstanding the discouraging reply, sustained her expectation; or there may have been something in the tone and manner of her son, something in the way he laid the emphasis as he pronounced the words, Mine hour is not *yet* come, which conveyed to her the impression that the hour was approaching, was near,—a

me,—common weaknesses and errors. Their faculties are such as I myself possess; there is no difference save in the use that we have made of them, in accordance with the different ends we had in view, our different countries and the circumstances of our times.

"It is not so with Christ. Everything in him amazes me; his spirit outreaches mine, and his will confounds me. Comparison is impossible between him and any other being in the world. He is truly a being by himself: his ideas and his sentiments, the truth that he announces, his manner of convincing, are all beyond humanity and the natural order of things.

"His birth, and the story of his life, the profoundness of his doctrine which overturns all difficulties, and is their most complete solution, his Gospel, the singularity of this mysterious being, his appearance, his empire, his progress through all centuries and kingdoms,—all this is to me a prodigy, an unfathomable mystery, which plunges me into a reverie from which there is no escape, a mystery which is ever within my view, a permanent mystery which I can neither deny nor explain.

"I see nothing here of man. Near as I may approach, closely as I may examine, all remains above my comprehension, great with a greatness that crushes me; it is in vain that I reflect—all remains unaccountable."—*Sentiments de Napoléon sur le Christianisme, par le* CHEVALIER DE BEAUTERNE.

speedy compliance shining through the apparent refusal. But why did she give that order to the servants, or how could she anticipate that it was through their instrumentality that the approaching supply was to be conveyed? Without some hint being given, some word or look of Jesus pointing in that direction, she could scarcely have conjectured beforehand what the mode of his action was to be.

Leaving the mystery which arises here unresolved, as being left without the key to open it, let us look at the simple, easy, unostentatious way in which the succeeding miracle was wrought. There stand—at the entrance, perhaps, of the dwelling—six water-pots of stone; Jesus saith to the servants, Fill the water-pots with water. They do so, filling them to the brim. Jesus saith, Draw out now, and bear to the governor of the feast. They do so; it is not water, but choicest wine they bear. The ruler of the feast at once detects it as better wine than they had previously been drinking, and addresses the bridegroom. The latter gives no reply, for he does not know whence or how this new supply of better wine has come. As little know the guests who partake of it; nor, perhaps, till the feast is over, and the servants tell what had been done, is it known by what a miracle of power the festivities of that social board had been sustained. What a veiling this of the hand and power of the operator! Imagine only that Jesus had asked the servants, while the water was water still, to draw it out and fill each goblet,—had asked each guest to lift up his cup and taste, and see what kind of liquid it contained,—and then, by a word of his power, had turned the crystal water into the ruddy wine. With what gaping wonder would every one have then been filled! Instead of this, ordering it so that what came to the guests appeared to come through the ordinary channel, without word or touch, aught said or done, in obedience to an inward volition of the Lord, the water hidden in the vessels is changed instantaneously into wine. There was the same dignified ease and simplicity, the same absence of ostentation, about all Christ's miracles, proper to him who used not a delegated but an intrinsic power.

Struck with the manner in which Christ met the domestic need and protected the family character, we must not overlook the largeness of the provision that he made. At the most moderate computation, the six water-pots must have held far more than enough to meet the requirements of the marriage-feast; enough of wine for that household for many months to come. In the overflowing generosity of his kindness, he does so much more than Mary would have asked or could have conceived. And still, to all who feel their need and come to him to have their spiritual wants supplied, he does exceedingly abundantly above all that they ask, and all that they can think.

When the governor of the feast had tasted the new-made wine, he called the bridegroom, and said to him, " Every man at the beginning doth set forth good wine; and when men have well drunk, then that which is worse; but thou hast kept the good wine until now." He knew not whence that better wine had come; he knew not to whom it was they owed it; he knew not that, in contrasting as he did the custom of keeping the best wine to the last, with that commonly followed at marriage-feasts, he was but showing forth, as in a figure, the way in which the Spiritual Bridegroom acts to all those who are called to the Marriage Supper of the Lamb. Not as the world giveth, gives Jesus to his own. The world gives its best and richest first. At the board which it spreads the viands may not fail; nay, may even grow in number and improve in quality, but soon they pall on the sated appetite, and the end of the world's feast is always worse and less enjoyable than the beginning. Who has found it so of the provisions of a Saviour's grace; of those quiet, soothing, satisfying pleasures, that true faith in him imparts? The more of these that any one receives, the more he enjoys them. The appetite grows with the food it feeds upon; the relish increases with the appetite; better and better things are still provided, and of each new cup of pleasure put into our hands, turning to the heavenly Provider, we may say, Thou hast kept the good wine even until now.

This, the beginning of his miracles, did Jesus

in Cana of Galilee. The miracle lay in the instantaneous transmutation of water into wine. And yet the water with which those water-pots were filled, and in which this change was wrought, might have been drawn from the well of a vineyard, and instead of being poured into these stone vessels, might have been poured out over the soil into which the vine-plants struck their roots, and by these roots might have been drawn up into the stem, and through the branches been distilled into the grapes, and out of the grapes been pressed into the vat, and in that vat have fermented into wine. And thus, by the many steps and secret processes of nature might that water without a miracle, as we say, have been converted into wine. But is each step or stage of that natural transmutation less wonderful? does it show inferior wisdom? is it done by a feebler power? Just as little can we explain the process as spread out into multiplied details in the great laboratory of nature, as when condensed into one single act. And just as much should we see the divine hand and power in the one as in the other. He who sees God in the one—the miracle, and not in the other, the processes of nature—has not the right faith in God. If we did not believe that God was operating throughout, working everywhere; his will and power the spring and support of every movement in the material creation, we should not believe that he is operating here or there, in this miracle or in that. It is because we believe in the universal agency of the living God, that we are prepared to believe in that agency in any singular form that it occasionally may take. There is, indeed, a difference between a miracle and any of the ordinary operations of nature; a difference not in the agent, not in the power, but simply in the manner in which the power and agency are employed. In the one, the hand of the Great Operator works, slowly, uniformly, doing the same things always in the same way; his footsteps follow each other so surely and so regularly, that, by a delusion of the understanding, we come to think that the things that follow each other so uniformly are not only naturally but necessarily linked to one another, —the one by some imagined inherent power drawing the other after it; needing no power but their own to bind them together at the first, or keep them bound together afterwards. Wherever there is orderly succession—and it pervades the whole universe of material things—we can classify the different processes that go on, and so reach what we call the laws of nature, which, after all, are but expressions of the orderly manner in which certain results are brought about; but to these laws, as if they were living things, and had a vital power and energy belonging to them, we come to attribute the actual accomplishment of the results. It happens thus that the works of his hands in the midst of which we live, and which, for his glory and our good, the Great Creator and Sustainer makes to move on with such fixed and orderly, stately and beautiful array, instead of being a clear translucent medium through which we see him, become often as a thick obscuring veil, hiding him from our sight. Hence the use of miracles, that He who worketh all in all, and worketh thus, should sometimes break as it were this order, that through the rent we might see the hand which had been hidden behind that self-constructed veil.

And yet when we speak thus of a miracle as a breaking-in upon the ordinary and established course of nature, let us not think of it as if it were discord thrust into a harmony; something loose, irregular, disjointed, coming in to mar the beautiful and orderly progression. In that harmonious progression, the lower ever yields to the higher. The vital powers, for instance, in plants and animals, are ever modifying the mechanical powers, the laws of motion; the will of man comes in, in still more striking manner, to do the same thing with all the powers and processes of nature. You do not say that such crossings and counteractions of lower by higher laws disturb the harmony of nature; they go to constitute it. And we believe that just as falsely as you would say that the order of nature was broken, the law of gravitation was violated, when the sap ascends in the stem of the tree, and is distributed upwards through its branches; just as falsely is it said of the miracles of Christianity, that they break that order, or violate any of nature's laws; for did we but know enough of that spiritual kingdom for whose establishment and advancement they were wrought, we should perceive that here too there was law and order, and that what we now call miracles were but instances of the lower yielding to the higher; that the grand, unbroken harmony of the vast universe, material, mental, moral, spiritual, may be sustained and promoted.

This beginning of miracles did Jesus in Cana of Galilee, and manifested forth his glory. The glory that was thus revealed lay not so much in the forthputting of almighty power (for it is an inferior glory that the bare exercise of any power, though it be divine, displays), as in the manner in which the power is exercised, the ends it is put forth to accomplish. Power appears here as the handmaid and minister of Loving Kindness, and gathers thus a richer glory than its own around it. Never let us forget that the first act of our Lord's public life was to grace a marriage by his presence. By doing so, he has for ever consecrated that and every other human bond and relationship. And the first exercise of his almighty power was to minister to the enjoyment of a marriage-feast. He who would not in the extremity of hunger employ his power to procure food for himself, put it forth to increase the comforts of others. By doing so, he has for ever consecrated all the innocent enjoyments of life. It will not do to say, that his example here is no pattern to us; that what was safe for him might be injurious to us; for he not only accepted the invitation for himself, but took his disciples along with him to the marriage-feast. There is something peculiarly striking and instructive in our Lord coming so directly from consort with the austere ascetic preacher of the wilderness, and carrying along with him these first disciples, the majority of whom had been John's disciples before they were his, and seating them by his side at this festive board. Does it not teach what the genius and spirit of his religion is? That it affects not the desert; that it shuns not the fellowship of man; that it frowns not on social joys and pleasures; that it rejoices as readily with those who rejoice as it weeps with those who weep; ready to be with us in our hours of gladness, as well as in our hours of grief. Let no table be spread to which He who graced the marriage-feast at Cana could not be invited;

let no pleasure be indulged in which could not live in the light of his countenance. Let his presence and blessing be with us and upon us wherever we go and however we are engaged; and is the way not open by which the miracle of Cana may, in spirit, be repeated daily still, and the water of every earthly enjoyment turned into the very wine of heaven ?

XII.

THE CLEANSING OF THE TEMPLE.[1]

THE miracle at the marriage-feast drew a marked line of distinction between Jesus, the Baptist, and the austere Essenes, those eremites who dwelt apart, shut up in a kind of monastic seclusion, and who renounced the use of wine, condemned marriage, and denounced all bodily indulgence as injurious to the purity of the spirit. By acting as he did at Cana, Jesus at the very outset of his career placed himself in direct opposition to the strictest class of pietists then existing,—in direct opposition to the spirit and practice of those in all ages who have sought, by withdrawal from the world and estrangement from all objects of sense, to cultivate communion with the unseen, to rise to a closer intercourse with and nearer resemblance to the Deity.

[1] John ii. 12-21 ; Matt. xxi. 10-17.

One effect of this first display by Jesus of his supernatural power was a strengthening of the faith of the men who had recently attached themselves to him. "His disciples," it is said, "believed in him." They had believed before, but they believed more firmly now. The ground of their first faith had been the testimony of the Baptist. Their faith had grown during the few days of private intercourse with Jesus which succeeded, and now by the manifestation of his power and glory, it was still more strengthened. It was still, as later trial too clearly proved, weak and imperfect. But their minds and hearts were in such a condition that they lay open to the influence of additional light as to their Master's character, additional evidence of his authority and power. But there were other spectators of the miracle upon whom it exerted no such happy influence. After the marriage-feast at Cana broke up, "Jesus and his mother, and his brethren, and his disciples went down to Capernaum." This is the first mention of those brethren of Christ who appear more than once in the subsequent history, always associated with Mary, as forming part of her family, carefully distinguished from the apostles and disciples of the Lord. They are represented on one occasion as going out after him, thinking he was beside himself; and when he was told that Mary and they stood at the outskirts of the crowd desiring to see him, he exclaimed, "Who is my mother, and who are my brethren? Whosoever shall do the will of my Father who is in heaven, the same is my brother, and sister, and mother." On another occasion, the Nazarenes referred to them when, astonished and offended, they said to one another, "Is not this the carpenter's son? is not his mother called Mary, and his brethren, James, and Joses, and Simon, and Judas? And his sisters, are they not all with us?" John tells that at a still later period, in the beginning of the last year of our Lord's ministry, these relatives taunted him, saying, "If thou do these things, show thyself to the world; for neither did his brethren believe in him." Had we been reading these passages for the first time, we should scarcely have understood them otherwise than as referring to those who were related to Jesus as children of the same mother. This would of course imply that Mary had other children than Jesus, an idea to which from the earliest period there seems to have been the strongest repugnance. Resting upon the well-known usage which allowed the term brother and sister to be extended to more distant relationships, and upon the acknowledged difficulty which arises in connexion with the names of our Lord's brothers as given by the Evangelists, both the Greek and the Latin Churches, though adopting different theories as to the exact nature of the relationship, have indignantly repudiated the idea of Mary's having any but 'one child, and have regarded those spoken of as his brothers as being either his half-brothers, sons of Joseph by another marriage, or his cousins, the children of Mary's sister, the wife of Alphæus or Cleophas. It would be out of place here to enter upon the discussion of this difficult question. I can only say that, after weighing all the objections which have been adduced, I can see no sufficient reason for rejecting the first and most natural reading of the passages I have referred to, for not believing that they were brothers and sisters of Jesus, who grew up along with him in the household at Nazareth. Perhaps our readiness to admit this may partly spring from our not sharing the impression that there is anything in such a belief either derogatory to the character of Mary, or to the true dignity of her first-born Son.

Whoever they were, and however related to him, these brethren of the Lord, his nearest relatives, who had all along been living, if not under the same roof, yet in close and intimate acquaintance with him, sat beside his disciples at that marriage-feast, and saw the wonder that was done, and they did not believe. As months rolled on, they saw and heard of still greater wonders wrought in the presence of multitudes. Residing with Mary at Capernaum, they lived in the very heart of that commotion which the teaching and acts of Jesus excited. Neither did they then believe. Their unbelief may have been in part sustained by Christ's having ceased to make their home his home, and chosen twelve strangers as his close and constant companions and friends. Nor did any of them believe in Jesus all through the three years of his ministry. But it is pleasing to note that, though so long and so stubbornly maintained, their unbelief did at last give way; you see them in that upper room to which the apostles retired after witnessing the ascension: "And when they were come in, they went up into an upper room, where abode both Peter and James, and John and Andrew, Philip and Thomas, Bartholomew and Matthew, James the son of Alphæus, and Simon Zelotes, and Judas the brother of James. These all continued with one accord in prayer and supplication, with the women, and Mary the mother of Jesus, and with his brethren." How many an apt remark on the peculiar barriers which the closer ties of domestic life often oppose to the influence of the one Christian member of a household, and on the peculiar encouragement which such a one has to persevere, might be grounded upon the fact that it was not till after his death that our Lord's own immediate relatives believed in him.

When the marriage-feast at Cana was over, Jesus and his mother, and his brethren, and his disciples went down to Capernaum. Of this town we shall have more to say hereafter, when it became the chosen centre of our Lord's Galilean ministry. One advantage of the short visit that Jesus now paid to it was, that it put him on the route along which the already gathering bands of visitors from Northern Galilee passed southwards to the capital. The Passover was at hand, and Jesus went up to Jerusalem. Hitherto, though some time had passed (two or three months perhaps, but there are no materials for exactly determining) since his baptism, and the public proclamation of his Messiahship, Jesus had taken no public step, none implying any assumption on his part of the office to which he had been designated. Of the few men who attended him, there was but one whom he had asked to follow him; nor was it yet understood whether he and the rest were to accompany him for more than a few days. The miracle at Cana was rather of a private and domestic than of a public character. Nothing that we know of was said or done by Jesus at Capernaum, or throughout the short visit to Galilee, to indicate his entrance on a public career.

But now he is in Jerusalem, in the place where

most appropriately the first revelation of himself in his new character is made. Let us acknowledge that it is not in the form in which we should have expected it; nor in that form in which any Jew of that age would ever have imagined that the Messiah should first show himself. We may be able, by meditating a little upon it, to see more of its suitableness than at first sight appears. But even a first glance reveals how utterly unlike it was to the popular Jewish conception of the advent of the Messiah. One of the first things our Lord does at Jerusalem is to go up into the Temple. He passes through one of the gates of its surrounding walls. He enters into the large open area which on all sides encompasses the sacred edifice. What a spectacle meets his eye! There all round, attached to the walls, are lines of booths or shops in which money-changers are plying their usurious trade. The centre space is crowded with oxen and with sheep exposed for sale, and between the buyers and the sellers all the turbulent traffic of a cattle-market is going on. It goes on within the outer enclosure, but close upon the inner buildings of the Holy Place;

so close that the loud hum from the crowded court of the Gentiles must have been heard to their no small disturbance by the priests and worshippers within. How comes all this? and who is responsible for this desecration of the Temple? The origin of it in one sense was natural enough. At all the great festivals, but especially at the Passover, an almost inconceivable number of animals were offered up in sacrifice. Josephus tells us of more than two hundred thousand victims sacrificed in the course of a single Passover celebration. The greatest proportion of these were not brought up from the country by the offerers, but were purchased on their arrival at Jerusalem. An extensive traffic, yielding no inconsiderable gain to those engaged in it, was thus created. Some open area for conducting it was needed. The heads of the priesthood, to whom the custody of the Temple was committed, saw that good rents were got for any suitable market-ground which the city could supply. They were tempted to fill their own coffers from this source. Jerusalem could furnish no place so suitable for the exposure of the animals as the Court of the Gentiles. What more convenient than that the victims should be purchased in the very neighbourhood of the place where they were to be offered up? The greed of gain prevailed over all care for the sanctity of the Temple. The Court of the Gentiles was let out to the cattle-dealers, and a large amount was thus added to the yearly revenue of the Temple. Still another source of gain lay open, and was taken advantage of. Every one who came up to the Passover, and desired to take part in the festival, had to present a half-shekel of Jewish money to the priests. This kind of money was not now in general use; it was scarce even in Judea, unknown beyond that land. Nothing, however, but the half-shekel of the sanctuary would be taken at the Temple. To supply themselves with the needed coin, visitors had to go to the money-changer. And where can he find a fitter place to erect his booth and set out his table than within the very area in which the larger traffic was going on? He offers so much to the priesthood to be permitted to do so; the bribe is taken, and the booth and the tables are erected. And so, amid a perfect

Babel of tongues, and thronging, jostling crowds of men and beasts, the buying and the selling and the money-changing are all going on.

Into the heart of this tumultuous throng Jesus enters. Of the many hundreds there, few have ever seen him before; few know anything about him, either about his baptism in the Jordan, or his late miracle at Cana. He appears as a stranger, a young man clad in the simple garb of a Galilean peasant, without any badge of authority in his hand. He looks around with an eye of indignant sorrow, pours out the changers' money, overthrows their tables, forming a scourge of small cords drives the herds of cattle before him, and, mingling consideration with his zeal, says to them who sold the doves, "Take these things hence; make not my Father's house a house of merchandise." Why is it that at the touch of this slender scourge, and the bidding of this youthful stranger, buyers and sellers stop their traffic, the money-changers suffer their money to be rudely handled, and their tables to be overturned? The slightest resistance of so many against one would have been sufficient to have arrested the movement. But no such resistance is attempted, no opposition is made, by men not likely from their occupation to be remarkable for mildness of disposition or pliability of character. How are we to explain this? We can understand how, at the last Passover, at the close of his ministry, when Jesus, then so well known, so generally recognised by the people as a prophet, repeated this cleansing of the Temple, there should have been a yielding to his authoritative command. But what are we to say of such an occurrence taking place at the very commencement of his ministry, his first public act in Jerusalem? It is a mysterious power which some men, in time of excitement, by look and word and tone of command, can exercise over their fellowmen. But grant that rare power in its highest degree to Jesus, it will scarce account for this scene in the Court of the Gentiles at Jerusalem. It would seem as if, in eye and voice and action, the divine power and authority that lay in Jesus broke forth into visible manifestation, and laid such a spell upon those rough cattle-drivers and those cold calculators of the money-tables, that all power of resistance was for the time subdued. It would seem as if it pleased him to exert here within the Temple the same influence that he did afterwards in the Garden, when he stepped forth from the darkness into the full moonlight, and said to the rough band that advanced with their lanterns and swords and staves to take him, " I that speak unto you am he ;" and when at the sight and word they reeled backward and fell to the ground. The effect in both cases was but temporary. High priests and officers were soon upon their feet again; and, wondering at their own weakness in yielding to a power which at the moment they were impotent to resist, proceeded to lay hold upon Jesus, and lead him away unto Caiaphas. So was it also, we believe, in the Temple court. A sudden, mysterious, irresistible power is upon that crowd. They yield, they know not why. But by and by the spell would seem to be withdrawn. They soon recover from its effect. Nor is it long till, wondering at their having allowed a single man, and one who had no right whatever, to interfere with arrangements made by the chief authorities, and to lord it over them, they return, resume their occupations, and all goes on as before.

It was with no intention or expectation of putting an end in this way to the desecration of the Holy Place that Jesus acted. What, then, was the purpose of his act? It was meant to be a public proclamation of his Sonship to God; an open assertion and exercise of his authority as sustaining this relation; a protest in his Father's name against the conduct of the priesthood in permitting this desecration of the Holy Place. It was far more for the priesthood than for the crowd in the market-place that it was meant. They were not ignorant that the chief object of the ministry of the Baptist, with which the whole country was ringing, was to announce the immediate coming of the Messiah. They had not long before sent a deputation to the banks of the Jordan to ask John whether he himself were not the Messiah whose near advent he was foretelling. The members of that deputation heard of the baptism of Jesus; in all likelihood they had not left the place when Jesus came back from the temptation in the Wilderness, and was publicly pointed to by John as the greater than himself who was to come after him, the Lamb of God, the Son of God. From the lips of the men whom they had sent, or from the lips of others, they must have known all about what had happened. And now here among them is this Jesus of Nazareth; here he is come up to the Temple, speaking and acting as if it were his part and office authoritatively to interpose and cleanse the building of all its defilements. What else could the priesthood who had charge of the Temple understand than that here was claimed a jurisdiction in regard to it superior to their own? What else could they understand when the words were heard, or were repeated to them, " Make not my Father's house a house of merchandise," than that here was one who claimed a relationship to God as his Father, and a right over the Temple as his Father's house, which none but *One* could claim? They go to him, therefore, or they call him before them, and entering, you will remark, into no justification of their own deed in hiring out the Temple court as they had done,—entering into no argument with him as to the rightness or wrongness of what he had done, rather admitting that if he were indeed a prophet, as his acts showed that he at least pretended to be, his act was justifiable; they proceed upon the assumption that he was bound to give to them some proof of his carrying a Divine commission, and they say to him, "What sign showest thou unto us, seeing thou doest those things?"

He had shown a good enough sign already, had they read it aright. He was about to show signs numerous and significant enough in the days that immediately succeeded; but to such a haughty challenge as this, coming, as he knew, from men whom no sign would convince of his Messiahship, he had but this reply: "Destroy this temple, and in three days I will raise it up." A truly dark saying; one that, not only they did not and could not at the time understand, but that they were almost certain to misunderstand, and, misunderstanding, to turn against the speaker, as if he meant to claim the possession of a power which he never could be called upon to exercise. Then said the Jews, interpreting, as they could scarce fail to do, his words as applicable to the material

Temple : "Thirty-and-six years has this Temple been in building, and wilt thou rear it up in three days."[1]

Jesus made no attempt to rectify the error into which his questioners had fallen. He could not well have done so without a premature disclosure of his death and resurrection, a thing that he carefully avoided till the time of their accomplishment drew near. He left this mysterious saying to be interpreted against himself. It seems to have taken a deep hold, to have been widely circulated, and to have fixed itself very deeply in the memory of the people. Three years afterwards,

---

[1] It is curious that, in saying so, they have left to us one of the few fixed and certain data upon which we can determine the year when the public ministry of our Lord began. We know that the building, or rather rebuilding of the Temple, was commenced by Herod in the eighteenth year of his reign ; that is, speaking according to the Roman method of counting their years from the foundation of Rome, during the year that began in the spring of 734, and ended in that of 735. Forty-six years from this would bring us to the year 780-781. Historical statements and astronomical calculations conspire to prove that it must have been between the 13th March and the 4th April, in the year 750, that Herod died. If Christ were born a few months before that death, thirty years forward from that time brings us to the year 780, as that in which our Lord's ministry commenced ;—the two independent computations thus singularly confirming one another.

when they were trying to convict him of some crime in reference to religion, this first saying of his was brought up against him, as one uttered blasphemously against the Temple, but the two witnesses could not agree about the words. And when the cross was raised, those who passed by railed on him, saying, "Ah, thou that destroyest the Temple, and buildest it in three days, save thyself." Whatever differences there were in the remembrances and reports of the people, in one thing they agreed, in the attributing the destrucsion of the Temple that Jesus had spoken of here, to himself. But he had not spoken of the destruction as effected by his own hands, but by those of the Jews themselves. And he had not had in his eye the material Temple on Mount Moriah, but the temple of his body, which they were to destroy, and which he, three days afterwards, was to raise from the dead. All this became plain afterwards, and went, when his real meaning stood revealed in the event, mightily to confirm the faith of his followers. And in one respect it may still go to confirm ours, for does not that saying of Jesus, uttered so early,—his first word, we may say, to the leaders of the people at Jerusalem,—does it not, along with so many other like evidences, go to prove how clearly the Lord saw the end from the beginning?

The Temple at Jerusalem has long been in ruins. In its stead there stands now before us the Church of the body of Christ, the society of the faithful. In her corporate capacity, in her corporate actings, has the Church not acted over again what the Jews did with their Temple, when she has made merchandise of her offices and her revenues, and sold them to the highest bidder, as you would sell oxen in the market or meat in the shambles? The spirit which prompts such open sacrilegious acts, such gross making gain of godliness, is the self-same spirit which our Lord rebuked; and how often does it creep into and take hold and spread like a defiling leprosy over the house of God? It does so in the pulpit, whenever self, in one or other of its insidious forms, frames the speech and animates the utterance; it does so in the pew, when in the hour hallowed to prayer and praise, the chambers of thought and imagery within are crowded with worldly guests. Know ye not, brethren, that ye are the temple of God; and that the temple of God is holy, which temple ye are? Would that half the zeal the Saviour showed in cleansing the earthly building were but shown by each of us in the purifying and cleansing of our hearts! Truly it is no easy task to drive out thence everything that defileth in his sight, to keep out as well as to put out; for, quick as were those buyers and sellers of old in coming back to their places in the Temple, and resuming their occupations there, quicker still are those vain and sinful desires, dispositions, imaginations, which in our moments of excited zeal we have expelled from our hearts, in returning to their old and well-loved haunts. The Lord of the temple must come himself to cleanse it; come, not once or twice, as in the case of the Temple at Jerusalem; come, not as a transient visitor, but as an abiding guest; not otherwise than by his own indwelling shall these unhallowed inmates be ejected and kept without, and the house made worthy of Him who deigns to occupy it.

XIII.

THE CONVERSATION WITH NICODEMUS.[1]

CHRIST'S first visit to Jerusalem, after his baptism, appears to have been a brief one; not longer, perhaps, than that usually paid by those who went up to the Passover. Besides the cleansing of the Temple he wrought some miracles which are left unrecorded, but which we may believe were of the same kind as his subsequent ones, and these were generally miracles of healing. Many believed on him when they saw those miracles performed; believed on him as a wonder-worker, as a man who had the great power of God at his command; but their faith scarcely went further, involved in it little or no recognition of his true character and office. Although they believed in him, Jesus did not believe in them (for it is the same word which is used in the two cases).

[1] John iii. 1-21.

Knowing what was in them, as he knew what was in all men, undeceived by appearance or profession, he entered into no close or friendly relations with them; made no hasty or premature discovery of himself.

But there was one man to whom he did commit himself on the occasion of this first and short residence in Jerusalem, to whom he did make such a discovery of himself, as we shall presently see he never made to any other single person in the whole course of his ministry. This was a man of the Pharisees, one of the sect that became the most bitter persecutors of Christ; a ruler too of the Jews, a man well educated, of good position, and in high office; a member of the Sanhedrim. He was one of the body that not long ago had sent the deputation down to the Jordan to inquire about the Baptist. He knew all about John's ministry, about his announcing that the kingdom of God was at hand, that there was One coming after him who was to baptize not with water but with the Holy Ghost. He had been wondering what this ministry of John could mean, when Jesus appeared in the city, cleansed the Temple, wrought those miracles. He saw that among the class to which he belonged, the appearance and acts of the young Nazarene, who had assumed and exercised such an authority within the Courts of the Temple, and when challenged had given such an unsatisfactory reply, had excited nothing but distrust and antipathy; a distrust and antipathy, however, in which he did not, could not share. He could not concur with those who spake of him as an ignorant rustic, a mere blind zealot, whom a fit of fanaticism had driven to do what he did in the Temple; still less could he agree with those who spake of him as an impostor, a deceiver of the people. We do not know what words of Christ's he heard, what acts of his he witnessed; but the impression had come upon him, whencesoever it came, that he was altogether different from what his fellow-rulers were disposed to believe. Could this indeed be the man of whom John spake so much; could this be indeed the Christ, the Messiah for whom so many were longing? If he was, what new and higher truths would he unfold, what a glorious kingdom would he usher in! Restless and unsatisfied with things as they were, all his Pharisaic strictness in the keeping of the law having failed to quiet his conscience, and give comfort to his heart, Nicodemus was looking about and longing for further light. Perhaps this stranger, who has come to Jerusalem, may be able to help him. He may be poor and mean, a Galilean by birth, without official rank or authority; but what of that, if he be really what he seems, one clothed with a Divine commission; what of that, if he can quench in any way this thirst of heart and soul which burns within? If he could be seen by him alone, Jesus would surely lay aside that reserve which he appeared to maintain, and instruct him fully as to the mysteries of the coming kingdom. But how could such a private interview be brought about? He might send for him; and sent for by one in his position, Jesus might not refuse to come. But then it would be noised abroad that he had been entertaining the Nazarene in his dwelling. Or he might go to him when he was teaching in public, but then it would be seen and known of all men that he had paid him an open mark of respect. He was not prepared to face either of these alternatives; he was too timid, thought too much of what his companions and friends and the general public of the city might think or say. Yet he is too eager to throw the chance away. He must see Jesus, and as his fears keep him from going to or sending for him by day, he goes by night, breaks in upon his retirement, asks and obtains the audience.

There was something wrong, no doubt, in his choosing such a time and way for the interview. It would have been a manlier, more heroic thing for him to have braved all danger, and risen above all fear of man. But whatever blame we may choose on this ground to attach to Nicodemus, let it not obscure our perception of his obvious honesty and earnestness, his intense desire for further enlightenment, his willingness to receive instruction. He came by night, but he was the only one of his order who came at all. He came by night, but it was not to gratify an idle curiosity, but in the disquiet of a half-awakened conscience to seek for peace. Rabbi, he says, as soon as he finds himself in Christ's presence. He salutes him with all respect. The

Rabbis of the Temple would have scorned the claim of one so young in years, unknown in any of their schools, who had given no proof of his acquaintance with their laws and their traditions, —to be regarded as one of them. But the Ruler, in all likelihood by many years Christ's senior, and one who on other grounds might have counted on being the saluted rather than the saluter, does not hesitate to address him thus: "Rabbi, we know that thou art a teacher come from God: for no man can do those miracles that thou doest except God be with him." He shows at once his respect, his candour, his intelligence, and his faith. He does not doubt that those are real miracles which Jesus has been working; he is ready to trace to its true source the power employed in their accomplishment; he is prepared at once to acknowledge that the worker of such miracles must be one sent and sanctioned by God. In saying so, he knows that he is saying more than perhaps any other man of his station in Jerusalem would be ready to say. He thinks that he says enough to win for himself a favourable reception. Yet, he is speaking far below the truth, much under his own half-formed conceptions and beliefs. It is but as a teacher, not as a prophet, much less the great Prophet, that he addresses Jesus.

One might have expected that, having addressed him as such, he would go on to put the questions to which he presumed that such a teacher could give replies. But he pauses, perhaps imagining that, gratified by such a visit, pleased at being saluted thus by one of the rulers, Jesus will salute him in return, and save him the trouble of inquiry by making some disclosures of the new doctrine which, as a teacher sent from God, he had come to teach; or by telling him something more about that new kingdom which so many were expecting to see set up. How surprised he must have been when so abruptly, yet so solemnly, without exchange of salutation or word of preface, Jesus says, "Verily, verily, I say unto you, Except a man be born again, he cannot see the kingdom of God." Such a man as Nicodemus could scarcely have been so stupid as to believe that, in speaking of being born again, Jesus meant a second birth of the body. He is so disconcerted, however, disappointed, perplexed, besides being perhaps a little irritated, by both the manner and the substance of the grave, emphatic utterance,—one which, however general in its terms, was obviously spoken with a direct and personal reference,—that, in his confusion, he seizes upon the expression as the only one that had as yet conveyed any definite idea to his mind. As affording him some ground of exception, some material for reply, and taking it in its literal sense, he says: How can a man be born again when he is old, old as I am? Can he enter the second time into his mother's womb, and be born? The wise and gentle teacher in whose hands he now is, takes no notice of the folly or the petulance of the remark. He reiterates what he had said, modifying, however, his expressions, so that Nicodemus could not fail to see of what kind of second birth it was that he was speaking: "Verily, verily, I say unto you, Except a man be born of water and of the Spirit, he cannot enter into the kingdom of God."

Had Nicodemus only had time at first to collect his thoughts, he would have remembered that it was no new term, framed now for the first time, that Jesus had been employing in speaking of a second birth; it being a proverbial expression with his countrymen with reference to those who became proselytes to the Jewish faith, and were admitted as such into the Jewish community, that they were as men new-born. The outward mode of admitting such proselytes to the enjoyment of Jewish privileges was by baptism, by washing with water. John had adopted this rite, and by demanding that all Jews should be baptized with the baptism of repentance, as a preparation on their part for the coming of the kingdom, he had in fact, already proclaimed, that, as every heathen man became as a new man on entering into the commonwealth of Israel, so every Jewish man must become a new man before entering into that new kingdom which the Messiah was to introduce and establish. It was virtually to symbolize the importance and necessity of repentance,—that change of mind and heart which formed the burden of his preaching, as a qualification in all candidates for admission into the kingdom—that John came baptizing with water. But he took great pains to inform his hearers that, while he baptized with water, there was One coming immediately, who was to baptize with the Holy Ghost. Was it likely then, or we may even say, was it possible that, when Nicodemus now heard Jesus say, "Except a man be born of water and of the Spirit, he cannot enter into the kingdom of God," he could fail to perceive the allusion to the water-baptism of John and the Spirit-baptism of the Messiah? In common with all his countrymen, Nicodemus had assumed that, be it what it might, come how or when it might, the Messianic Kingdom would be one within which their very birth as Jews would entitle them to be ranked. The popular delusion John had already, by his baptism and his teaching, done something to rectify. The full truth it was reserved for Jesus to proclaim, and he does it now to Nicodemus. This master in Israel has come to Jesus to be taught; let him know then that it is not a new doctrine, but a new life which Jesus has come to proclaim and to impart. It is not by knowing so much, or believing in such truths, or practising such duties, that a man is to qualify himself for becoming a subject of the spiritual kingdom of Jesus Christ. First of all, as a necessary preliminary, he must be born again ; born of the Spirit, have spiritual life imparted, before he can see so as to apprehend its real nature, before he can enter so as to partake of its true privileges, the kingdom of God. This kingdom is not an outward or a national one, not the kingdom of a creed, or of an external organized community. It is a kingdom exclusively of the new-born—of those who have been begotten of the Spirit—of those who have been born again, not of blood, nor of the flesh, nor of the will of man, but of God. For that which is born of the flesh is flesh, and that which is born of the Spirit is spirit.

A mystic thing it looks to Nicodemus, this second birth,—this birth of the Spirit; secret, invisible, impalpable ; its origin and issues hidden, remote. Marvel not, says Jesus, at its mysteriousness. The night is quiet, around you, not a sound of bending branch or rustling leaf comes from the neighbouring wood; but now the air is stirred as by an invisible hand; the sigh of the night-breeze comes through the bending branches and rustling leaves; you hear the sound; but who can take you to that breeze's birthplace, and show you where and how it was begotten; who can carry you to its place of sepulchre, and show you where and how it died? Not that the wind, —the air in motion,—is a whit more wilful or capricious, or less obedient to fixed laws than any other elements, or is chosen upon that account to represent the operations of God's Spirit on the souls of men. All its movements are fixed and orderly; but as the movements of an invisible agent, they elude our observation; nor, if you sought for a material emblem of that hiddenness with which the Holy Spirit works, could you find in the whole creation one more apt than that which Jesus used, when he said to Nicodemus, "The wind bloweth where it listeth, and thou hearest the sound thereof, but canst not tell whence it cometh or whither it goeth: so is every one that is born of the Spirit."

Already a dim apprehension of that for which he was being apprehended of Christ has begun to dawn upon Nicodemus. He receives the truth as affirmed by Jesus as to the necessity of the new birth. He begins even to understand something as to its nature. Yet a haze still hangs over it. He wonders and he doubts,—giving expression to his feelings in the question, "How can these things be?"

If Christ's answer may be taken as the best interpretation of this question, Nicodemus was now troubling himself not so much either with the nature or the necessity of the new birth, as with the manner of its accomplishment; the kind of instrumentality by which so great an inward change was to be effected; for, read aright, our Lord's reply is not only a description of that instrumentality, but an actual employment of it. First, however, a gentle rebuke must be given: Art thou a master of Israel, and knowest not these things? Hast thou forgotten all that is written in the book of the law and in the prophets, about the coming of those days in which the Lord would pour out his Spirit upon all flesh; about the new covenant that the Lord would then enter into with his people, one of whose two great provisions was to be this: " I will give them one heart, and I will put a new spirit within you; and I will take the stony heart out of their flesh, and will give them an heart of flesh?" (Ezek. xi. 19.) What had so often and so long beforehand been thus spoken of was now about to be executed. The Spirit of God was waiting to do his gracious work, in begetting many sons and daughters to the Lord. Let Nicodemus be assured of this, on the testimony of one whose knowledge of the spirit-world was immediate and complete. He had spoken very confidently about his knowledge of Jesus. We know, he had said, thou art a teacher sent from God. Let him listen now to words of equal confidence, which no mere human teacher, though he were even sent by God, could well, upon such a subject, have employed: "Verily, verily, I say unto thee, We speak that we do know, and testify that we have seen; and ye receive not our witness." 'This work of the Spirit in regenerating is connected with another—my own—in redeeming. The one is but an earthly operation; a work performed within men's souls: but the other, how high have you to rise to trace it to its source;

how far to go to follow it to its issues? "If I have told you these earthly things, and ye believe not, how shall ye believe if I tell you of heavenly things."

'And yet who can speak of these heavenly things as I can do? You take me, Nicodemus, to be a teacher sent from God, perhaps you might even acknowledge me as a prophet; but know me that I am no other than He, the Son of man, the Son of God, coming down from heaven, ascending to heaven, but leaving not heaven behind me in my descent, bringing it along with me; while here on earth, being still in heaven. "No man, I say unto thee, hath ascended up to heaven, but he that came down from heaven, even the Son of man which is in heaven."'

And having thus proclaimed the ground and certainty of his knowledge of all the earthly and all the heavenly things pertaining to the kingdom, Jesus goes on to preach his own gospel beforehand to Nicodemus, taking the lifting-up of the serpent in the wilderness, as the type to illustrate his own approaching lifting-up on the cross, declaring this to be the great and gracious design of his death, that whosoever believeth in him might not perish, but have eternal life: "For God so loved the world, that he gave his only begotten Son; that whosoever believeth in him should not perish, but have everlasting life."

It does not fall within our scope to illustrate at large or attempt to enforce the great truths about the one and only manner of entering into Christ's spiritual kingdom; about the universal need of the Spirit-birth in order to make this entrance; about his own character and office; the manner and objects of his death; the faith which, trusting to him, brings with it everlasting life; the moral guilt that lies in the act of rejecting him as a Redeemer; the true character of that temper of mind and heart which prompts to faith on the one side, and to unbelief on the other, which are all brought out in the discourse of our Lord to Nicodemus. But it does fall precisely within our present design that I ask you to reflect a moment or two,—first, upon the Time at which this discourse was delivered; and next, as to its Effect upon him to whom it was addressed.

It was delivered weeks or months before the

Sermon on the Mount, or any other of Christ's public addresses to the people. Standing in time the first, it stands in character alone. You search in vain through all the subsequent discourses of our Lord for any such clear compendious comprehensive development of the Christian salvation: of its source in the love of the Father; its channel in the death of his only begotten Son; and of the great Agent by whom it is appropriated and applied. You search in vain for any other instance in which the three persons of the Trinity were spoken of by our Lord consecutively and conjunctly; to each being assigned his proper part in the economy of our redemption. It may even be doubted whether in the whole range of the apostolic epistles there be a passage of equal length in which the manner of our salvation through Christ is as fully and distinctly described.

Delivered thus at the very beginning of our Lord's ministry, it utters a loud and unambiguous protest against the error of those who would have us to believe that there was a decided and essential difference between the earlier and later teachings of our Saviour; between the doctrine taught by Christ, and that taught afterwards by his apostles. It is quite true, that until within a few months of the final decease accomplished at Jerusalem, our Lord studiously avoided all reference to his death. It is quite true that, in not a single instance—not even where one would most naturally have expected it—in the prayer that he taught to his disciples,—is there an allusion by Jesus to that death, as supplying the ground of our forgiveness. But that this marked silence is misinterpreted, when it is inferred that he did not assign to it that place and importance given to it afterwards, we have here, in this discourse to Nicodemus, the most convincing proof. I shall have occasion hereafter to refer to those considerations by which our Saviour was obviously influenced during the course of his personal ministry in not publicly unfolding the doctrine of the Cross. Let those, however, who delight to dwell on the simple and pure morality of the Sermon on the Mount, and to contrast it with the doctrinal theology of the apostles, declaring their preference for the teachings of the Master above that of his disciples, but ponder well this first of all our Lord's discourses, and they will see that instead of any conflict there is a perfect harmony.

But if he never afterwards unfolded his gospel so plainly or so fully, why did he do so now; why reveal so much to Nicodemus that he appears to have withheld from the multitude? Am I wrong in regarding this as due in part to the very circumstance that this was a nocturnal and a solitary interview with Nicodemus? No one but this ruler of the Jews may have heard the words that Jesus spake that night, and he would be the last man to go and repeat them to others. There is good reason to believe that the Gospel of St. John was written and published some years after those of the other Evangelists. It is in the Gospel of St. John alone that the interview with Nicodemus is recorded. The other Evangelists appear to have been ignorant of it. How the beloved disciple came to his knowledge of it, it is not necessary for us to inquire. He may have received it from the lips of Nicodemus himself. Enough for us to know that it was not currently reported in the Church till St. John gave it circulation. At any rate we may be sure that it remained unknown all through the period of our Lord's own life. It was not, then, in violation of the rule that he acted on afterwards that he spoke now so plainly and fully as he did to Nicodemus. It was a rare opportunity, one that never perhaps returned, to have before him one so qualified by capacity, by acquirement, by honesty, by earnestness, to receive the truth; and the very manner in which the Saviour hastened to reveal it, is to us the proof that he saw good soil here into which to cast the seed, and the proof too how grateful to him the office of his hand in sowing it.

He knew indeed that the seed then sown was long to be dormant. For three years there was no token of its germination. Nicodemus never sought a second interview with Jesus, but kept studiously aloof. Once, indeed, and it is the only sight throughout three years that we get of him, he ventured to say a word in the Council against a hasty arrest and condemnation of Jesus, but he met with such a sharp rebuff that he never opened his lips again. The memorable words, however, of the midnight meeting at Jerusalem had not been forgotten. There was much in them that he could not understand. Who was He who had spoken of himself as the Son of man, the Son of God; of his ascending and descending to and from heaven; of being in heaven even when he stood there on earth? He had spoken of his being lifted up, that men might believe in him, and, believing, might not perish, but have everlasting life. What could that lifting up of Jesus be, and how upon it could there hang such issues? Much to perplex here, yet much to stimulate; for that life, that eternal life, of which Christ had spoken, was the very life that above all things he was longing to possess and realize. In this troubled state of mind and heart, with what an anxious eye would Nicodemus watch the after-current of our Lord's history! For a year and a half he had disappeared from Judea; was heard of only as saying and doing wonders down in Galilee. Then came the final visit to the capital, the great commotion in the Temple, the raising of Lazarus, the seizure, the trial, the condemnation. Was Nicodemus present, with the rest of that Council of which he was a member, on the morning of the crucifixion? If he was, he must ingloriously have kept silence, for the vote was unanimous. I would rather believe, from what happened on the after part of that day, that he was not present, did not obey the hasty summons. With him or without him, the verdict is given. The license to crucify is extorted from the vacillating Governor; the cross is raised. At last, the words that three years before had sounded in the ruler's listening ear, and which had since been frequently recalled, the mystery of their meaning unrevealed, are verified and explained. The cross is raised; Jesus is lifted up. The darkened heavens, the reeling earth, the prayer for his crucifiers, the promise to the penitent who dies beside him, the voice of triumph at the close, proclaim the death of that only begotten Son of God, whom He had given to be the Saviour of the world. The scales drop off from the eyes they so long had covered. Fear goes out, and faith comes into Nicodemus' breast, a faith that plants him by Joseph's side in the garden, and unites their hands in the rendering of the last services to the body, which they buried in the new sepulchre.

What a flood of light fell then on the hitherto mysterious words of the Crucified; what a rich treasure of comfort would the meditation of them unfold all his life long afterwards to Nicodemus: and what an honour to him that he was chosen as the man to whom were first addressed those words which have comforted so many millions since, and are destined to comfort so many millions more in the years that are to come: " God so loved the world, that he gave his only begotten Son, that whosoever believeth in him should not perish, but have everlasting life!"

XIV.

THE WOMAN OF SAMARIA.[1]

COMING, as he did, to a community that had long been accustomed to act in its corporate capacity as a nation in covenant with God; coming to be nationally received or nationally rejected as the Messiah; a reception or rejection which could only be embodied in some decisive expression of the will of the nation, made through its authorized heads and representatives,—our natural expectation is that Christ's public manifestation of himself would be made principally in Judea and at Jerusalem. And the actual opening of his public ministry convinces us that had no check or hindrance been interposed, had any readiness been shown by the rulers of the people to look favourably on his character and claims, Judea and Jeru-

[1] John iv.

salem would have been the chief scene of his labours. For before he opened his lips as a teacher sent from God, to any Galilean audience, or in any provincial synagogue, he presented himself in the capital, and by a bold and striking act, fitted to draw all eyes upon him, asserted his authority within the Temple, as the house of his Father, which it became him to cleanse. The bold beginning was well sustained both by word and deed, but no favourable impression was made. The only one of the Rulers who made any approach came to him by night, and went away to lock up deep within his breast the wonderful revelation that was made to him. Jesus retired from Jerusalem, but lingered still in Judea, spending the summer months which succeeded the Passover in some district of the country, not far from that in which John was baptizing.[1] It seems strange to us that after the sign from heaven had been given that the greater than he

---

[1] As yet all attempts have failed to identify the Ænon near Salim, to which from the banks of the Jordan John had now removed. It will, in all probability, be discovered somewhere north-east of Jerusalem, so situated that the way from it into Galilee lay naturally through Samaria.

had appeared, instead of joining himself to Jesus, as one of his disciples, John should have kept aloof, and continued baptizing, preserving thus a separate following of his own. And it seems equally strange, that now for a short time, and for this short time only, our Lord's disciples— the men who had voluntarily attached themselves to him, none of whom had as yet been separated from their earthly callings, or set apart as those through whom a new order of things was to be instituted—should also have engaged in baptizing, if not at the suggestion, yet by the permission and under the sanction of their Master. Whatever reasons we may assign for the separate baptisms of John and Jesus being for this short season contemporaneously sustained, they serve to bring out fully and in striking contrast the character and disposition towards Jesus of the Pharisees on the one hand, and of the Baptist on the other. At first, in Judea as in Galilee, the common people heard Christ gladly, and came in great numbers to be baptized. This for the Pharisees is a new matter of offence, out of which, however, they construct an implement of mischief, which they hasten to employ. There can be little doubt that the question which arose between John's disciples and the Jews was stirred by the latter, had respect to the relative value of the two baptisms, and was intended to sow the seeds of dissension between the two discipleships. Fresh from the dispute, and heated by it, some of John's disctples came to him, and said unto him, evidently with the tone of men complaining of a grievance by which their feelings have been hurt: "Rabbi, he that was with thee beyond Jordan, to whom thou barest witness, behold, the same baptizeth, and all men come to him."

We may be all ready enough to acknowledge the superiority of another to ourselves in regard to qualities or acts in which we never sought for prominence or praise. Even as to those qualities and acts in which we may have ourselves excelled, we may not be unwilling to confess the superiority of another, provided that we do not come into direct comparison with him, in presence of those who embody the expression of their preference in some marked piece of conduct. But it does subject our weak nature to an extreme trial when, by his side, in the very region in which he has attained extraordinary and unlooked for success, a man sees another rise whose success so far outstrips his own as to throw it wholly into the shade. Remember, now, that the Baptist was but a man, with all the common infirmities of our nature clinging to him; that up to the time he had baptized Jesus, his course had been one of unparalleled popularity; that from that time the tide of the popular favour began to ebb away from him, and to rise around this other, till at last he hears the tidings, He baptizeth, and all men now go to him. And then, listen to his answer to the complaint of his disciples: "A man," he said, "can receive nothing, except it be given him from heaven." 'This growing baptism of Jesus, this lesser baptism of mine, are both as Heaven has willed. The multitudes that once flocked to me were sent by God; the power which I had over them I got from God; and if the Lord who sent and gave is pleased now to withdraw them from me, to bestow them upon another, still will I adore his name. Nor is it bare submission to his will I cherish. I hear of and I rejoice at the success of Christ. " Ye yourselves bear me witness, that I said, I am not the Christ, but that I am sent before him. He that hath the bride is the bridegroom : but the friend of the bridegroom, which standeth and heareth him, rejoiceth greatly because of the bridegroom's voice. This my joy therefore is fulfilled. He must increase, but I must decrease."' Rare and beautiful instance of an unenvying humility; all the rarer and more beautiful as occurring not in one of weak and gentle nature, but in a character of masculine energy, in which are often to be found only the stronger passions of humanity. A rare and beautiful sight it is to see the gentle Jonathan not only give way to David, as successor to his father's kingdom, but content to stand by David's side, and live under the shadow of his throne; but a rarer, I believe, and still more beautiful thing it is to see the strong-willed Baptist not only make room for Jesus, but rejoice that his own light, which had "shone out so brilliantly, enlightening for a season the whole Jewish heavens, faded away and sunk out of sight in the beams of the rising Sun of righteousness." And John's final testimony upon this occasion to the character and office of Jesus is as striking as the involuntary display that he makes of his own character, going much beyond what he had said before, and containing much that bears a singular likeness to what Jesus had shortly before said of himself to Nicodemus: "He that cometh from above is above all; he that is of the earth is earthly, and speaketh of the earth; he that cometh from heaven is above all: and what he hath seen and heard, that he testifieth; and no man receiveth his testimony. He that hath received his testimony hath set-to his seal that God is true. For he whom God hath sent speaketh the words of God: for God giveth not the Spirit by measure unto him. The Father loveth the Son, and hath given all things into his hand. He that believeth on the Son hath everlasting life: and he that believeth not the Son shall not see life; but the wrath of God abideth on him."[1]

[1] John iii.

Such was the testimony elicited from John on being told of the large concourse of people which had gathered round Jesus and his disciples. Very different was the effect which this intelligence produced in Jerusalem. It fanned the hostile feeling already kindled in the breasts of the Pharisees. How that feeling might have manifested itself had Jesus continued in Judea, his disciples gone on baptizing, and the people kept flocking to them, we cannot tell. As from one quarter there burst about this time on the head of John the storm that closed his public career, so from another quarter might a storm have burst on the head of Jesus with like effect.

Foreseeing the peril to which he might be exposed, Jesus, "when he knew how the Pharisees had heard that he made and baptized more disciples than John, left Judea, and departed again into Galilee." His nearest and most direct route lay through the central district of Samaria. This district was inhabited by people of a foreign origin, and with a somewhat curious history. When the king of Assyria carried the Ten Tribes into captivity, it is said that, in order to fill the void which their exile created, he brought "men from Babylon, and from Cuthah, and from Ava, and from Hamath, and from Sepharvaim, and placed them in the cities of Samaria instead of the children of Israel; and they possessed Samaria, and dwelt in the cities thereof."[1] These certainly were idolaters, worshippers of a strange medley of divinities, and brought with them their old faiths to their new home. Shortly after their settlement, a frightful plague visited them, and it occurred to themselves, or was suggested by the neighbouring Israelites, that it had fallen upon them because of their not worshipping the old divinity of the place. In their alarm they sent an embassy to their monarch, who, either humouring or sharing their fears, sent one of the captive Jewish priests to instruct them in the Israelitish faith. This faith they at once accepted and professed, combining it with their old idolatries: "They feared the Lord," we are told, "and served their graven images."[1] Gradually, however, they were weaned

[1] 2 Kings xvii. 24.

from their ancient superstitions. When, under the decree of Cyrus, the captives of Judah and Benjamin, returning from Babylon, set about rebuilding the Temple at Jerusalem, the Samaritans proposed to join them in the work. The proposal was haughtily rejected, and that rejection was the first of a long series of disputes. A fresh ground of offence arose when Manasseh, a grandson of one, and brother of another High Priest, had, contrary to the laws and customs of the Jews, married a daughter of Sanballat, the governor of the province of Samaria. Called upon to renounce this alliance and repudiate his wife, Manasseh, rather than do so, fled from Jerusalem, and put himself under the protection of his father-in-law. A considerable number of the Jews who were dissatisfied with the great strictness with which Nehemiah was administering affairs at Jerusalem, followed him. The Samaritans, thus strengthened in numbers, and having now a member of one of the highest families of the priesthood among them, erected a rival temple on Mount Gerizim, and set up there a ritual of worship in strict accordance with the Mosaic institute. Their history from this time to the time of Christ is a very chequered one. Their territory was invaded by John Hyrcanus, one of the family of the Maccabees, who plundered their capital, and razing the stately temple on Mount Gerizim from its foundations, left it a heap of ruins, so that when Jesus passed that way, an altar reared upon these ruins was all that Gerizim could boast.

Notwithstanding all these vicissitudes, and all the harsh hostilities to which they were exposed, the Samaritans became purer and purer in their faith, till all relics of their Medo-Persian idolatries had disappeared. They received, as of Divine authority, the five Books of Moses, the Pentateuch, but they rejected all the books of history and prophecies which followed, and which were full, as the Jews believed, of intimations of the future subjection of the whole world to Israelitish sway, and the establishment of Jerusalem, as the central place of worship, and the seat of universal empire.

But though the Jews despised the Samaritans as a people of a mixed origin and a mutilated faith, and the Samaritans repaid the contempt, we are not to think that the two communities lived so much apart that there was no traffic or intercourse between them. There was little or no interchange of kindly or social feeling; but it was quite within the limits of the common usage for the disciples to go into a Samaritan town, to buy bread for themselves and their Master by the way.

Their morning's walk had carried Jesus and his disciples across or along the plain of Mukhna to the entrance of that narrow valley which lies between Mounts Ebal and Gerizim. Here, upon a spur of the latter height, which runs out into the plain, was Jacob's Well,—the town of Sychar, the ancient Shechem, the modern Nablous lying about a mile and a half away, up in the valley, at the base of Gerizim. It was the sixth hour —our twelve o'clock—and the Syrian sun glared hotly upon the travellers. Wearied with the heat of the day and the toil of the morning, Jesus sat down by the well-side, while his disciples went on to Sychar to make the necessary purchases. As Jesus is sitting by the well alone, a woman of Samaria approaches. He fixes his eye upon her as she comes near; watches her as she proceeds to draw the water, waiting till the full pitcher is upon the well-mouth, and then says to her, "Give me to drink." He is a Jew; she knows it by his dress and speech. Yet, as one willing to be indebted to her, he asks a favour at her hands; a favour for which, if his look do not belie him, he will be grateful. Not as one unwilling to grant the favour, but surprised at its being asked, her answer is: "How is it that thou, being a Jew, askest drink of me, who am a woman of Samaria?" He will answer this question, but not in the way that she expects. The manner of his dispensation of the great gift he came from heaven to bestow stands embodied in the words: "Thou wouldest have asked, and I would have given thee the living water."[1]

The woman has taken him to be a common Jew,

---

[1] There is no doubt that the well still shown to travellers near Nablous, is the well of Jacob. Its position near to Sychar; its importance as inferred from its dimensions, being a well of nine feet in diameter and seventy-five in depth; cut out of the solid rock, with sides hewn and smooth as Jacob's servants may be sup-

an ordinary wayfarer, whom thirst and the fatigue of travel have overcome, forcing him perhaps unwillingly to ask for water to drink. He will fix her attention upon himself; he will stir up her feminine curiosity by telling her that he who asks has something on his part to give; that if she only knew who he was, and what that living water was which he had at command, instead of stopping to inquire why he had asked water of her, she would be asking it of him, and what she asked he without question would have given. Living water!—better

---

posed to have left them,—go far, of themselves, to determine its identity; and the conclusion is confirmed by an undivided, unbroken tradition,—Jewish, Samaritan, Arabian, Turkish, Christian.

Besides the absence of all doubt as to its identity, there is another circumstance which surrounds it with a peculiar sacredness. It is the one and only limited and well-defined locality in Palestine that you can connect with the presence of the Redeemer. You cannot in all Palestine draw another circle of limited diameter within whose circumference you can be absolutely certain that Jesus once stood, except round Jacob's Well. I had the greatest possible desire to tread that circle round and round, to sit here and there and everywhere around that well-mouth; that I might gratify a long-cherished wish. But never was disappointment greater than the one which I experienced when I reached the spot. Close by it, in early Christian times, they built a church, whose ruins now cover the ground in its immediate neighbourhood. Over the well itself they erected a vaulted arch, through a small open-water than that which she has in her pitcher. Could it be by going deeper down, and getting nearer to the bubbling spring beneath, that he could get such water, or was it water of superior quality from some other well than this of Jacob. Sir, she says, addressing him with awakening interest and an increasing respect : " Sir," she says, in her ignorance and confusion, " thou hast nothing to draw with, and the well is deep : from whence then hast thou that living water ? Art thou greater than our father Jacob, who gave us the well, and

---

ing in which, travellers, a hundred years ago, crept down into a chamber ten feet square, which left but a narrow margin on which to stand and look down into the well. This vaulted covering has now fallen in, choking up so completely the mouth of the well, that it is only here and there, through apertures between the blocks of stone, that you can find an entrance into the well. I speak of it as I found it last year. It must have been more accessible to travellers even a few years ago ; but year by year the rubbish that is constantly being thrown into it accumulates, and the opening at the top is becoming more closed. The Mussulmans of the neighbourhood, seeing the respect in which it is held by Christians, appear to take a pleasure in obstructing and defiling it. You cannot sit, then, by Jacob's Well, or walk around it, or look down into its waters. It is stated upon good authority, that recently the well, and the site around it, have been purchased by the Russian Church. Let us hope that they will clear away all the stones and rubbish, and leave it clear and open, as Jesus found it, when, weary and way-worn, he sat down beside it.

drank thereof himself, and his children, and his cattle?" Her thoughts are wandering away back to the first drinkers at this well, when its waters first burst out in their freshness, imagining that it must be of them, or of the water of some other neighbouring well, that this stranger had been speaking. Again, waiving as before all direct reply to her question, Jesus with increased solemnity says: "Whosoever drinketh of this water shall thirst again: but whosoever drinketh of the water that I shall give him shall never thirst; but the water that I shall give him shall be in him a well of water springing up into everlasting life." It is not this water, then; it is no common water; it is water that this man alone can give; water which is not to be taken in draughts, with which you may quench your thirst now, and then wait till the thirst comes back again ere another draught be taken; but water of which a man should constantly be drinking, and if he did so would be constantly satisfied, so that there would be no recurring intervals of desire and gratification,—this water as received turning into a well within the man himself, springing up into everlasting life. Beginning to understand a little, seeing this at least, that it was of some element altogether different from any water that she had ever tasted, yet clinging still to the notion that it must be some kind of material water that he means,—she says: " Sir, give me this water, that I thirst not, neither come hither to draw."

One part of Christ's object has now been gained; he has awakened not an idle, but a very eager curiosity; he has forced the woman's attention on himself as having some great benefit in his hand which he is not unwilling to bestow. Through a figurative description of what this benefit is, he will not or cannot carry her further at present. Abruptly breaking the conversation off at this point, he says to her: "*Go, call thy husband*, and come hither." With great frankness she says, "I have no husband." Jesus said to her, "Thou hast well said, thou hast no husband, for thou hast had five husbands, and he whom thou now hast is not thy husband; in that saidst thou truly." In the past domestic history of this woman there had been much that was peculiar, though up to the last connexion she had formed there may not have been anything that was sinful. Christ's object, however, was not so much to convict her of bygone or existing guilt, as to convince her that he was in full possession of all the secrets of her past life, and so to create within her a belief in his more than human insight. Not so much as one overwhelmed with the sense of shame, but rather as one surprised into a new belief as to the character and capabilities of the stranger who addresses her, she replies, "Sir, I perceive that thou art a prophet." If she had been a woman of an utterly abandoned character, whose whole bygone life had been one series of flagrant offences, whose conscience, long seared with iniquity, Christ was now trying to quicken,—very curious would it appear that so soon as the quickening came, waiving all questions about her own character, she should so instantly have put the question about the true place of religious worship, whether here at Gerizim, or there at Jerusalem.

There may have been an attempt to parry conviction, and to turn aside the hand of the convincer, by raising questions about places and forms of worship; but I cannot think, had this been the spirit and motive of this woman's inquiries, that Jesus would have dealt with them as he did; for, treating them evidently as the earnest inquiries of one wishing to be instructed, assuming all the dignity of that office which had been attributed to him, he says to her: Woman, believe me, the hour cometh—(I speak as one before whose eye the whole history of the future stands revealed; the hour cometh,—I came myself into the world to bring it on)—when that strong bias to worship, that lies so deep in the hearts of men, shall have found at last its one only true and worthy object in that God and Father of all, who made all, and who loves all, and has sent me to reveal him to all; when, stripped of all the restraints that have hitherto confined it to a single people, a single country, a single town; relieved of all the supports that were required by it in its weak and tottering childhood,—the spirit of a true piety shall go forth in freedom over the globe, seeking for those —whatever be the places they choose, the outward forms that they adopt,— for those who will adore and love and serve him in spirit and in truth, and wherever it finds them, owning them as the true worshippers of the Father. Woman, believe me, the hour cometh, when neither in this mountain nor yet in Jerusalem, nor here, nor there, nor anywhere exclusively, shall men worship the Father. "God is a Spirit; and they that worship him, must worship him in spirit and in truth." The newness, the breadth, the sublimity, if not also the truth of his teaching, at once suggested to the mind of the listener the thought of that Messiah for whom every Samaritan and Jew alike were looking. I know, she said, that Messias cometh. When he is come he will tell us all things. Jesus saith to her: "I that speak to thee am he."

Why was it that that which he so long and studiously concealed from the Jewish people, that which he so strictly enjoined his disciples not to make known to them, was thus so simply, clearly, and directly told? In the woman herself to whom the wonderful revelation was made, there may have been much to draw it forth. The gentle surprise with which she meets the request of the Jewish stranger; the expression of respect she uses so soon as he begins to speak of God, and some gift of his she might enjoy; her guileless confession when once she found she was actually in a prophet's presence; her instant readiness to believe that Jew though he was—apparently of no note or mark among his brethren—he was yet a prophet; her eager question about the most acceptable way of worshipping the Most High; the quick occurrence of the coming Messiah to her thoughts; the full, confiding, generous faith that she at once reposed in him when he said, I that speak unto thee am he; her forgetfulness of her individual errand to the well; her leaving her pitcher there behind her; her running into the city to call all the men of Sychar, saying, Come, see a man who told me all things that ever I did, is not this the Christ?—all conspire to convince us that, sinful though she was, she was hungering and thirsting after righteousness, waiting for the consolation of Israel, we trust prepared to hail the Saviour when he stood revealed.

But besides her individual character, there was also the circumstance that she was a Samaritan. It is the first time that Jesus comes into close, private, personal contact with one who is not of the seed of Israel; for though she claimed Jacob as her father, neither this woman nor any of the tribe she belonged to, were of Jewish descent. "I am not come," said Jesus, afterwards defining the general boundaries of his personal ministry, "but to the lost sheep of the house of Israel." When he sent out the Seventy, his instructions to them were: "Go not into the way of the Gentiles, and into any city of the Samaritans enter ye not." And yet there were a few occasions, and this is the first of them, in which Christ broke through the restraints under which it pleased him ordinarily to act. I believe that there are just four instances of this kind recorded in the Saviour's life: that of the woman of Samaria, of the Roman Centurion, of the Canaanitish woman, of the Greeks who came up to Jerusalem. All these were instances of our Lord's dealings with those who stood without the pale of Judaism, and as we come upon them in the narrative, we shall be struck with the singular interest which Jesus took in each; the singular care that he bestowed in testing and bringing out to view the simplicity and strength of the desire towards him, and faith in him, that were displayed; the fulness of the revelations of himself that he made, and of that satisfaction and delight with which he contemplated the issue. It was the great and good Shepherd, stretching out his hand across the fence, and gathering in a lamb or two from the outfields, in token of the truth that there were other sheep which were out of the Jewish fold, whom also he was in due time to bring in, so that there should be one fold and one shepherd.

Our idea, that it was this circumstance,—her Samaritan nationality,—which lent such interest, in our Saviour's own regard, to his interview with this woman by the well-side, is confirmed by casting a glance at its result. Jesus at their entreaty turned aside, and abode two days with the Sycharites. You read of no sign or wonder wrought, no miracle performed, save that miracle of knowledge which won the woman's faith.

Though no part of it is recorded, his teaching for those few days in Sychar was, in its general character, like to his teaching by the well-mouth, and on the ground alone of the truthfulness, the simplicity, the purity, the spirituality, and the sublimity of that teaching, many believed on him, declaring they knew that this was indeed the Christ, the Saviour of the world.

The phrase is so familiar to the Christian ear, that we may fail to mark its singularity as coming from the lips of these rude Samaritans. No Saviour this for Jew alone, or Samaritan alone; for any one age or country. Not his the work to deliver from mere outward thraldom, to establish either in Jerusalem or elsewhere any temporal kingdom : his the wider and more glorious office to emancipate the human spirit, and be its guide to the Father of the spirits of all flesh. Compare the notions which these simple villagers had of the Messiah, with those prevalent among the Jews; compare with them any of the most intelligent of our Lord's apostles up to the day of Pentecost, and your very wonder might create doubt, did you not remember that it was not from the books of Daniel and Zechariah and Ezekiel, the books from which the Jews by false interpretations derived their ideas of the Messiah's character and reign, that the Samaritans derived theirs, but from the Pentateuch alone, the five books of Moses; and when you turn to the latter, and look at the prophecies regarding Christ which they contain, you will find that the two things about him to which they point,—that he should be a prophet sent from God, and that his office should have respect to all mankind, that to him should the gathering of the people be, and that in him should all families of the earth be blessed,—were the very two things that the faith of these Samaritans embraced when they said, "We know that this is indeed the Christ, *the Saviour of the world.*"

The conversation by the well, the two fruitful days at Sychar, what is the general lesson that they convey? That wherever Christ finds an open listening ear, he has glad tidings that he is ready to pour into it; that wherever he finds a thirsting soul, he has living waters with which he delights to quench its thirst; that to all who are truly seeking him, he drops disguise, and says, "Behold, even I that speak unto you, am he;" that wherever he finds minds and hearts longing after a revelation of the Father, and the true mode of worshipping him, to such is the revelation given. Had you but stood by Jacob's well, and seen the look of Jesus, and listened to the tones of his voice; or had you been in Sychar during those two bright and happy days, hearing the instructions so freely given, so gratefully received, you would have had the evidence of sense to tell you with what abounding joy to all who are waiting and who are willing, Jesus breaks the bread and pours out the water of everlasting life. Multiplied a thousandfold is the evidence to the same effect now offered to the eye and ear of faith. Still from the lips of the Saviour of the world, over all the world the words are sounding forth: "If any man thirst, let him come to me and drink." Still the manner of his dispensation of the great gift stands embodied in the words: "Thou wouldest have asked, and I would have given thee the living water." And still these other voices are heard catching up and re-echoing our Lord's own gracious invitation: "And the Spirit and the bride say, Come. And let him that heareth say, Come. And let him that is athirst come. And whosoever will, let him take the water of life freely."

XV.

THE JEWISH NOBLEMAN AND THE ROMAN CENTURION.[1]

SEATED by the side of Jacob's well, and seeing the Samaritan woman draw water out of it, Jesus seizes on the occasion to discourse to her of the water of life. So soon as she hears from his own lips that he is the Messiah, this woman leaves her water-pot behind her, and hurries into the neighbouring city to announce to others the great discovery which has been made to her. She has scarcely left the Saviour's side, ere his disciples present themselves with the bread which they had bought in Sychar, offering it, and saying to him, "Master, eat." But, as if hunger had gone from him, and he cared not now for food, he answers, "I have meat to eat that ye know not of." Wondering at his manner, his appearance,

[1] John iv. 46-54; Luke vii. 1-10.

his speech, so different from what they had expected, the disciples say to one another—it is the only explanation that occurs to them—"Hath any man brought him ought to eat?" Correcting the false conception, our Lord replies: "My meat is to do the will of him that sent me, and to finish his work." He had been eating that meat, he had been doing that will, while they were away; and so grateful had it been to him to be so engaged, so happy had he been in instructing a solitary woman, and sending her away, in full belief in his Messiahship, to go and bring others to him, that, in the joy of a spirit whose first desire had been granted to it, the bodily appetite ceases to solicit, and the hunger of an hour ago is no longer felt. She is gone, but already foreseeing all, he anticipates her return,—hears and acts upon the invitation given, has the fruit of these two productive days at Sychar before his eyes, looking upon the few sheaves then gathered in as the first-fruits of a still wider, richer harvest. The idea of that harvest filling his mind, he looks over the fields around him, and blending the natural and the spiritual together, he says to his disciples: "Say not ye, There are yet four months, and then cometh harvest? Behold, I say unto you, Lift up your eyes, and look on the fields, for they are white already to harvest. And he that reapeth receiveth wages, and gathereth fruit unto life eternal: that both he that soweth and he that reapeth may rejoice together. And herein is that saying true, One soweth, and another reapeth." How many contrasts as well as analogies between the husbandry of nature and the husbandry of grace do these words set forth! The sower in the fields of nature has always four months to wait; such is the interval in Palestine between seed-time and harvest. In those other fields in which Jesus is the chief sower, as in the very corner of them at Sychar, sometimes the seed has scarcely sunk into the soil ere it springs up ready for the reaper's hands. Then not seldom the ploughman overtakes the reaper, and the reapers and the sowers go on together. And yet there is often, too, an interval; nor is it always even generally true that it is he who sows who reaps. Nowhere is the common proverb, that one soweth and another reapeth, oftener verified than here. In the spiritual domain it is the lot of some to do little else all their lives than sow, to sow long and laboriously without seeing any fields whitening unto the harvest; it is the lot of others to have little else to do than gather in the fruits of others' labours ; or, looking at the broad history of the world and of the church, can we not mark certain epochs which we would particularly characterize as times of sowing, others as times of reaping, sometimes separated by wide intervals, sometimes running rapidly into one another? But whether they be the same or different agents that are employed in the sowing and in the reaping ; whether longer space intervene, or the sowing and the reaping go together, one thing is true, that when the harvest cometh, and the everlasting life, towards which all the labour has been tending, is reached, then shall there be a great and a mutual rejoicing,—the gladness of those to whom it is given to see that their labour has not been in vain in the Lord.

It has always been a question whether there was any allusion made or intended by Christ to the actual condition of the fields around him as he spake. I cannot but think, though it be in opposition to the judgment of some of our first scholars, that there was. Jesus was speaking at the time when there were as yet four months unto the harvest. If it were so, then we have good ground for settling at what period of the year this visit of our Lord to Sychar took place. The harvest in Palestine begins about the middle of April. Four months back from that time carries us to the middle of December, the Jewish seed-time. If so, the interval between the first Passover at which our Lord had his conversation with Nicodemus, which took place, as we know, at the commencement of the early harvest, and the conversation with the woman of Samaria, an interval of no less than eight months, were spent by Jesus in Judea, giving to the rulers of the people a privileged opportunity of considering Christ's character and claims. Nothing but disappointment, neglect, indifference, or alienation, having been manifested, Jesus retired to Galilee, taking Samaria by the way. The two days at Sychar presented a striking contrast to his reception in Judea. How will they stand in comparison with the reception that awaits him in Galilee?

Cana lies farther north than Nazareth. The road to the one would lead close to, if not through the other. On this occasion Jesus appears to have passed by Nazareth. Perhaps it was to avoid such a reception as he knew to be awaiting him there, or it may have been simply because Mary and the family had shifted their residence, and were now living near their relatives at Cana. The rumour of the first miracle which he had wrought there some months before may have spread widely in the neighbourhood. It was done, however, so quietly, and in such a hidden manner, that one can well conceive of different versions of it going abroad. It was different with those reports which the Galileans who had been up at the last Passover brought back from Jerusalem. Our Lord's miracles there, whatever they were, were done openly; many had believed because of them. The Galileans who were at the feast had seen them all, and on their return home had filled the country with the noise of them, all the more gratified, perhaps, that he who had drawn all eyes upon him at Jerusalem was one of themselves. And now it is told abroad that he has come back from Judea and is at Cana.

The tidings reach the ear of a nobleman in Capernaum, a Jew of high birth connected with the court of Herod Antipas, at the very time that a grievous malady is on his son, and has brought him to the very brink of death. He had not heard, perhaps, that Jesus had restored the dying to health; so far as we know, the healing of his son may have been the first miracle of that kind which Jesus wrought; but he has heard of his turning the water into wine, he has heard of the wonders wrought at Jerusalem. He by whom such miracles had been done should be able to rebuke disease. It is at least worth trying whether he will or can. The distance to Cana is but a short one, some twenty miles or so. He will send no servant, he will go himself, and make the trial. He went, saw Jesus, told him his errand, and besought him that he would come down and heal his son. Why was it that before Jesus made any reply, or gave any indication of his purpose, he said, as the fruit of some deep inward thought which the application had suggested, "Except ye see signs and wonders ye will not believe?" It was because he saw all that was in that man, all the motives by which he had been prompted to this visit; the strong affection for his son, which Jesus will not rebuke; his willingness to be at any pains on his behalf, to seek help from any quarter; his partial faith in Christ's power to help—for without some faith of this description, he would not have come at all; yet the absence of all deeper faith springing from a sense of spiritual disease, which should have brought the man to Jesus for himself as well as for his son, and which should have taught him to look to Jesus as the healer of the soul. It was because he saw in this nobleman a specimen of his countrymen at large, and in his application a type and prelude of the multitude of like applications afterwards to be made to him.

It may have served to suggest this the more readily to Christ's thoughts, and give the greater intensity to the emotion excited within his breast, that he had just come from Sychar, where so many had believed in him without any sign or wonder done, believed in him as a teacher sent from God, believed in him as the Messiah promised to their fathers. What a contrast between those simple-minded, simple-hearted Samaritans, whose love and wonder, faith and penitence, joy and gratitude had been so quickly, so purely, so exclusively awakened, and this nobleman of Capernaum and his Galilean fellow-countrymen! We know that Jesus never returned to Sychar, though he must more than once have passed near to it on his way to and from Jerusalem. We know that he gave positive instructions to the Seventy to go into no city of the Samaritans. It was in fulfilment of his design that his personal ministry should be confined to the lost sheep of the house of Israel, that he laid this restraint upon himself and his disciples. But can we think that it cost him no self-denial, that it was with no inward pang that Jesus turned away from those who showed themselves so willing to receive, to those who were for ever asking a sign from heaven, and who, " after he had done so many miracles, yet believed not in him?" (John xii. 37.) Why was it then, that when the Pharisees came forth, and began to question him, seeking of him a sign from heaven, "he sighed deeply in his spirit, and said, Why doth this generation seek after a sign?" (Mark viii. 12.) The deep sigh came from the depth of a spirit moved and grieved at this incessant craving for outward seals and vouchers, this unwillingness to believe in him simply on the ground of his character and his doctrine. Though he did not meet the peculiar demand of the Pharisees, who, unsatisfied even with his other works, sought from him a special sign from heaven, our Lord, we know, was lavish in the performance of miracles, supplied willingly and largely that ground of faith which they afforded, appealed often and openly to the proof of his divine mission which they supplied. Yet all this is consistent with his deploring the necessity which required such a kind of evidence to be supplied, and his mourning over that state of the human spirit out of which the necessity arose. "The works that I do, bear witness of me, that the Father hath sent me." "If I do not the works of my Father, believe me not. But if I do, though ye believe not me, believe the works."[1] Such was Christ's language openly addressed to the rulers of the people at Jerusalem. Nor was it differently that he spoke to his disciples in private: "Believe me that I am in the Father, and the Father in me: or else believe me for the very works' sake."[2] Jesus would rather have been believed in without the works, would rather that he had not had the works to do in order to win the faith. It is not, then, a faith in the reality of miracles, nor in him simply as the worker of them, nor in anything he was or said or did that rests exclusively upon his having performed them, which constitutes that deeper faith in himself to which it is his supreme desire to conduct us. And when we read of Jesus sighing when signs were asked, and sighing as miracles were wrought by him, we cannot interpret his sighing otherwise than as the expression of the profound grief of his spirit over those who are so little alive to the more spiritual evidence that his character and works carried along with them, as to need to

[1] John v. 36; x. 37, 38.   [2] John xiv. 11.

have these outward props and buttresses supplied. There are two different kinds of faith,—that which you put in what another is, or in what another has said, because of your own personal knowledge of him and your perception of the intrinsic truthfulness of his sayings, and that which you cherish because of certain external vouchers for his truthfulness that he presents. Jesus invites us to put both these kinds of faith in him, but the latter and the lower in order to lead on to the former and the higher, the real abiding, life-giving faith in Him as the Saviour of our souls.

"Except ye see signs and wonders, ye will not believe." We are scarcely surprised that the nobleman of Capernaum, when his eager entreaty was met in this way, by the utterance of so broad an aphorism, should have felt somewhat disappointed and chagrined. There was some hope for him, indeed, had he reflected on it, in the words that Christ had used; for if Jesus had not meant to do this sign and wonder, he would not have spoken as he did. But the father is in no mood to take up and weigh the worth and meaning of Christ's words. What he wants is that

Christ should go down with him immediately to Capernaum; he has some hope, that if there, he may be able to cure his son. He has no idea of a healing wrought at a distance, effected at Cana by a word of the Lord's power, an act of the Lord's will. "Sir," he says, "come down ere my child die:" a tinge of impatience, perhaps of pride, yet full of the good compensatory element, strong parental love. "Jesus saith unto him, Go thy way; thy son liveth." It is the first time, it is one of the few instances in which Jesus stood face to face with earthly rank and power. Perhaps this nobleman presumed on his position, when he said, with something of an imperative tone, "Sir, come down ere my child die." If so, he must have been not a little astonished to find the tone of command rolled back upon him thus: "Go thy way, thy son liveth." How high above the nobility of earth rises the royalty of heaven! This is the style and manner of Him who saith, and it is done; who commandeth, and creation throughout all its borders obeys. None ever did such works on earth as Jesus did; none ever did them in such a simple, easy, unaffected manner;

the manner becoming one who was exerting not a delegated but a native power.

The manner and the substance of the declaration told alike at once upon the nobleman. It satisfied him that the end of his visit was gained. He believed in the word of Jesus, that the death he dreaded was not to come upon his son, that the child he loved so tenderly was to be spared to him. How exactly this had been brought about he did not as yet know. Whether the cure had been instantaneous and complete, or whether the crisis of it had passed, and the recovery had begun; whether it had been by his possession of a superhuman knowledge, or by his exercise of a superhuman power, that Jesus had been able to announce to him the fact, "Thy son liveth,"—he neither stayed, nor did he venture to ask any explanation. It was enough for him to be assured of the fact, and there was something in the manner in which that *Go thy way* had been spoken, which forbade delay. He meets his servants by the way, bearers of glad tidings. With them he can use all freedom. He asks all about the cure, and learns that it had not been slowly but instantaneously that the fever had gone, and that the time at which it had done so was the very time at which these words of Jesus, "Thy son liveth," had been spoken at Cana. He had gone out to that village but half a believer in Christ's power in any way to help, limiting that power so much in his conception that it had never once occurred to him that Jesus could do anything for him unless he saw the child. But now he feels that he has been standing in the presence of One, the extent of whose power he had as much underrated as the depth and the tenderness of his love. Awe, conviction, gratitude, fill his soul. A double sign and wonder has been done in Israel. A child has been cured of a fever at Capernaum by one standing miles away at Cana, and a father has been cured of his unbelief,—the same kind of power that banished the disease from the body of the one, banishing distrust from the heart of the other.

How far above all that he had ever asked! His child was dying when the father left Capernaum, was still nearer death when he arrived at Cana; had Jesus done what the father wanted, and gone down with him to Capernaum, his son might have been dead ere they got there. The word of power is spoken, and just as the disease is clasping its victim in a last embrace, it has to relax its grasp, take wings, and fly away. The father has gone unselfishly, affectionately, on an errand of love, seeking simply his child's life, not asking or caring to get anything himself from Christ. But now in this Jesus he recognises a higher and greater than a mere healer of the body: spiritual life is breathed into his own soul. Nor is this all; he returns to Capernaum to tell all the wonders of the cure; tells them to the healed child, who also believes,—and strange would be the meeting afterwards between that child and Jesus,—he tells them to the other members of his family, and each in turn believes. He himself believed, and with him all his house, —the first whole household brought into the Christian fold.

Let us compare for a moment this case with that of the Centurion. Both plead for others; the one for his child, the other for his servant, and the pleading of both is signally successful;

the compliance prompt and generous. Such honour does Jesus put on all kindly intercession with him on behalf of those to whom we are bound by ties of relationship and affection. In both the cases, too, Christ adopts the unusual method of curing at a distance, curing by a word. But the treatment of the two applicants is different: suited to the state, the character, the necessities of each. The one's faith is limited and weak, and needs to be expanded and strengthened; the other's is strong, and waits only to be exhibited in combination with that humility which covers it as with a crown of .glory. The one man, little knowing what Christ can do for him, and impatient at what looks like a repulse, says in his haste, Sir, come down ere my child die. The other, having a boundless faith in Jesus, ventures not at first to prescribe any special mode of cure, but contents himself with sending some elders of the Jews to ask that Christ's healing power should be exercised on behalf of his servant. Jesus goes not with him who asks him to do so, having a far greater thing to do for him than to comply with his request. But he no sooner gets the message delivered by deputy from the other, than he says, I will come and heal him, and sets off instantly on the errand. But he knew that he should be arrested by the way. He knew that the Roman Centurion had such a sense of his own unworthiness that he shrank from receiving him into his house; he knew that he had such confidence in his power, that all he wanted was that Jesus should will it and his servant should be cured. He knew that there was a humility and a faith in the breast of this Gentile officer —the first Gentile that ever applied to him— such as was not to be found in any Israelitish bosom. It was to bring these before the eyes of his fellow-countrymen, and to hold them up for admiration and rebuke, that he did not at the first act as he had done at Cana, but made that movement towards the Centurion's dwelling. Wonderful, indeed, the faith embodied in the message which the Centurion sent: I, a Roman officer, have a limited authority, but within its limits this authority is supreme. I can say unto one of my soldiers, Go, and he goeth; to another, Come, and he cometh; to my servant, Do this, and he doeth it. But thou, Jesus, art supreme over all. As my soldiers are under me, so under thee are all the powers and processes of nature. Thou canst say—to this disease, Come, and it cometh; to that other disease, Go, and it goeth; to thy servants Life and Death, Do this, and they do it. Say thou then but the word, and my servant shall be healed. And Jesus marvelled when he heard the message, and he turned about and said to the people that followed him,—it was very much for their sakes that he had arranged it so, that so many peculiarities should attend this miracle, and such a pre-eminence be given to this first exhibition of Gentile faith in him,—I say unto you, I have not found so great faith, no, not in Israel. It was the highest exercise of human faith in him that Jesus had yet met with, and he wondered and rejoiced that it should be found beyond the bounds of Israel. Midway between the Gentile and the Jew stood the woman of Samaria; outside the bounds of Judaism stood this Roman Centurion. Was it to prefigure the great future of the gathering-in of all people, and nations, and tongues, and tribes, that so early in his ministry such manifestation of a faith in the Saviour was made?

But while wondering with Christ at the beautiful exhibition of humility and faith in a quarter so unlooked-for, let us take home the warning with which Jesus followed up the expression of his approval and admiration: "And I say unto you, that many shall come from the east and west, and shall sit down with Abraham, and Isaac, and Jacob, in the kingdom of heaven; but the children of the kingdom shall be cast into outer darkness, there shall be wailing and gnashing of teeth." Surely from the lips of the living and compassionate Redeemer words of such terrible import never would have passed, had the warning they convey not been needed. Let it then be the first and most earnest effort of each of us to enter into this kingdom, of which nominally and by profession we are the children, in all humility, and with entire trust in Christ our Saviour, lest the opportunity for entering in go past, and the door be shut—shut by Him who shutteth, and no man openeth.

XVI.

THE POOL OF BETHESDA.[1]

COULD we ascertain what the feast was to which Jesus went up, and at which he healed the man beside the Pool of Bethesda, it would go far to settle the question as to the length of our Lord's public ministry; but after all the labour that has been bestowed on the investigation, it remains still uncertain whether it was the Passover, or one of the other annual festivals. If it was the Passover—as, upon the whole, we incline to think it was, as John mentions three other Passovers, one occurring before, and two after this one— Christ's ministry would come to be regarded as covering a space of about three years and a half; if it were one or other of the lesser festivals, a year or more, according to the festival which is fixed upon, must be deducted from that period.

[1] John v.

This much, at least, appears certain, that it was our Lord's second appearance in Jerusalem after his baptism, and that it occurred at or near the close of a year, the most of which had been spent in Judea. On the occasion of this second visit, Jesus went one Sabbath-day to walk through the cloisters or colonnades that were built round a large swimming bath, called the Pool of Bethesda. Tradition has for many ages pointed to a large excavation 360 feet long, 130 feet broad, and 75 feet deep, lying outside the north wall of the Harem enclosure, and near to St. Stephen's Gate, as having been this pool. The peculiar character of its masonry establishes the fact that it must have been intended originally as a reservoir for water. At one of its corners there are two arched openings or vaults, one twelve, the other nineteen feet wide, extending backward to an unknown distance, forming part, it may have been, of the porches of which the Evangelist speaks. These porches, on the day on which Jesus visited them, were crowded. They formed one of the city resorts; and besides numbers of others that frequented them for the ordinary use of the waters, there lay around a great multitude of the blind, the halt, the withered, waiting for the moving of the water.

If we accept the account given in the fourth verse of the fifth chapter, the moving of the water, and the healing virtue temporarily bestowed upon it during the period of its commotion, were due to angelic agency. The verse, however, is wanting in many of the most ancient manuscripts, and has come now to be very generally regarded as an interpolation very naturally inserted by the early transcribers of the Gospel, as embodying the expression of what was then the popular belief. We are disposed the rather to go in with this view, when we consider how unlike to angelic influence is the kind of agency here attributed to it as elsewhere described in Holy Writ, and how singular it would have been had the healing power been so bestowed that it should be restricted to the single person who first stepped in. Of itself this would not be sufficient ground on which to reject the idea of a supernatural agency having been employed, but if the verse alluded to did not form part of the original

THE POOL OF BETHESDA.

writing of the Evangelist, then we are left at liberty to believe that this was a pool supplied by an intermittent spring, which at certain seasons, owing to the sudden formation of particular gases, bubbled up, throwing the whole water of the reservoir into commotion, impregnated for the time with qualities which had a healing power over some forms of disease—a power of course greatly magnified in the popular idea. But whether the verse, and the explanation which it contains of the moving of the water, be accepted or rejected, the narrative of what Jesus said and did remains untouched.

Wandering through these crowded porches, and looking at the strange array of the diseased waiting there for the auspicious moment, the eye of Jesus rests on one who wears a dejected and despairing look, as if he had given up all hope. Thirty-eight years before, the powers of life and motion had been so enfeebled that it was with the greatest difficulty, and at the slowest pace, he could creep along the ground. His friends had got tired perhaps of helping him otherwise, and as their last resource, had carried him to the porches of the pool, and left him there to do the best for himself he could. And he had done that best often and often, yet had failed. Every time the troubling of the water came, he had made the effort; but every time he had seen some one of more vigour and alertness, or better helped, get in before him and snatch the benefit out of his hands. Jesus knew all this: knew how long it had been since the paralytic stroke first fell on him; how long it was since he had been brought to try the efficacy of these waters; how the expectation of cure, at first full and bright, had been gradually fading from his heart. To rekindle the dying hope, to fix the man's attention on himself, Jesus bends over the bed on which he lies, looks down at him, and says, Wilt thou be made whole? Were the words spoken in mockery? That could not be; a glance at the speaker was sufficient to disprove it. But the question surely would not have been asked had the speaker known how helpless was he to whom it was addressed. He said, "I have no man, when the water is troubled, to put me into the pool, but while I am coming another steppeth down before me." As he gives this explanation, he looks up more earnestly into the stranger's face—a face he had never seen before—and gathers a new life and hope from the expression of sympathy, the look of power that countenance conveys.

"Jesus saith unto him, Rise, take up thy bed, and walk." The command was instantly obeyed. The cure was instantly complete. The short time, however, that it had taken for him to stoop and lift the mattress on which he lay, had been sufficient for Jesus to pass on, and be lost among the crowd. The stopping, the question, the command, the cure, all had been so sudden, the man has been so taken by surprise, that he doubts whether he would be able to recognise that stranger if he saw him again. Lifting his bed, and rejoicing in the new sensation of recovered strength, he walks through the city streets in search of his old home and friends. The Jews —an expression by which, in his Gospel, John always means, not the general community, but some of the ecclesiastical heads and rulers of the people—the Jews see him as he walks, and say to him: "It is the Sabbath-day; it is not lawful for thee to carry thy bed." No answer could be more natural, as no excuse could be more valid, than that which the man gave when he said: "He that made me whole, the same said unto me, Take up thy bed, and walk." His challengers do not ask him anything about the healing—as soon as they hear of it, they suspect who the healer was—but fixing upon the act in which the breach of the Sabbath lay, and as if admitting the validity of the man's defence, in throwing the responsibility of that act upon him who had ordered him to do it, "They asked him, What man is that which said unto thee, Take up thy bed and walk?" He could not tell, and so the conversation by the wayside dropped.

Soon after, the healed man is in the Temple, thanking God, let us believe, for the great mercy bestowed upon him. Jesus, too, is there; but they might have passed without the healed recognising the healer. It was not the purpose, however, of our Lord that it should be so. Finding the man among the worshippers, he says to him, "Sin no more, lest a worse thing come unto thee." Nothing more seems to have been said; nothing more to have passed between the two; but that short sentence, what a light it threw upon the distant past!—reminding the man that it had been to the sins of his youth that he had owed the eight-and-thirty years of infirmity that had followed; and what a solemn warning did they carry as to the future!—reminding him that if, on being restored to strength, he should return to sin, a still worse thing than so many years of bodily infirmity might be in store for him. Jesus gives this warning, and passes on. Recognising him at once as he who had cured him beside the pool, the man inquires about him of the bystanders, and learns now who he is. And he goes and tells the Jews; not, let us hope, from any malicious motive, or any desire to put an instrument into the hands of Christ's enemies. Considering where and how he had so long been lying, he may have known so little of all that had recently happened, as to imagine that he was at once pleasing the rulers, and doing a service to Jesus, by informing them about his cure. But it was no new intelligence that he conveyed. The Jews, we presume, knew well enough who had effected this cure. But it was the first instance in which they had heard of Jesus healing on the Sabbath-day—of itself in their eyes a violation of its sanctity; and as it would appear that, not content with this offence, he had added another in ordering the man to carry on that day a burden through the streets —a thing strictly and literally prohibited by the law,—it may have gratified the Jews to be able to convict Jesus of a double breach of the Sabbath law by direct and indubitable evidence from the man's own lips. You can imagine the secret though malignant satisfaction with which they got and grasped this weapon, one at once of defence and of assault; how they would use it in vindicating their rejection of Christ as a teacher sent from God, for could God send a man who would be guilty of such flagrant breaches of his law? how they would use it in carrying out those purposes of persecution already brooding in their breasts. Their hostility to Jesus, which had been deepening ever since his daring act of cleansing the Temple, now reached its height. From this time forth—and it deserves to be especially noted as having occurred at so early a stage, inasmuch as it forms the key to much of our Lord's subsequent conduct—they sought to slay him, because he had done those things on the Sabbath-day. But though the purpose to slay him was formed, it was not expressed, nor attempted to be carried out. Things were not yet ripe for its execution. Jesus might be convicted as a Sabbath-breaker, and all the opprobrium of such a conviction be heaped upon his head; but as things then stood, it would not be possible to have the penalty of death inflicted on him upon that ground. They must wait and watch for an opportunity of accusing him of some crime which will carry that penalty even in the eyes of a Roman judge.

Though not serving them much in this respect, they have not to wait long till, in their very presence—so that they have no need to ask for other proof—Jesus commits a still higher offence than that of violating the Sabbath. Aware of the charges that they were bringing against him as to his conduct at the Pool of Bethesda, he seizes upon some public opportunity when he could openly address the rulers; and in answer to the special accusation of having broken the Sabbath, he says to them, '"My Father worketh hitherto, and I work." The rest into which my Father entered after his work of creation, of which your earthly Sabbatic rest is but a type, was not one of absolute inactivity—of the suspension, cessation of his agency in and over the vast creation he had formed. He worketh on still; worketh on continuously, without distinction of days, through the Sabbath-day as through all days, sustaining, preserving, renewing, vivifying, healing. Were this work Divine to cease, there would not be even that earthly Sabbath for you to rest in. And as he, my Father, worketh, so work I, his Son, knowing as little of distinction of days in my working as he. By process of nature, as you call it—that is, by the hand of my Father—a man is often cured on the Sabbath-day. And it is only what He thus does that I have done, and my authority for doing so is this, that I am his Son.'

Whatever difficulty the men to whom this defence of his alleged Sabbath-breaking was offered, may have had either in understanding its nature or appreciating its force, one thing is clear, that they did at once and most clearly comprehend that in speaking of God as his Father in the way he did, Jesus was claiming to stand to God, not simply in the relationship of a child—such a relationship as that in which we all, as the creatures of his power and the preserved of his providence, may be regarded as standing—but in that of a close, personal, peculiar sonship belonging to him alone, involving in it, as all true filiation does, unity of nature between the Father and the Son. It was thus that the Jews understood Jesus to speak of the Father and of himself, when he so associated himself with the Father, as to imply that if his Father was not a breaker of the Sabbath in healing men upon that day, neither was he, his Son; and so they sought the more to kill him, because he had not only broken the Sabbath, but said also that God was his own Father, making himself equal with God.

If the Jews had misunderstood Jesus, what was easier than for him to have said so; to have denied and repudiated the allegation that he had intended to claim anything like equality with God? Instead of this, what does Jesus do? He go on to reassert, to explain, and to expand what had been implied in the compendious expression he had employed. Anything like such distinction between the Father and the Son as that the one would or could judge, or will, or act independently of the other—without or against the other—he emphatically and reiteratedly repudiates: "Verily, verily, I say unto you, the Son can do nothing of himself;" "I can of my own self do nothing." The very nature of the relationship forbade it that the Son ever would or could assert for himself any such independence of the Father as the creature, in its wilfulness and sinfulness, is apt to assert for itself. But though all such separation and independence of council and of action is here precluded, so complete is the concert that what things soever the Father doeth the same doeth the Son likewise. Some things that the great Divine Master Workman does, a superior scholar may copy or imitate. But Jesus does not say, what things the Father does, the Son does other things somewhat like them; but the same things, and whatever things the Father doeth, the same doeth the Son, and doeth them likewise, *i.e.*, in the very same manner, by the exercise of the same power, for the furtherance of the same ends.

In far greater works than that simply of healing, will the unity of action between them be made to appear. One of these greater works is that of quickening the dead, by the incommunicable prerogative of the Creator. This prerogative the Father and the Son have equally. As he wills, and by his will, the Father quickeneth; so too does the Son. The highest form of life is that which is breathed into souls spiritually dead. This life is of the Son's imparting equally as of the Father. It comes through the hearing of Christ's word; through a believing in the Father as he who sent the Son. Verily, verily, I say unto you, the hour is coming, and now is, when the dead—the spiritually dead—shall hear the voice of the Son of God, and they that hear shall live. Another work peculiar to Divinity is that of judging; approving, condemning, assigning to every man at last, in strict accordance with what he is, and has been, and has done, his place and destiny. Who but the all-wise, all-just, all-gracious God is competent for such a task? but that task, in the outward execution of it, the Father has devolved upon the Son, giving him authority to execute it, because he is not simply the Son of God, in which character he needs not such authority to be conveyed to him; but because he is also the Son of man, and it is in that complex or mediatorial office with which he is invested, that he is to sit upon the Throne of Judgment at the last, when all the inhabitants of the earth shall stand before his tribunal. Should this then be a subject for marvel? for the hour was coming, though not yet come, when all that are in their graves shall hear Christ's voice and shall come forth; they that have done good to the resurrection of life, and they that have done evil to the resurrection of condemnation. Having thus unfolded the great truth of the unity of will, purpose, and action, between the Father and the Son, Jesus ceases to speak of himself in the third person, and proceeds onwards to the close of his address, to speak in the first person, and that in the plainest way,[1] of the testimonies that had been borne to him, that of the Father, that of John, that of his own works, that of the Holy Scriptures, all of which these Jews had wilfully

[1] "I can of mine own self do nothing: as I hear, I judge: and my judgment is just; because I seek not mine own will, but the will of the Father which hath sent me. If I bear witness of myself, my witness is not true. There is another that beareth witness of me; and I know that the witness which he witnesseth of me is true. Ye sent unto John, and he bare witness unto the truth. But I receive not testimony from man :- but these things I say, that ye might be saved. He was a burning and a shining light; and ye were willing for a season to rejoice in his light. But I have greater witness than that of John : for the works which the Father hath given me to finish, the same works that I do, bear witness of me, that the Father hath sent me. And the Father himself, which hath sent me, hath borne witness of me. Ye have neither heard his voice at any time, nor seen his shape. And ye have not his word abiding in you : for whom he hath sent, him ye believe not. Search the scriptures; for in them ye think ye have eternal life : and they are they which testify of me. And ye will not come to me, that ye might have life. I receive not honour from men. But I know you, that ye have not the love of God in you. I am come in my Father's name, and ye receive me not : if another shall come in his own name, him ye will receive. How can ye believe, which receive honour one of another, and seek not the honour that cometh from God only? Do not think that I will accuse you to the Father: there is one that accuseth you, even Moses, in whom ye trust. For had ye believed Moses, ye would have believed me : for he wrote of me. But if ye believe not his writings, how shall ye believe my words?"

rejected. Now the accused becomes the accuser. Now he who had been charged as a Sabbath-breaker, rises to the height of that very elevation which they had regarded him as a profane and blasphemous man for venturing to claim; and he tells these unbelieving Jews, as one knowing the hearts of all men, and entitled to judge, and exercising that very authority with which, as the Son of man, he had been clothed,—he tells them, that they had not the love of God in them, nor his word abiding in them; that they did not believe Moses when he wrote of him; that, much as they reverenced their Scriptures, they only believed in them so far as they tallied with their own thoughts and fancies. Still further, he declares that there was this great obstacle in the way of their receiving one who came to them as Jesus did, in the name of the Father, to do alone the Father's will, that they were all too busy seeking after the honour that came from man, minding earthly things, and seeking not the honour that came from the one only living and true God; attributing thus all their perverseness to moral causes, to motives operating within, over which they should have had control; this being their condemnation, that they would not come to him that they might have life. He would, but they would not.

If Jesus Christ were but a man, what are we to make of such a discourse as this? What are we to make of the first part of it, in which he speaks of the Father and his connexion with him? What of the second part of it, in which he speaks to the Jews and of their treatment of him? We know not which would be the worst,—the arrogance in the one direction, or the presumption and uncharitableness in the other,—if this were but a man speaking of the Creator, and to his fellows. It can alone relieve him from the guilt of profane assumption towards God, and unlicensed liberty with man, to believe that Jesus was really that which the Jews regarded him as claiming to be, the Son of, the equal with, the Father, whom all men should honour even as they honour God.

But let me ask now your particular attention to the circumstances under which this marvellous discourse was spoken, and to the object which, in the first instance, as at first delivered, it was intended to serve. Jesus voluntarily, intentionally, created the occasion for its delivery. The miracle here,—the healing of the impotent man at the Pool of Bethesda,—was a wholly secondary or subordinate matter, intended to bring Christ into that relationship with the Jewish rulers, which called for and gave its fitness and point to this address. Why did Jesus choose a Sabbath-day to walk in the porches of Bethesda? Why did he do what only on one or two occasions afterwards he did, instead of waiting to be applied to, himself single out the man and volunteer to heal him? Why did he not simply cure the man, but bid him also take up his bed and walk? He might have chosen another day, and then, in the story of the cure, we should have had but another instance added to the many of the exertion of our Lord's divine and beneficent power. He might have simply told the man to rise up and walk, and none could have told how the cure had been effected, or turned it into any charge. He chose that day, and he selected that man, and he laid on him the command he did, for the very purpose of bringing himself front to front with the Jewish rulers. At first the question between them seems to refer only to the right keeping of the Sabbath. Had Jesus as a man, as a Jew, broken the Sabbath law in curing a man upon that day? Had he broken it in telling the man he healed to carry his bed through the city? Had the Jews not misunderstood, overstrained the law, sticking to its letter, and violating its spirit? These were grave questions, with which, as we shall find, Jesus afterwards did deal, when on another Sabbath he volunteered another cure. But here Christ waives all lesser topics—that, among the rest, of the right interpretation of the Sabbath law—and uses the antecedent circumstances as the basis on which to assert, and then amplify and defend, the truth of his true and only sonship to the Father. His ministry in Judea was now about to close. Aware of the design against his life which had now been formed, and wishing to baffle it for a season, he retires to Galilee. But he will not leave Jerusalem till he has given one full and public testimony as to who and what he is, so that the Jews in continuing to reject him, shall not have it in their power to say that he has not revealed his own character, nor expressed to them the real grounds upon which their opposition to him is based.

Such was the special drift and bearing of the address of Jesus as originally delivered to the Jews. But is there nothing in its close applicable to ourselves and to all men in every age? The same kind of obstacles that raised such a barrier in the way of the Jews believing in Jesus, do they not still exist? If the spirit of pride and worldliness, a conventional piety and an extreme thirst for the applause and honour that cometh from man, occupy and engross our hearts, shall they not indispose and render us unable to believe simply, heartily, devotedly, on Jesus Christ? Of one thing let us be assured, that whatever be our disposition and conduct towards him, his towards us is ever a longing desire to have us, keep us, bless us, save us; and that the one and only thing that stands in the way of our enjoying all the benefits of his salvation, is our own unwillingness; his lament over all that wander away from him, being ever this, Ye will not come to me, that ye might have life.

XVII.

THE SYNAGOGUE OF NAZARETH.[1]

IN the route commonly taken from Jerusalem to the Sea of Galilee, one of the most interesting day's travel is that which carries you from Jenin across the three valleys into which, at its upper extremity, the great plain of Esdraelon divides, and up to Nazareth, as it lies embedded in the southern ridge of the hills of Galilee. Crossing the first valley, we skirted the base of the mountains of Gilboa, and paused for a few moments upon a gentle elevation, now occupied by a few houses of the humblest description, on which Jezreel, the ancient capital of Israel, once stood, with the palace of Ahab in its centre, and the vineyard of Naboth in its outskirts. Our eye wandered along the twelve or fourteen miles of

[1] Luke iv. 16-31.

dead-level that run from Jezreel to Carmel, and the figure of the great prophet running before the king's chariot rose before us. We turned round and gazed upon the slopes of Gilboa, and the tide of Saul's last battle seemed to roll over them, and the sounds of the funeral dirge of David to be lingering still among the hills. The crossing of the next valley carried us to the base of Little Hermon, where a small hamlet lies, consisting of a few miserable-looking hovels, surrounded by ill-kept gardens. This was the Shunem in which the house once stood which had in it the prophet's chamber; and these were the gardens in one of which the widow's son once sickened unto death. Leaving behind us the place which, in the old prophetic times, saw the dead child given back to his mother, climbing Little Hermon and descending on the other side, we entered another village which witnessed another dead son given back to another widowed mother, by him who touched the bier, and said, "Young man, I say unto thee, arise." Here, in this village of Nain, we came for the first time on the traces of our Lord's Galilean ministry. The third plain passed, a steep ascent carried us to the summit of that range of hills which forms the north-eastern boundary of the plain of Esdraelon. Descending, we came upon a circular, basin-shaped depression, girdled all round by a dozen or more swelling hill-tops that rise from three to four hundred feet above the valley they enclose. Near to the foot of the highest of these surrounding hills, nestled in a secluded upland hollow, lies the village of Nazareth. No village in Palestine is liker what it was in the days of Jesus Christ, and none more fitting to have been his residence during the greater part of his life on earth. The seclusion is perfect, greater even than that of Bethany, which on one side looks out openly upon the country that stretches away to the shore of the Dead Sea. Nazareth is closed in on every side, offering to us an emblem of the seclusion of those thirty years which were passed there so quietly. Pure hill breezes play over the village, and temper the summer heat. The soil around is rich, and yields the fairest flowers and richest fruits of Palestine. You seem shut out from the world, and yet you have but to climb a few hundred feet to the top of the overlooking hill, and one of the widest, finest prospects in all the Holy Land bursts upon your view. Away in the west, a sparkling light plays upon the waters of the Mediterranean, revealing a portion of the Great Sea that formed the highway to the isles of the Gentiles. The ridge of Carmel runs out into the waters, closing in the bold promontory on the top of which Elijah stood and discomfited the prophets of Balaam. Southward, below your feet, stretches the great battle-plain of Palestine, behind which rises the hilly district of Samaria, through the opening between which and the mountains of Gilboa the eye wanders away eastward across the whole breadth of the Holy Land, till it rests upon that range, the everlasting eastern background of every Syrian prospect—the mountain range of Bashan and Gilead and Moab. Turning northward, the whole hill-country of Galilee lies spread out before us, the Sea of Gennesaret hidden, but a glimpse of Safed obtained, the city set upon a hill, above and beyond which there rise the snowy heights of Hermon, called by the Arabs the Sheikh of the Mountains.

Up to the hill-top which commands this magnificent prospect, how often in childhood, youth, and early manhood must Jesus have ascended, to gaze—who shall tell us with what thoughts?—upon the chosen scene of his earthly ministry, and upon that sea over whose waters the glad tidings of salvation were to be borne to so many lands. It pleases us to think that so many years of our Lord's life were spent in such a home as that which Nazareth supplied; one so retired, so rich in natural beauty, with glimpses of the wide world around for the morning or evening hours. There it was, in the fields below the village, that he had watched how the lilies grew, and seen with what a gorgeous dress, in colouring above that of kingly purple, their Creator clothed them. There, in the gardens, he had noticed how the smallest of all seeds grew into the tallest of herbs. There, outside the house, he had seen two women grinding at one mill; inside, a woman hiding the leaven in the dough. There, in the market-place, he had seen the five sparrows sold for the two farthings. The sheep-walks of the hills and the vineyards of the valleys had taught him what were the offices of the good shepherd and the careful vine-dresser; and all the observations of those thirty years were treasured up to be drawn upon in due time, and turned into the lessons by which the world was to be taught wisdom.

No means are left for ascertaining what impression was made during these thirty years upon the inmates of his home, the playmates of his boyhood, the associates of his youth, the villagers generally in midst of whom he grew up. It may readily be believed that the gentleness, the truthfulness, the lovingness displayed by him, must have won respect. Yet we can imagine, too, that the unearthly purity and sanctity of such a childhood and such a manhood may have created an awe, a sense of distance and separation, which in meaner spirits might deepen into something like aversion and dislike. At last he leaves them, and is not seen in Nazareth for many months. But the strangest tidings about him are afloat through the village. First, they hear of what happened at his baptism in the Jordan, then of what he did a few miles off at Cana, then of his miracles in Jerusalem, then of his curing the nobleman's son of Capernaum; and now he is once more among them, and the whole village is moved. The Sabbath-day comes round. He had been in the habit all through these thirty years of attending in the synagogue; sitting there quietly and unobtrusively, taking part in the prayers and praises, listening to the reading of the Law and of the Prophets, and to the explanations of the passages which were read, with what kind and amount of self-application none of all around him knew. But how will he comport himself in the new character that he has assumed? The synagogue is crowded with men among whom he has been brought up, all curious to see and hear. The earlier part of the service goes on as usual. The opening prayer is recited; the opening psalm is chanted; the portion from the Law, from the Book of Moses, is read by the ordinary minister; the time has come for the second reading—that of some portion of the Prophets—when Jesus steps forth and stands in the reader's place. There is no challenging of his right to do so. It is not a right belonging exclusively to priest or Levite;

any Jew of any tribe might exercise it. But there was a functionary in every synagogue regularly appointed to the office. This functionary, in this instance, at once gives way, and hands to Jesus the roll of the prophet out of which, according to the calendar, the reading for the day is to be taken. It is the roll of the prophet Isaiah. Jesus opens it, and whether it was that the opening verses of the 61st chapter were those actually appointed for that day's service, or whether it was that the roll opened at random and these verses were the first that presented themselves, or that Jesus, from the whole book, purposely selected the passage, he read as follows: "The Spirit of the Lord is upon me, because he hath anointed me to preach the gospel to the poor; he hath sent me to heal the broken-hearted, to preach deliverance to the captives, and recovering of sight to the blind, to set at liberty them that are bruised; to preach the acceptable year of the Lord." And stopping there, in the middle of the sentence, he closed the book, gave it to the minister, and sat down upon the raised seat of the reader, taking the attitude usually assumed by Jewish teachers.

There was a breathless stillness. The eyes of all that were in the synagogue were fastened on him. "This day," said Jesus, "is this scripture fulfilled in your ears."

It was a scripture universally understood to be descriptive of the coming Messiah, his office, and his work. Jesus gives no reason for appropriating and applying it to himself; he offers nothing in the shape of argument or evidence in favour of his being indeed the Christ, the Anointed of the Holy Ghost. He contents himself with the simple authoritative assertion of the fact. We have indeed but the first sentence given that he spoke on this occasion. What followed, however, we may well believe to have been an exposition of the passage read, as containing an account of the true character, ends, and objects of his mission as the Christ of God; the telling who the poor were to whom he brought good tidings, who the bruised and the broken-hearted were whom he came to heal, who the bound were that he came to liberate, who the blind whose eyes he came to open, what that year was he came to usher in—the long year of grace which still runs on, in the course of which there is acceptance for all of us with God, through Christ. As Jesus spake of these things—spake with such ease, such grace, such dignity—the first impression made upon the Nazarenes, his old familiar friends, was that of astonishment and admiration. He had got no other, no better education than that which the poorest of them had received. He had attended none of the higher schools in any of the larger towns, had sat at the feet of none of their chief rabbis to be instructed in the law; yet no rabbi of the schools could speak with greater fluency, greater authority, greater confidence. Soon, however, as from the mere manner, they began to turn their thoughts to the substance of this discourse, and began to realize what the position really was which Jesus was assuming,—that it was nothing short of the very highest that ever any son of man was to reach; that it was as the Lord's anointed Christ that he was speaking, and speaking to them as the poor, the blind, the captives, to whom he was to render such services, —the admiration turns into envy. Who is he that is arrogating to himself all this dignity, authority, and power? who is speaking to them as so immeasurably his inferiors, as needing so much his help? Is not this the son of honest, plain, old Joseph, whom we all so well remember as our village carpenter? His brethren and his sisters, are they not here beside us in the synagogue, listening, apparently with no great delight or approval, to this new strain in which their brother has begun to speak? He the Messiah, the opener of our eyes, the healer of our hearts, our deliverer from bondage! Before he asks us to believe any such thing of him, let him show us some sign from heaven; do some of those miracles that they say he has done elsewhere, particularly at Capernaum. If he wanted us, who have all known him so well from his childhood, to believe in him as a prophet, he should have come to us first, convinced us first, unfolded his credentials to us first, wrought his first miracles here in Nazareth. Jealousy heightens the offence that envy had created, and ere long the whole company in that synagogue is looking at him askance. Jesus sees this, and turning from his former subject of discourse, tells them that he sees and knows it, lays open their hearts to them, puts the very words into their lips that they were ready to utter, and proceeds to vindicate himself for not showing any special sign to his fellow-townsmen, by quoting two instances in which Elijah and Elisha, the two great workers of miracles among the prophets, passed over all their fellow-countrymen to show favour to the Sidonian widow and the Syrian officer. There is nothing that men dislike more than that the evil and the bitter things hidden in their breasts should be brought to light. It aggravates this dislike when the discoverer, and revealer of their thoughts, is the very person against whom the malignant sentiment is cherished. Should he remain calm and unimpassioned, neither taken by surprise, nor betraying irritation, they are so much the more incensed. So felt the Nazarenes under the address of our Lord; and when he proceeded to assume the mantle of Elijah and Elisha, as if he were of the same order with these great prophets of the olden time, it is more than they can any longer bear. They will be lectured no more in such a way by the son of the carpenter. They rise, they rush upon him, they thrust him out of the village, and on to the brow of a precipice over which they would have hurled him; but it pleased him to put forth that power, and to lay upon them that spell which he laid upon the high-priest's band in the garden of Gethsemane. They are hurrying him to the brow of the hill; he turns, he looks, the spell is on them, their hands drop powerless by their sides; he passes through the midst of them, they offer no resistance, and before they recover themselves he is gone.

About two miles from Nazareth, there is a hill which shows, upon the side facing the plain of Esdraelon, a long and steep descent. The monks of the middle ages—the determiners of most of the sites of the holy places in Palestine—fixed on this as the precipice over which the angry Nazarenes designed to throw our Saviour, and gave it the name of the Mount of Precipitation. The very distance of this mount from the village, goes far to disprove the tradition regarding it. But though this distance had been less, it could not have been the place, for it is distinctly stated by the Evangelist that it was a brow of the hill on which the city was built from which they intended to cast him. Modern travellers are all agreed that it must have been from some part of the rocky cliff which overhangs the oldest quarter of the present village of Nazareth that Jesus was about to have been thrown. This rocky cliff extends for some distance along the hill on which Nazareth is built, and shows at different points perpendicular descents of from thirty to forty feet, which, as they have been filled up below with accumulations of rubbish, must originally have been much deeper. Any one of these would so far answer to the description given by the Evangelist. In taking this view, however, it is necessary to suppose that on leaving the synagogue, with the deliberate intention of killing him, the infuriated Nazarenes either forced Jesus up the height from which they designed afterwards to cast him, or made a circuit up and round the hill, in order to reach the intended spot. The same ascent which it must have been needful thus to make, I made, in company with the Rev. Mr. Zeller, who for some years has been resident as a missionary in Nazareth. On getting to the top of the ridge, we found ourselves on a nearly level plateau of considerable extent. There were no houses on this plateau, but Mr. Zeller pointed out to us, here and there, those underground cisterns which are the almost infallible signs of houses having once been in the neighbourhood. Here, then, on this plateau, a portion, if not the whole, of the ancient Nazareth may have stood. If it was so, if even a few houses of the old village were here, then, as we know it to have been the rule that, wherever it was possible, the synagogue was built on the highest ground in or near the city or village to which it belonged, it must have been on this elevated ground that the synagogue of Nazareth stood, not far from the brow of the hill. It seems more likely that the Nazarenes should, in the phrensy of the moment, have attempted to throw our Lord from a precipice quite at hand, than that, acting on a deliberate purpose, they should have spent some time, and climbed a hill in order to its execution.

But turning now from the locality and outward circumstances of this event in our Saviour's life, let us try to enter into its meaning and spirit. So far as we know, this was the first occasion on which Jesus addressed an audience of his countrymen in the synagogue on the Sabbath-day; it would appear indeed to have been the only one on which he took the duty of the reader as well as that of the exhorter. It was a common enough thing for any one, even a stranger, to be asked, when the proper service of the synagogue was over, to address some words of instruction or encouragement to the audience. The Gospels tell us how frequently Jesus made use of this opportunity; and you may remember how at Antioch in Pisidia, after the reading of the Law and the Prophets, the rulers of the synagogue sent unto Paul and Barnabas, saying, "Men and brethren, if ye have any word of exhortation for the people, say on." The peculiarity of the incident now before us lay in this, that Jesus first read the passage from the Prophets, and then grounded directly upon it the address which he delivered. In this respect we might regard it as the first sermon ever preached; the text chosen, and the discourse uttered by our Lord himself. Had these Nazarenes, who, in their insatiate and zealous craving after signs and wonders, wanted him only to do the same or greater things than he had done in Capernaum, but known how highly honoured, far above that of its being made a mere theatre for the exhibition of divine power, their synagogue was, in being the first place on earth in which that instrument was employed which has been so mighty through God to the pulling down of the strongholds of the ungodly, and the upbuilding of the Church, their vanity might have been gratified; but they slighted the privilege thus enjoyed, and so lost the benefit.

The body of the first synagogue sermon of our Saviour has been lost. The text and introductory sentence alone remain, but how much do they reveal to us of the nature, the needfulness, the preciousness of those spiritual offices which our Divine Redeemer came on earth to execute, and which he still stands waiting to discharge towards our sinful humanity! It was to a company of a few hundreds at the most that the words of Jesus were spoken in the synagogue at Nazareth; but that desk from which they were spoken, was turned into the centre of a circle whose bounds are the ends of the earth, and that audience has multiplied to take in the whole family of mankind. To the men of every land in every age, Jesus has been thus proclaiming what the great ends are of his mission to this earth. To open blinded eyes, to heal bruised and bleeding and broken hearts, to unlock the doors, and unloose the fetters of the imprisoned and the bound; to announce to the poor, the meek, the humble, that theirs is the kingdom of heaven; and to proclaim to all that this is the year of our Lord, the long year of Christ that takes in all the centuries down to his Second Coming, the year in every day and every hour and every moment of which our heavenly Father waits to forgive, receive, accept, all contrite ones who come to him. Such, our Saviour tells us, is that great work of grace and power for whose accomplishment he has been anointed of the Father and replenished by the Spirit. In that high office to which he has thus been set apart, and for which he has been thus qualified, we all need his services. There is a spiritual blindness which Jesus only can remove; a spiritual imprisonment from which he only can release; a deadly spiritual malady eating in upon our heart which he alone can heal. And shall he not do all this for us, if we feel our need of its being done, since the doing of it is the very design of his most gracious ministry among the sinful children of men? Let us not do him the injustice to believe that he will be indifferent to the accomplishment of the very errand of mercy on which he came, or that he will refuse in ours or in any case to enlighten and emancipate, bind up and heal.

It seems to us to throw a distinct, and, though not a very broad, yet a very clear and beautiful beam of light on the graciousness of our Lord's character, that instead of reading the number of verses ordinarily recited, he stopped where he did in his quotation from Isaiah. Had he gone on, he should have said, "to proclaim the acceptable year of the Lord, and the day of vengeance of our God." Why not go on, why pause thus in the middle of the sentence? not assuredly that he meant either to deny or hide the truth, that the day of vengeance would follow upon the acceptable year, if the opportunities of that year were abused and lost; but that then and now, it is his chosen and most grateful office to throw wide open the arms of the heavenly mercy, and invite all to throw themselves into them and be saved.

But though he came in the Spirit to those among whom he had been brought up, though he came thus to his own, by his own he was not received, by his own he was despised and rejected. His treatment at Nazareth was a foreshadowing of the treatment given generally to him by his countrymen, and terminating in his crucifixion on Calvary. The rude handling in the Galilean village, the binding, the scourging, the crucifying in the Jewish capital, were types of that still rougher spiritual handling, that crucifying of our Lord afresh which the world, in every age, has gone on repeating. It was their very familiarity with him in the intercourse of daily life which proved such a snare to the Nazarenes, and tempted them into their great offence. Let us fear lest our familiarity with him of another kind—the frequency with which we hear about him, and read about him, and have him in one way or other set before us—blind our eyes and blunt our heart to the wonders of his redeeming love, and exceeding riches of his grace and power.

XVIII.

FIRST SABBATH IN CAPERNAUM, AND FIRST CIRCUIT OF GALILEE.[1]

THE first eight months of our Lord's ministry were spent, as we have seen, in Judea. By the sign from heaven, by the Baptist's proclamation, by Christ's own words and deeds, he was presented to the rulers and to the people as the Son of God, the Messiah. His character was misunderstood; his claims were rejected. At Jerusalem a plot against his life was formed; it was no longer safe for him to reside where the Jewish authorities had power. Jesus retired to Galilee (John iv. 1-3). Besides the purpose of placing himself beyond the reach of the Scribes and Pharisees of Jerusalem, another circumstance seems to have had its influence in directing Christ's footsteps into Galilee. He heard that

[1] Matt. iv. 12-22, 23-25; Mark i. 21-39; Luke iv. 42-44.

John was cast into prison. The Baptist's work was over; the labours of the Forerunner were closed; the ground was open for Jesus to occupy. Hitherto, in his earlier Judean ministry, he had neither publicly taught in the synagogues, nor openly and indiscriminately healed the sick, nor called any other disciples to his side than those who voluntarily and temporarily followed him.[1] We may safely say, then, that prior to his appearance in Galilee, he had taken no steps either to proclaim the advent of the kingdom, or, by the selection of a band of chosen adherents, to lay the foundation of that new economy which was to take the place of the one which was now waxing old, and was ready to vanish away. It looks

[1] His disciples, indeed, in imitation of John's practice, had begun to baptize, but as soon as "the Lord knew how the Pharisees had heard that Jesus had made and baptized more disciples than John (though Jesus himself baptized not, but his disciples), he left Judea, and departed again into Galilee" (John iv. 1-3). It would seem to have been a sudden impulse of zeal in their Master's cause which led those first disciples to engage so eagerly in baptizing,—a zeal which, instead of checking or rebuking, Jesus dealt with by quietly cutting off the occasion for its display. By his own removal to Galilee, an entirely new state of things was ushered in, and by John's imprisonment his baptisms ceased; nor do we read anywhere of a Galilean baptism by the disciples of Jesus.

as if, before fully and openly entering on the task of providing a substitute for that Judaic economy which his own kingdom was to overturn, Jesus had gone up to Jerusalem, and given to the head and representatives of the Jewish commonwealth the choice of receiving or rejecting him as their Messiah. It was not, at least, till after he had been so rejected in Judea, that he began in Galilee to preach the gospel of the kingdom (Matt. i. 15), and to plant the first seeds of that tree whose leaves were to be for the healing of the nations. This helps to explain at once the marked difference between Christ's course of conduct during the period which immediately succeeded his baptism, which was passed in Judea, and the laborious months in Galilee which followed, and the marked silence regarding the former which is preserved by the first three Evangelists, who all make our Lord's ministry begin in Galilee, and contain no allusion to anything as happening between the temptation in the wilderness and the opening of his ministry there. Nor do they allude to any visits of Jesus to Jerusalem prior to those which he made after his final departure from Galilee, and which preceded his crucifixion. With them, up to that time, Galilee appears as the exclusive theatre of our Lord's labours. It is to the supplemental Gospel of St. John that we are indebted for all our knowledge of the memorable incidents in Judea, which preceded the first preaching in the synagogue of Nazareth. We can understand this singular silence of the first three Evangelists, if we regard our Lord's earlier appearance and residence in Judea as constituting rather a preliminary dealing with the Jews, in the way of testing their disposition and capacity to welcome him as their own last and greatest prophet, than as forming an integral part of that work whereby the foundations of the Christian church were laid.

Rejected by the chiefs of the people in the capital, Jesus comes to Galilee. There, in the synagogue of that town in which he had lived so many years, he first publicly proclaims his office and his work, as the healer of the broken-hearted, the restorer of sight to the blind, the deliverer of the captives, the preacher of the gospel to the poor—an office and a work which had nothing of confinement in it, nothing restricting it to any one age or country. But there, too, by his fellow-townsmen at Nazareth, as by the rulers of the capital, he is rejected, and so he descends to the shores of the Sea of Galilee. Walking by these shores, he sees first Andrew and Peter casting a net into the sea. He says to them, " Follow me, and I will make you fishers of men. Straightway they leave all and follow him." A little farther on, another pair of brothers, James and John, are in their boat mending their nets. He calls them in the same way, and they leave their boat and their nets, their father and the hired servants, and follow. He was not speaking to strangers, to those previously ignorant or indisposed to follow him. Andrew was one of the two disciples of John who had heard the Baptist say, " Behold the Lamb of God," and who had followed Jesus. The other of these two disciples was John. Andrew had brought his brother Peter to Jesus; and though it is not said that John had done the same with his brother James, the latter must already have been acquainted with Christ. Andrew, Peter, and John had followed Jesus from

Bethabara to Cana, and had witnessed there the first of his miracles. They had been up at Jerusalem, and seen the miracles which Jesus wrought at the first Passover which he attended. They may have taken part in the baptizing, may have been with Jesus at the well of Jacob. Mention is made of disciples of Jesus being there with him, and who so likely to be among them as those who first followed him from Bethabara? But they do not appear as yet to have attached themselves permanently to his person, nor to have attended him on his return from his second visit to the metropolis, nor to have been with him at Nazareth. The stopping of the baptisms, the imprisonment of John, the scattering of his disciples, may have thrown them into some doubt as to the intentions of the new Teacher. For a time at least they had returned to their old occupation as fishermen, and were busily employed at it when Jesus met them; but his voice fell upon ears that welcomed its sound, his command upon spirits that were ready to obey. Not that they understood as yet that the summons was one to relinquish finally their earthly calling. The present was but a preliminary invitation to follow Jesus, —and chiefly by hearing what he said, and watching what he did, to be instructed by him in the higher art of catching men. It was not till weeks afterwards that they were solemnly set apart as his apostles.

In the meantime, however, they accompanied him into Capernaum. The entrance of Jesus, attended by the two well-known brothers,—who, from the mention of hired servants belonging to one of them, we may believe, ranked high among their craft,—was soon known throughout all the town. The inhabitants of Capernaum had already heard enough about him to excite their liveliest curiosity. That curiosity had the keenest edge put on it by the manner in which the cure of the nobleman's child had been effected. And now he is amongst them. It would be a crowded synagogue on the Sabbath-day when he stood up there to preach for the first time the gospel of the kingdom of God. Nothing of what he said upon this occasion has been preserved. The impression and effect upon his auditors are alone recorded : " They were astonished at his doctrine; for he taught them as one having authority, and not as the scribes;" "his word was with power" (Mark i. 22; Luke iv. 32). The scribes, the ordinary instructors of the people, presented themselves simply as expositors of the law, written and traditional, claiming no separate or independent authority, content with simply discharging the office of commentators, and resting their individual claims to respect on the manner in which that office was fulfilled. But here is a teacher of quite a new order, who busies himself with none of those difficult or disputed questions about which the rabbis differed; who speaks to the people about a new kingdom—the kingdom of God—to be set up among them, and that in a tone of earnestness, certainty, authority, to which they were unaccustomed. What can this new kingdom be, and what position in it can this Jesus of Nazareth occupy?

Of one thing they are speedily apprised, that it is a kingdom opposed to that of Satan, intended to destroy it. For among them was a man possessed with a devil, who, as Jesus stood speaking to them, broke in upon his discourse, and, with a voice so loud as to startle the whole synagogue, cried out, addressing himself to Jesus, "Let us alone; what have we to do with thee, thou Jesus of Nazareth; art thou come to destroy us? I know thee who thou art, the Holy One of God." He speaks in the name of others, as representing the whole company of evil spirits, to whom, at that time, here and there, it had been allowed to usurp the seat of will and power in human breasts, and so to possess the men in whom they dwelt as to strip them of their volition and conscious identity, and to turn them into human demons. But how came this human demon into the synagogue, and what prompted him to utter such cries of horror and of spite? Was this devil as much beside himself as the poor man in whom he dwelt? Had the presence, the look, the words of Jesus such a power over him that as the man could not regulate or restrain his own actions, so neither could the devil regulate or restrain his thoughts and words? His exclamations sound to our ear like the mad, involuntary, impotent outcries of the vassals of a kingdom who feel that the reins of empire are passing out of their hands, but who cannot give them up without telling who the greater than they is who has come to dispossess them of their power.

Whatever may be thought of the kind of pressure under which the devil who possessed this man acted; whether the testimony he gave to our Lord's character be regarded as free and spontaneous, intended rather to injure than to honour; or whether it be regarded as unwillingly drawn forth by close personal contact with the Holy One, the testimony so given was not welcomed by Christ. It came unsuitably from a quarter whence no witness should be borne to him, nor was wished for, as it came unseasonably, when premature revelations of his true character were not desired. In other instances as well as this Jesus did not suffer the devils to speak, "because they knew him," acting as to them on the same principle on which he often cautioned those whom he healed and his own disciples, not to make him known, seeking by such repression to prevent any hurrying forward before its time of what he knew would be the closing catastrophe of his career. But though refused thus, and as it were rejected by our Lord, its first wild impatient utterances all that it was permitted to give forth, this voice is most striking to us now as a testimony from the demon-world, through which a knowledge of who Jesus truly was seems so rapidly to have circulated. The Prince of Darkness, in his temptation of our Lord a year before, seems himself to have been in some doubt, as he put the question so often, "If thou be the Son of God." But no doubt was entertained by the devils who came, as Luke tells us, "out of many, crying out and saying, Thou art Christ, the Son of God" (Luke iv. 41). Some have thought that those demoniacs whom Christ cured were lunatics, and nothing more; men whose deranged and disordered intellects were soothed down into calmness and order by the gentle yet firm voice and look and power of Christ. But what are we to make of the unique testimony that so many of them gave to Christ's Messiahship and Sonship to God, and that at the very commencement of his ministry? Were lunatics the only ones who knew him? or whence got they such knowledge and such faith?

Accepting, with whatever mystery the whole subject of demoniac possession is clothed, the simple account of the Evangelists, it does appear most wonderful,—the quick intelligence, the wild alarm, the terror-striking faith that then pervaded the demon-world, as if all the spirits of hell who had been suffered to make human bodies their habitation, grew pale at the very presence of Jesus, and could not but cry out in the extremity of their despair.

"Hold thy peace," said Jesus to the devil in the synagogue, "and come out of him." The man was seen to fall, torn as by violent convulsions; a loud, inarticulate, fiendish cry was heard to issue from his lips;[1] hale and unhurt, the devil gone, the man himself again, he rose to converse with those around, and to return to his home and friends. Amazement beyond description seized at once on all who saw or heard of what had happened. Men said to one another, in the synagogue, on the streets, by the highways, What thing is this, what a word is this! for with authority he commandeth even the unclean spirits

[1] Mark i. 36; Luke iv. 35.

and they do obey him. And immediately (it could scarce well have been otherwise), the fame of him went out into every place of the country, and spread abroad throughout all the region round about Galilee."[1] Chiefly, however, in Capernaum did the excitement prevail, begun by the cure of the demoniac in the synagogue, quickened by another cure that followed within an hour or two. The service of the synagogue closed before the mid-day meal. At its close Jesus accepted an invitation to go to the house of Simon and Andrew. These brothers, as we know, were natives of Bethsaida, and had hitherto resided there. But recently they had removed to Capernaum. Peter having married, and perhaps taken up his abode in the house of his mother-in-law, James and John were also of the invited guests. Jesus did not know that the house he went to was one of sickness, and his ignorance in this respect creates the belief that it was the first time he had entered it. But soon he hears that the great fever (it is the physician Luke who in this way describes it) has seized upon Simon's wife's mother. They tell

---

[1] Mark i. 27, 28; Luke iv. 36, 37.

him of it; he goes to, bends kindly over her, takes her by the hand, rebukes the fever. The cure is instantaneous and complete. She rises, as if no disease had ever weakened her, with glad and grateful spirit to wait upon Jesus and the rest. And so within that home, kindly hands were provided, like those of Martha at Bethany, to minister to the Saviour's wants during the busiest, most toilsome period of his life, when, in season and out of season, early in the morning, and far on often in the night, he came and went, living longer under that roof of Peter's house at Capernaum, than under any other that sheltered him after his public ministry had begun. This cure, too, was noised abroad through the city. Here was an opportunity not to be lost, for who could tell but that next morning Jesus will be gone? Though it was the Sabbath, Jesus had not scrupled to eject the devil and rebuke the fever; but the people could not so easily get over their scruples. They wait till the sun has set before they apply to this new and strange physician. But meanwhile all that were diseased in Capernaum, and all that were possessed were brought. All the city has gathered together at the door of Peter's house. The sun goes down, and Jesus steps out into that bustling, anxious crowd; he lays his hand on every one of the diseased,[1] and heals them, and casts out all the spirits with his word. The stars would be shining brightly in the heavens ere the busy blessed work was done, and within a few hours a city which numbered many thousand inhabitants saw disease of every kind banished from its borders.

After the excitement and fatigue of such a day, Jesus may lay his head peacefully on his pillow, and take the rest that such labour has earned. But long before the others—while yet they are all sleeping in Simon's house around him—rising up a great while before day, he goes out into a solitary place to pray. Was it on his own account that Jesus thus retired? Was his spirit too much under the distracting influence which such a scene of bustle and excitement as he had passed through the day before, was fitted to exert? Did he feel the need to calm the inward tumult, by silent and solitary communion with Heaven? As

[1] Luke iv. 40.

we follow his footsteps, let us be careful to notice and to remember in what circumstances it was that Christ resorted to special, solitary, continued prayer. But in leaving Capernaum, alone and so early, Jesus had in view the state of others as well as his own. He was well aware how apt, in his case, the office of the healer, the wonder-worker, was to overshadow that of the teacher, the preacher of the glad tidings; how ready the inhabitants of Capernaum already were to hail and honour him in this one character, however little they might be disposed to regard or obey him in the other. He had done enough of the one kind of work, had got enough of that one kind of homage, there. And so, when, after an eager search for him, he is found,—and Simon and the disciples tell him that all men were seeking for him, and the people when they came up entreat him that he should not depart from them,[1]—Jesus says to the one, "Let us go into the next town, that I preach there also;" and to the other, "I must preach the kingdom of God to other cities also, for therefore am I sent." He

[1] Compare Mark i. 36, 38, and Luke iv. 42, 43.

did not, indeed, forsake the city that had treated him so differently from his own Nazareth. He chose it as the place of his most frequent residence, the centre of his manifold labours, the scene of many of his most memorable discourses and miracles. But now he must not rest on the favour which the healings of this wonderful day have won for him. And for a time he left Capernaum, and "went about all Galilee, teaching in their synagogues, and preaching the gospel of the kingdom, and healing all manner of sickness, and all manner of disease, among the people. And his fame went throughout all Syria: and they brought unto him all sick people that were taken with divers diseases and torments, and those which were possessed with devils, and those which were lunatic, and those that had the palsy; and he healed them. And there followed him great multitudes of people from Galilee, and from Decapolis, and from Jerusalem, and from Judea, and from beyond Jordan."[1]

We read of nine departures from and returns to

[1] Matt. iv. 23-25.

Capernaum in the course of the eighteen months of our Lord's Galilean ministry; of three extensive tours through all the towns and villages of the district as the one now described; and of five or six more limited ones. Had the three Evangelists not been so sparing in their notices of time and place; had they not often shown such entire disregard to the mere order of time, in order to bring together incidents or discourses which were alike in character; could we have traced, as we cannot do, the footsteps of our Saviour from place to place, from month to month, as he set forth on these missionary rounds through Galilee, made, let us remember, all on foot, we should have had a year and a half before us of varied and almost unceasing toil, the crowded activities of which would have filled us with wonder. As it is, a general conception of how these months were spent is all that we can reach. To give distinctness to that conception, let us remember what, in extent of surface and in the character and numbers of its population, that district of country was to which these pedestrian journeys of our Saviour were confined.

Galilee, the most northern of the three divisions of Palestine, is between fifty and sixty miles in length, and from thirty to forty in breadth. A three-days' easy walk would take you from Nain, on the south, to Cæsarea Philippi in the north,—which seem to have been the limits in these directions of our Saviour's circuits. Less than two days' travel will carry you from the shores of the Sea of Galilee to the coasts of Tyre and Sidon. Galilee presented thus an area somewhat larger than Lancashire, and somewhat smaller than Yorkshire. So far, therefore, as the mere distances were concerned,. it would not take long —not more than a week or two—to travel round and through it. But then, in the Saviour's days, it was more densely populated than either of the English counties I have named. Josephus, who knew it well, speaks of 204 towns and villages, the smallest of them containing above 15,000 inhabitants. Making an allowance for exaggeration, the population of the province must have been about three millions,—as crowded a population as any manufacturing district in any of the western kingdoms of Europe now presents. And this population was of a very mixed character. If the majority were of Jewish descent, there were so many Phœnicians, Syrians, Arabs, Greeks, and others mingled with them, that we may be almost certain that Jesus never addressed any large assembly in which there were not Gentiles as well as Jews. There cannot be a greater mistake than to imagine that, in selecting Capernaum, on the shores of the Lake of Gennesaret, as his head-quarters, and Galilee as his chosen field of labour, Jesus was retiring from the populous Judea to a remote and unfrequented region. In those days there was much more life and bustle in Galilee than in Judea. So far as both the numbers and character of its population were concerned, it was a much better, more hopeful theatre for such evangelistic labours as those of Jesus. The people, though no less national in their spirit, were much less infected with ecclesiastical prejudice. The seed had thus a better soil to fall upon. Though a Roman governor was placed over them, the Scribes and Pharisees had great power in Jerusalem, as they proved in effecting the crucifixion. Herod Antipas, who ruled over Galilee, had none of the jealousies of the Jewish Sanhedrim; and, in point of fact, does not appear till the last to have taken much interest in, or in any way to have interfered with the proceedings of Jesus. So long as he confined himself to the work of a religious teacher, Herod had no desire to meddle with his doings; and even if he had, Jesus had but to cross the Lake of Galilee to put himself beyond his power, by placing himself under the protection of Philip, the gentlest and most humane of the Herods.

Well adapted every way as Galilee was for our Lord's peculiar work,—the laying of the first foundations of the Christian faith, a faith which was to spread over the whole earth,—Capernaum was equally fitted to be the centre whence his labours were to radiate. Looked at, as you find it marked upon the map of Galilee, it does not occupy anything like a central position. But looked at in relation to the population and to the means of transit, a better centre could not have been selected. Wherever its site was, it lay on the north-western shore of the Sea of Galilee, close upon, if not within, the plain of

Gennesaret.[1] This plain,—three miles long, and two miles broad,—was then dotted with villages, teeming with population, and of the most exuberant fertility. "One may call the place," says the Jewish historian, "the ambition of nature, where it forces those plants that are naturally enemies to one another, to agree together; it is a happy contention of the seasons, as if every one of them laid claim to this country." While all round its shores the Sea of Galilee saw towns and villages thronged with an agricultural and manufacturing population, itself teemed with a kind of wealth that gave large occupation to the fishermen. How numerous the boats were that once skimmed its surface, and how large the numbers employed as fishermen, may be gathered from the fact, that in the wars with the Romans, two hundred small vessels were once collected for the only naval action in which the Jews ever engaged. Remembering that the Lake is only thirteen miles long and five or six miles broad, it is not too much,

---

[1] After visiting the ruins at Khan Mineyeh and Tell Hum, the writer had no hesitation in deciding in favour of the latter as more likely to have been the site of Capernaum.

perhaps, to say that never did so small a sheet of water see so many keels cutting its surface, or so many human habitations circling round and shadowing its waves, as did the Sea of Galilee in the days of Jesus Christ.

Now all is silent there; lonely and most desolate. Till last year but a single boat floated upon its waters. On its shores, Tiberias in ruins, and Magdala composed of a few wretched hovels, are all that remain. You may ride round and round the empty beach, and, these excepted, never meet a human being, nor pass a human habitation. Capernaum, Chorazin, Bethsaida are gone. Here and there you stumble over ruins, but none can tell you exactly what they were. They knew not, those cities of the Lake, the day of their visitation; their names and their memory have perished.

EDINBURGH: T. CONSTABLE,
PRINTER TO THE QUEEN, AND TO THE UNIVERSITY.

www.ingramcontent.com/pod-product-compliance
Lightning Source LLC
Chambersburg PA
CBHW030543300426
44111CB00009B/840